D1634322

Strategically

New Perspectives in Organizational Learning, Performance, and Change

JERRY W. GILLEY, SERIES EDITOR

Strategically Integrated HRD, 2nd Edition by Jerry W. Gilley and Ann Maycunich Gilley

Critical Issues in HRD edited by Ann Maycunich Gilley, Jamie L. Callahan, and Laura L. Bierema

Ethics and HRD by Tim Hatcher

High Impact Learning by Robert O. Brinkerhoff and Anne M. Apking

Transforming Work *by Patricia E. Boverie and Michael Kroth*

Philosophy and Practice of Organizational Learning, Performance, and Change by Jerry W. Gilley, Peter Dean, and Laura L. Bierema

Assessing the Financial Benefits of Human Resource Development by Richard A. Swanson

The Manager as Change Agent by Jerry W. Gilley, Scott A. Quatro, Erik Hoekstra, Doug D. Whittle, and Ann Maycunich Gilley

Strategically Integrated HRD

2nd Edition

Six Transformational Roles in Creating Results-Driven Programs

Jerry W. Gilley and
Ann Maycunich Gilley

*New Perspectives in Organizational Learning,
Performance, and Change*

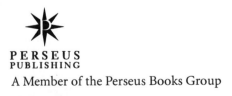

PERSEUS
PUBLISHING
A Member of the Perseus Books Group

Many of the designations used by manufacturers and sellers to distinguish their products are claimed as trademarks. Where those designations appear in this book and Perseus Publishing was aware of a trademark claim, the designations have been printed in initial capital letters.

Cataloging-in-publication Data is avaialable from the Library of Congress.
ISBN 0-7382-0762-4
Copyright © 1998, 2003 by Jerry W. Gilley and Ann Maycunich Gilley

Perseus Publishing is a member of the Perseus Books Group.

Find us on the World Wide Web at http://www.perseuspublishing.com

Perseus Publishing books are available at special discounts for bulk purchases in the U.S. by corporations, institutions, and other organizations. For more information, please contact the Special Markets Department at the Perseus Books Group, 11 Cambridge Center, Cambridge, MA 02142, or call (617) 252–5298. (800) 255-1514 or email j.mccrary@perseusbooks.com

Text design by Jeffrey Williams
Set in 10-point Minion by the Perseus Books Group

First printing, December, 2002
1 2 3 4 5 6 7 8 9 10—05 04 03 02

Publisher's Note

Organizations are living systems, in a constant state of dynamic evolution. *New Perspectives in Organizational Learning, Performance, and Change* is designed to showcase the most current theory and practice in human resource and organizational development, exploring all aspects of the field—from performance management to adult learning to corporate culture. Integrating cutting-edge research and innovative management practice, this library of titles will serve as an essential resource for human resource professionals, educators, students, and managers in all types of organizations.

The series editorial board includes leading academics and practitioners whose insights are shaping the theory and application of human resource development and organizational design.

Contents

Part A: Philosophy of HRD

Part B: Creating Credibility by Redesigning and Repositioning HRD

Part C: Six Transformational Roles in Results-Driven HRD

9 Change Champion 227

10 Political Navigator 265

List of Figures and Tables

Figures

Tables

Introduction

Human Resource Development (HRD) professionals enhance their credibility in organizations by embracing three fundamental activities. First, they need to reexamine their philosophy of HRD and adopt one that fosters results in organizations (Chapters 1 and 2). Second, they need a game plan for redesigning and repositioning HRD in their organization (Chapters 3 and 4). Third, HRD professionals need to adopt six transformational roles useful in creating result-driven HRD programs (Chapters 5–10).

For decades HRD professionals have been debating their philosophy of HRD. In the final analysis two different philosophies have emerged: activity-based and results-driven. The former philosophy embraces the uses of training activity as a way of enhancing organizational effectiveness. In Chapter 1, we examine six training beliefs that anchor HRD practitioners into an activity-based philosophy. We also explore the first four phases of the evolution of HRD: no HRD, one-person HRD, vendor-driven HRD, and customized vendor-driven HRD.

In Chapter 2, we direct our attention toward the explanation of results-driven HRD. Here we explore the last two phases of the evolution of HRD: operationally linked HRD and strategically integrated HRD. Additionally, we identify the barriers to adopting a strategically integrated HRD philosophy and provide suggestions for preparing for the journey to results-driven HRD.

In the second part of the book, we examine the way HRD professionals create credibility in their organizations. We believe that this can primarily be accomplished by redesigning and repositioning HRD within an organization. We contend that this requires HRD professionals to link their practice to the three domains of strategic HRD, which include organizational learning, performance, and change (Chapter 3). Next we provide a seven-step approach to the successful transformation of HRD. These are provided in Chapter 4 and include:

Step 1: Communicating the urgency for change
Step 2: Providing leadership for change
Step 3: Creating ownership and support for change
Step 4: Creating a shared vision for change
Step 5: Implementing and managing change
Step 6: Integrating change into the organization culture
Step 7: Measuring and monitoring change

At the heart of strategically integrated HRD are the six transformational roles required to create results-driven HRD (see Figure I.1). Each role enables HRD professionals to enhance their credibility within their organization. We have subdivided these six roles into three subroles focused on one's principal responsibilities. The subroles include partnership, professional, and leadership roles.

In the partnership role, HRD professionals serve as *relationship builders* (Chapter 5). They use communication and interpersonal strategies to build collaborative client relationships that enhance trust within the organization.

HRD professionals use one of three professional roles to demonstrate technical expertise that is valuable to the organization. First HRD professionals serve as *organizational architects* by demonstrating their understanding of the formal and informal organization, managing the organizational immune system, and understanding the organization as a system (Chapter 6). Second, they serve as *strategists* responsible for strategic planning initiatives (Chapter 7). Finally, HRD professionals serve as *performance engineers* responsible for performance improvement and performance engineering (Chapter 8).

Finally, HRD professionals need to demonstrate their leadership capabilities by serving in one of two leadership roles. As *change champions*, HRD professionals understand the purpose and phases of change management and the roles and competencies needed to apply the change management process. They need to understand the eight phases of implementing and managing change initiatives (Chapter 9). *Political navigators* demonstrate their professional and organizational competence and expertise as well as politically savvy strategies (Chapter 10). Both skills are critical in enhancing one's credibility in an organization.

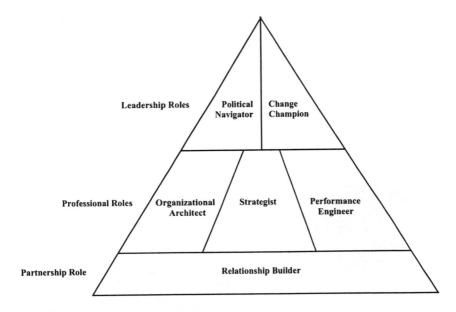

Figure I.1

PART A

Philosophy of HRD

Consider the following: Every morning many of us wake up and wonder how we evolved to our current status in life. Why do we do what we do and perform the activities and roles we do? We realize that we have charted a career path for ourselves but cannot remember the decisions that led us to it. Most of us spend little time thinking about how we got to this point. Consequently, many of us just accept our fate, realizing that the complexity of our lives is one of the reasons for our uncertainty. Occasionally curiosity gets the better of us, and we stop and ask a very simple but thought-provoking question, one question that changes our lives forever: "How did I get to this point in life?" When this occurs, we have begun the process of examining our personal philosophy.

The same could be said about the development of one's philosophy of HRD. It simply evolved. But your philosophy of HRD reflects what you believe to be the purpose of HRD. For some HRD professionals, their purpose is to provide training and development activities to enhance employees' skills and knowledge. Others believe that their purpose is to provide career development opportunities to advance employees' careers. Still others hold that their HRD purpose helps organizational leaders create environments that foster employee development and create a more responsive and humane workplace.

Although these are noble purposes, we believe that the primary purpose of HRD is to improve the organization and make it more effective, whether this is a large, total system or a small division or department within an organization. If HRD achieves this end, employees will ultimately benefit by having opportunities to

develop their careers
increase their financial position as a result of improved
    organizational profitability
enhance their sense of participation and belonging
improve their performance
engage in growth and development planning.

Unfortunately, defining organizational effectiveness is not easy. The most common definition of organizational effectiveness focuses on an organization's long-term ability to consistently achieve its strategic and operational goals (Fallon and Brinkerhoff 1996, 14). This approach (the goal method), although the oldest and most widely used evaluation approach for measuring organizational effectiveness, is by no means the only method.

At least three additional definitions of organizational effectiveness appear to be appropriate (Cameron 1980). First, organizational effectiveness can be measured by the ability of an organization to acquire needed resources to accomplish its desired goals. Using this definition, organizations are perceived to be successful when they are able to obtain the quantity and quality of resources appropriate, which could include financial, material, and/or human resources. Second, organizational effectiveness can be defined in terms of how smoothly the organization functions, especially the degree or absence of internal strain within the organization (Burke 1992, 8). When this definition is applied, it is often referred to as the process model of organizational effectiveness. Third, organizational effectiveness can be determined by the extent to which the organization is able to satisfy all of its internal and external clients. Internal clients include employees, managers, and executives, with satisfaction measured in terms of loyalty, motivation, esprit de corps, cooperation, and teamwork. External clients obviously include recipients of the organization's products and services. In this scenario, effectiveness can be measured in terms of customer satisfaction with those products and services, as well as their perception of the correctness of their decision to have an ongoing relationship with the organization.

Each of the previous definitions provides insight as to the importance of organizational effectiveness. Although it may be difficult to arrive at an agreed-upon definition, it is certainly an important aspect of organizational life. Consequently, you must strive to obtain an acceptable definition that relates to your organization, industry, or both. In this way, an agreed-upon target can be identified that all members of the organization strive to achieve.

Comparing Activity-Based and Results-Driven HRD

In Chapters 1 and 2, we compare and contrast two opposite philosophies of HRD: activity-based and results-driven. Although few if any HRD practitioners openly admit to maintaining an activity-based philosophy, their actions tell a different story. In Chapter 2, we provide a five-phase change model to help you examine your HRD philosophy. In this chapter, we provide a simple exercise to help transform your HRD philosophy to that of results-driven.

Activity-Based HRD

The journey of creating a results-driven HRD function cannot begin until you understand why HRD practitioners behave the way they do. The answer may be found in the assumptions and beliefs one holds about HRD. In other words, what is the practitioner's philosophy of HRD, and how does it affect his or her behavior and action?

Many HRD programs are perceived to be "outside" the mainstream of the organization because they are viewed as merely internal training houses for employees. Often, training is not considered critical to the success of the organization nor are HRD practitioners taken seriously. Moreover, little attention is given to the outcomes of training or the impact it has on employee performance. Another perceptual problem is that HRD practitioners are not viewed as credible because they don't live in the real world or face the problems other organizational members face. These perceptions often cause HRD practitioners to be treated with a lack of respect. Such perceptions also cause senior management to seriously question the value of HRD. As a result, HRD programs are the first to be eliminated during periods of financial difficulty. Thus, the image and credibility of HRD remain weak.

To compound the situation, many HRD practitioners spend much of their time designing classroom-based training events; others behave as if their mission were to conduct workshops, seminars, meetings, and conferences. Consequently, they view training as an end unto itself. Management reinforces this belief when they do not use HRD as a strategic tool in improving organizational performance and effectiveness. Moreover, training vendors, professional associations, and direct mail distributors reinforce this belief when they guarantee that they can fix every possible organizational ill using the latest ten-step format, the newest training games, or the "four-quadrant anything." With this type of reinforcement, it is not surprising that HRD practitioners fail to understand the importance of becoming strategic partners within an organization.

Some HRD programs are not linked to the strategic business goals of the organization (Brinkerhoff and Apking 2002; Brinkerhoff and Gill 1994). When this occurs, training is conducted in a vacuum. Little attention is paid to the problems facing the organization and how training can be used to address them. As a result, employees fail to receive the type of training and reinforcement needed to improve performance. Organizational performance cannot improve when training is not focused on the business needs of the organization. We call this type of training the "hit or miss" approach. Some training is on target, but most is not.

When HRD practitioners believe that the business of HRD is to deliver training for training's sake, all their energy is directed toward the number of training courses they deliver and the number of employees they train. Consequently, they rely on employees' responses to training as a means to justify HRD's existence rather than focusing on learning transfer or the impact of training. When this approach is present, HRD practitioners are embracing the activity-based HRD philosophy (Robinson and Robinson 1989). Is this philosophy of HRD the most appropriate way to help improve organizational performance and effectiveness? We will consider the parable of the sower to examine this question.

The Parable of the Sower

As the story goes, the sower threw his seed indiscriminately on top of the soil. Some of the soil was stony, and the seeds had difficulty producing a consistent crop. Some of the soil was full of thorns, which prevented the seeds from growing to maturity. Some of the soil was shallow, which allowed the seeds to take root but prevented the development of a strong root system; the crop soon withered away under the hot summer sun. Some of the soil was hard, preventing the seeds from taking root at all. However, some of the soil was fertile and prepared to accept the seeds, and consequently produced a bumper crop.

How does this parable relate to the field of HRD? The sower is the HRD practitioner. The seeds are performance improvement interventions that are designed to improve organizational performance and effectiveness. The different types of soil represent two things: the organization's readiness to provide growth and development opportunities, and the organizational barriers that prevent performance improvement, growth, and development.

Stony soil represents an organization that has a hot and cold relationship with HRD. Some divisions embrace HRD whereas others avoid it. Thorny soil is representative of organizations that allow their managers, structure, operations, and reward systems to get in the way of performance improvement and growth. Shallow soil represents organizations that do not encourage learning transfer. When learning does occur, it improves job performance only temporarily before it gets lost among hundreds of competing events. Hard soil is representative of organizations and people who believe that they have nothing to learn. Consequently, they resist learning altogether. Fertile soil represents organizations that are prepared to accept growth and development opportunities and are willing to support and encourage them.

Effective sowers have learned they cannot just throw their seed indiscriminately on top of the soil, go home, and wait for a bumper crop. They must prepare the soil for planting by removing the stones and thorns and tilling it. They must plant their seeds deep in the earth, fertilize the soil soon after planting, irrigate if Mother Nature does not cooperate, weed the growing crop to ensure maximum growth, continue to fertilize and water the crop during the long hot summer months, and finally harvest the crop and prepare the soil for winter.

Which sower is the most effective (productive)? The answer is obvious: the one who is willing to carefully prepare the soil to produce maximum yields. Likewise, improving organizational performance and effectiveness is not about better products, more capital, or even better business processes, but about growing and developing human resources. Unfortunately, even though they are the heart of every organization, people are the organizational asset least developed and cared for. Without their people, organizations are not able to operate or serve their customers. In essence, organizations cannot produce products or provide services without the input and effort of their employees.

Organizations are people, so why are people treated so poorly so much of the time? The answer is simple. Many organizations have an HRD philosophy similar to the planting strategy of the sower in the parable. They think that developing their human resources requires no effort. Their philosophy goes something like this: "We'll throw some training at our employees and hope that performance improves" or "We really don't have the time to train and develop our people because we're so busy" or "We'll get around to it as soon as we can; remember, the customer comes first" or "If they don't develop fast enough or produce well enough we will find someone else who will" (Gilley and Boughton 1996, 48).

Many HRD practitioners simply cannot see the damaging effects of the old HRD philosophy. Gill (1995, 27) believes that the old HRD philosophy is contributing to the destruction of organizations. He states, "at the end of the 20th century, our 17th century organizations are crumbling because the changes which are required to improve performance and productivity are simply not being made." High-performance organizations require a shift from the old HRD approach to a new philosophy of HRD, one that enables HRD practitioners to become strategic partners responsible for improving organizational performance and effectiveness.

Seven Beliefs that Anchor HRD Practitioners in Activity-Based HRD

Seven deeply held beliefs contribute to the activity-based (for example, training for training's sake) philosophy of HRD. These beliefs appear to anchor HRD practitioners into this philosophy, affecting their behavior, actions, and the decisions they make. The first five anchors were introduced by Gill (1995), and the last two surfaced by Clifton and Nelson (1992). They are as follows:

1. Training makes a difference.
2. Training is an HRD practitioner's job.
3. The trainer's purpose is to manage training programs.
4. Training's purpose is to achieve learning objectives.
5. Employees fear applying new skills or knowledge, so training should be fun.
6. Training is designed to "fix" employees' weaknesses.
7. Training is a missionary endeavor.

Anchor 1: Training Makes a Difference

Many HRD practitioners are true believers. They honestly think that training by itself changes an organization and improves its performance and effectiveness. When this belief is held, HRD practitioners think there is a direct cause-and-effect relationship between training and improving performance in the workplace. Yet nothing could be further from the truth. Employees are so bombarded with problems, circumstances, and decisions that little of the training they receive can penetrate their mental shields. Without careful and deliberate reinforcement on the job, most of what employees learn is forgotten and never applied.

Some HRD practitioners' lack of vision is one of their biggest problems. They believe that training is the answer to all organizational ills. Yet training can only correct problems caused by the lack of knowledge or skill. Training cannot by itself ensure improved organizational performance or effectiveness.

When HRD practitioners internalize this belief, many employees are left on their own immediately after participating in a learning intervention. This is because some believe that learning is a natural occurrence; hence, they are reluctant to adopt learning transfer strategies useful in the integration of learning on the job. Consequently, some practitioners fail to develop transfer of learning processes that encourage managers to reinforce new learning. They need to understand that before learning can be translated into value for the organization, it must be applied to the job. Unfortunately some practitioners fail to assist in integrating skills or knowledge on the job, which causes confusion and frustration for managers, employees, and HRD practitioners alike. Consequently, much of the learning is lost.

Additionally some present too much information to learners in too short a period of time under the false perception that the more information shared the more is retained. Such overload causes learners to become confused, overwhelmed, and bewildered, inhibiting their ability to use or apply skills. Consequently, employee performance fails to improve.

Anchor 2: Training Is an HRD Practitioner's Job

Many HRD practitioners have the attitude that training is their responsibility. Managers reinforce this belief by allowing their training responsibilities to be delegated to professional trainers. In other words, managers wash their hands of the responsibility of developing their employees.

Who should be responsible for training? We believe that the person held accountable for employee performance and productivity ultimately should be responsible for training. This individual should also be responsible for conducting employee performance reviews, providing feedback, and confronting poor performance. The person responsible for training should be held accountable when productivity declines or when the organization fails to meet its goals and objectives. The person an organization holds accountable for each of these activities is the manager. Managers lacking the skills essential to adequately train employees should be relieved of their managerial duties and responsibilities.

Because HRD practitioners are not truly responsible for employee performance and productivity, should they be responsible for providing employee training? The answer is no. Training should be the primary responsibility of managers because they are the only organizational players truly held accountable for employee performance and productivity. Organizations need to allow people who have real-world experience—managers—to deliver training, which is the only way learning transfer will be successful.

Unfortunately, many managers fail to adequately communicate expectations to their employees. This of course sets the stage for poor performance. To compound this problem, many managers fail to confront performance issues. Either they do not know how or they are uncomfortable doing so (conflict avoidance). Often, the problem becomes nearly insurmountable before being addressed.

To improve employee performance, managers should use an approach known as the theory of expectation/inspection. This approach is achieved by communicating to their employees exactly what and how they expect them to perform and how the quantity and quality of their performance will be measured. Second, managers are responsible for inspecting employee performance to determine if they meet or exceed established performance standards. Performance improvement will only take place when managers combine expectation and inspection.

Sadly, most managers fail to coach their employees to attain needed results, which prevents learning transfer. Accordingly, organizations need to enhance their managers' performance coaching skills to improve performance and manage change. In this way, managers become the champions of training rather than its gatekeepers.

Anchor 3: The Trainer's Purpose Is to Manage Training Programs

Many HRD practitioners spend a great deal of their time managing training events. They schedule courses, select training materials, manage enrollments, arrange conferences and workshops, and collect and analyze evaluation forms. In fact, so much of their time is spent doing these types of activities that they have little time to spend on the critical issues facing their organizations, such as building strategic relationships (Chapter 5), analyzing organizational dynamics (Chapter 6), performing strategic planning activities (Chapter 7), installing and managing performance management systems (Chapter 8), and facilitating change management activities (Chapter 9). As a result, HRD practitioners operate as though business issues have little effect on them and the role they perform in the organization. They are happy managing training and behave as if their department is tangential to other operational units.

As discussed previously, managers should primarily assume training responsibilities. When this occurs, what should HRD practitioners be responsible for within the organization? We believe that HRD practitioners should evolve from trainers, which we describe as a transactional role, into any one of six transformational roles (see Chapters 5–10). In any of the transformational roles, HRD practitioners support and supplement the efforts of managers as trainers by training them. Further, they transform the HRD program into a results-driven initiative and enhance organizational effectiveness by demonstrating their ability to build partnerships, influence organizational leaders, and lead the organization through the change process.

Anchor 4: Training's Purpose Is to Achieve Learning Objectives

Many HRD practitioners believe accomplishing learning objectives is their primary purpose. Learning objectives do provide structure and direction for a learning program, and they help define the purpose of learning interventions. Although they are important, they are not an end unto themselves.

As strange as this may sound, some practitioners fail to realize that the ultimate outcome of a learning intervention is the improvement in employee performance through the acquisition of new knowledge and skills—not simply achieving learning objectives in an artificial training setting. HRD practitioners, acting as trainers, rely too much on learning objectives and thus fail to recognize that employees may not be anxious to acquire new skills or apply new knowledge. Additionally, HRD practitioners cannot assume that employees possess the self-discipline to manage themselves and their work environment so that learning is transferred to the job. In the final analysis, learning often fails to be transferred to the job. Therefore, achieving learning objectives cannot improve organizational effectiveness. Only HRD interventions that help an organization achieve its strategic business goals can.

Anchor 5 : Employees Fear Applying New Skills and Knowledge, So Training Should Be Fun

Many HRD practitioners believe employees should enjoy training. This belief is evident by the type of training evaluations used, which are typically reactionary and are often referred to as "smile sheets." Many HRD practitioners rely on this type of evaluation form to determine whether employees enjoyed training. Consequently, training programs that produce stress or cause employees to feel uncomfortable may not be viewed as positively as those designed for enjoyment. Is it any wonder that most training programs are designed to satisfy employees?

Rather than focusing on making training enjoyable, practitioners need to concentrate on some of the most common reasons employees fail to transfer learning. These include delayed application, fear of change, and lack of confidence. When employees do not have an opportunity to apply what they have learned in a timely fashion, most of the knowledge or skills will be forgotten. This occurs because training is often provided without any immediate opportunity for application, which negatively affects learning transfer. To ensure that performance applications are provided, one needs to make certain that application is made during and after training. This guarantees that employees have an immediate use for what they have learned.

Some employees fear change because they do not want to jeopardize their current productivity and performance, even if there is a better way of performing a job. Consequently, many resist new technologies, changes, innovations, methods, techniques, skills, or knowledge. Moreover, change can cause employees to feel inferior, inadequate, and insecure. To overcome these feelings, encourage managers to reassure their employees by displaying confidence in their skills and abilities, at the same time providing emotional and technological support.

Some employees may not have developed sufficient confidence during training to try new skills or apply new knowledge. Others may fail in their first attempts to use the skills or apply the knowledge on the job, or they may fear negative feedback or criticism from managers. Other employees resist learning transfers because they lack confidence in their ability to use new skills or apply new knowledge. Such fears prevent them from transferring learning.

Some employees need to "relearn" skills in a safe environment, and others need a great deal of support and encouragement when using new skills or applying new knowledge for the first time. Effective HRD professionals encourage managers to offer training that helps employees gain confidence, help employees share how they have incorporated new skills or knowledge on the job, and provide support and feedback during initial application. You should also encourage employees to take risks by helping managers provide work environments that do not punish them for trying to improve. They should encourage managers to provide reasons (rewards and recognition) for trying new skills and knowledge and help them eliminate negative peer pressure by demonstrating the rewards for improving one's performance.

Training should be free from negative feedback that reduces employees' self-esteem. However, training has a greater purpose if done correctly. It should be designed to improve organizational performance and effectiveness. Sometimes this requires painful experiences, the type that develops employees as well as the organization.

Anchor 6: Training Is Designed to Fix Employees' Weaknesses

One of activity-based HRD practitioners' biggest problems is that they believe they are in the "business of fixing employees rather than discovering their uniqueness and the things they do well. Therefore, [learning and] career development activities are designed to correct weaknesses" (Gilley 1998, 68). Strategies such as this sabotage an organization's effort to improve employee performance and send the message that something must be wrong with its employees. As such, training interventions are designed to correct employees' weaknesses rather than build on their strengths and manage their weaknesses (Clifton and Nelson 1992). Such a philosophy undermines the efforts of HRD practitioners and conditions employees to enter training with a negative, defensive attitude. Consequently, organizational performance and effectiveness do not improve.

Managers often contend that employee weaknesses will take care of themselves through time, experience, or luck. This is another myth. Like any other organizational problems, weaknesses do not disappear, they must be addressed and minimized. Employees build expertise through continual practice and reinforcement; hence, effective learning and career development activities improve their existing competencies rather than fix their deficiencies.

Another common myth is that anything is possible regardless of difficulty or obstacles. Phrases such as "if at first you don't succeed, try, try again," "practice makes perfect," and "if I can do it you can do it" oversimplify potentially complex organizational issues. Statements like these are often frustrating or demotivating to those attempting to master an unattainable goal. In reality, certain things just are not feasible in spite of the effort expended. Furthermore, this belief erroneously assumes that all employees are the same, possessing identical talents, abilities, and competencies. As we all know, individuals have a finite and eclectic set of strengths, weaknesses, skills, knowledge, and competencies—they're not clones.

Improving organizational performance capacity and enhancing renewal requires a fundamental shift in philosophy—from fixing weaknesses to building on strengths and managing weaknesses (Buckingham and Clifton 2001; Buckingham and Coffman 1999; Clifton and Nelson 1992).

Identifying Strengths.   In certain occupations, individual expertise is easily demonstrated, measurable, or noticeable by others. Individuals recognized for their expertise have certain strengths upon which they capitalize, and are usually strategically placed to take advantage of these skills to the fullest. Identifying strengths challenges you to analyze employee behaviors to determine why some are successful and others are not. The keys to this analysis centers around four characteristics indicative of individual strengths:

- internal burnings—unwavering desire for something
- high satisfaction levels—receiving intrinsic pleasure each time one performs a certain task or activity
- rapid learning—something comes easily or is learned very quickly
- performance zones—performing at an extremely high level a task or series of tasks without any conscious awareness of the steps involved (Clifton and Nelson 1992).

Identifying Weaknesses.   Identifying weaknesses is the first step in managing them. *Slow learning* is the primary indication of a weakness (Clifton and Nelson 1992). A second indication of weakness is defensive behavior regarding one's performance. Some employees become obsessive, engaging in addictive behavior that overtakes them, or are overly focused on performance as they attempt to overcome weaknesses. Finally, negative statements made by employees often underlying weaknesses.

Managing Weaknesses.   Identifying weaknesses is only the first step; their management makes the difference. You can engage in four strategies to help employees minimize their weaknesses, including

1. delegating—assigning responsibilities/tasks to those in the organization who possess the necessary strengths
2. partnering—matching one person's strengths to another's weakness
3. preventing—encouraging employees to cultivate those tasks, activities, and jobs they are good at rather than accept ones that they are not
4. accepting alternatives—enabling employees to accomplish the required work using their strengths instead of demanding that all employees complete tasks exactly the same way (Clifton and Nelson 1992).

Anchor 7: Training Is a Missionary Endeavor

Many training practitioners enter the field for the purpose of converting others by providing the "truth" and a "better way" of performing, behaving, and thinking. Much like missionaries, these individuals spend their lives attempting to convert nonbelievers. Their attitude is often one of self-righteousness whereby they and they alone have a corner on truth—and unless others accept the message and convert they will forever be lost, unable to find their performance way. Because these individuals have a passion for what they believe they are very persuasive and steadfast in their efforts to save the organization from the apocalyptic doom awaiting it due to lack of performance understanding.

As a result of this philosophy, many HRD practitioners spend their organizational lives "preaching" their message. They truly believe the organization can be saved—if enough people hear the message and change their evil ways of performing. Precious little time is spent conducting needs assessments to determine what people really need because these practitioners possess the truth, and such activities interfere with their mission of spreading the word. Rarely do they conduct evaluations to determine the effects or impacts of their training, for they perceive themselves as the experts and think such feedback is unnecessary. Moreover, evaluation activities are not needed since the message they are spreading is sufficient to alter the behavior of the worst performance offender. Learning transfer procedures and processes are unnecessary since the training message is so powerful that it alone will transform people into exemplary performers. Consequently, employees are left on their own to make the learning transition and application on the job. Finally, in true missionary fashion, they fail to focus on other things affecting performance, such as the work environment, compensation system, managerial actions, or the learning support and reinforcement process needed to encourage the application of new skills and knowledge. These critical performance improvement variables are avoided by missionary practitioners who believe that the "training message" represents the one and only way to true performance expertise.

Evidence of Activity–Based HRD

Every day, HRD practitioners commit several conscious and unconscious acts that provide evidence of their activity-based orientation. Each of these prevents HRD programs from helping the organization achieve strategic business goals and objectives and hinders HRD practitioners in their quest to become influential partners within organizations. Finally, each of these acts continue to lock the HRD program into the training for training's sake philosophy (see Table 1.1).

The Evolution of HRD: The Journey from Activity to Results-Driven HRD

HRD programs evolve through six separate phases (see Figure 1.1), each with its own distinctive characteristics, purposes, and approaches (Gilley and Coffern 1994). As HRD programs evolve, their focus changes. In addition, management becomes more aware of its role in improving employee performance. As a result, HRD becomes less a separate department and more an integrated function within the organization. The phases of evolution are:

Activity-Based HRD Phases

1. no HRD
2. one-person HRD
3. vendor-driven HRD (VD-HRD)
4. vendor-customized HRD (VC-HRD)

Results-Driven HRD Phases

1. operationally integrated HRD (OI-HRD)
2. strategically integrated HRD (SI-HRD)

The first four phases of the evolution of HRD are activity-based whereas the last two are results-driven, which will be addressed in Chapter 2.

One clue used in determining the current phase of HRD is the types of interventions being offered within your organization. According to Silber (1992), five types of interventions can be offered. These include isolated training, isolated performance, total training, total performance, and total cultural. Each adds value to the organization; however, their impact is drastically different. Within each phase, we will identify the most common location of each intervention.

Other clues in determining the current phase are

**Conscious and Unconscious Acts that Provide Evidence
of an Activity-Based HRD Philosophy**

- Failing to develop a philosophy of HRD dedicated to achieving organizational results
- Failing to adopt a strategic approach to improving organizational performance and development
- Failing to think strategically before responding to a client's request for training
- Failing to develop an understanding of an organization and its businesses
- Failing to design, develop, and implement an organizational effectiveness strategy
- Failing to develop a systems approach to organizational change and development
- Failing to develop performance management systems
- Failing to become strategic business partners within organizations
- Failing to link HRD interventions and initiatives to an organization's strategic business and performance needs
- Failing to adopt a customer service approach with internal stakeholders
- Failing to let managers develop their employees
- Failing to develop a management development partnership to improve organizational performance capacity and effectiveness
- Failing to encourage managers to use performance appraisals as a vehicle for providing their employees with meaningful, specific, and timely feedback
- Failing to help managers develop performance coaching skills
- Failing to implement organizational development partnerships that will transform organizational effectiveness
- Failing to make the transition from a transactional role (trainer) to a transformational role (for example, partnership, influencer, and leadership roles)
- Failing to identify organizational and performance needs
- Failing to use organizational and performance needs as the foundation of all HRD interventions and initiatives
- Failing to design and develop performance improvement and change interventions that maximize organizational performance
- Failing to create a learning acquisition strategy
- Failing to eliminate barriers to learning transfer
- Failing to implement transfer of learning strategies
- Failing to measure the impact of performance improvement and organizational results achieved through HRD

TABLE 1.1   Conscious and Unconscious Acts that Provide Evidence of an Activity-Based HRD Philosophy

- the type of organizational effectiveness strategy employed by HRD practitioners
- the type of performance partnerships developed
- the way the HRD program is organized
- the application and sophistication of HRD practice within the organization.

Each of these clues will be examined more closely as we discuss each phase of the evolution of HRD.

Phase 1: No HRD

In many organizations no HRD program or activities exist. Thus, little or no formal training is provided to employees. Several reasons explain this condition. Typically, this condition exists among small businesses and most retail operations (for example, franchise operations, restaurants, retail stores, and automotive dealerships) that cannot afford a formal HRD program. If training does occur, it is either accidental or provided on the job by a manager or coworker.

Sometimes HRD is not valued by management and therefore is not offered. Under these conditions, HRD is not viewed as a way of improving organizational performance or effectiveness. Consequently, there is no organizational effectiveness strategy, performance partnerships, or HRD practice to examine. Employees and managers are on their own to improve organizational performance and quality.

Phase 2: One-Person HRD

When organizations realize that training might help them improve their effectiveness and increase their competitiveness, the HRD program evolves to the next phase. This period is known as one-person HRD. When an HRD program begins to emerge, it becomes externally attached to the organization in order to sustain itself (see Figure 1.1). At this point, the HRD program is totally dependent on the organization in order to survive (for example, money, human resources, recognition, and approval).

During this period, HRD practitioners are jacks-of-all-trades. In other words, a single person is responsible for identifying and analyzing employees' needs; designing, developing, and implementing training programs; and evaluating their success (philosophy of HRD). Because each of these tasks is very complex, it is impossible for a single person to do them all well. There-

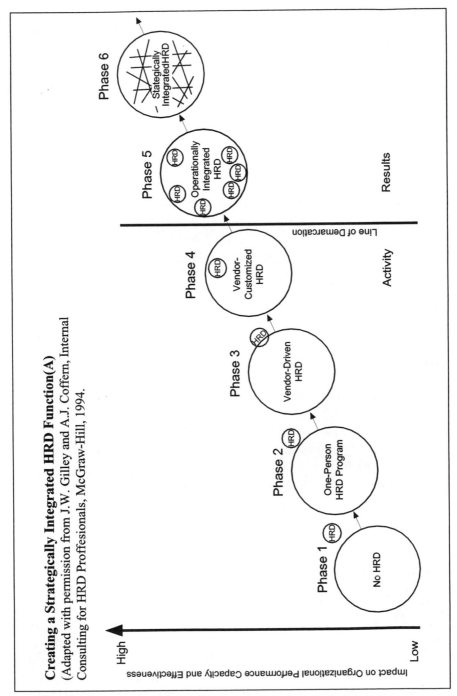

Creating a Strategically Integrated HRD Function(A)
(Adapted with permission from J.W. Gilley and A.J. Coffern, Internal Consulting for HRD Proffesionals, McGraw-Hill, 1994.

FIGURE 1.1   Creating a Strategically Integrated HRD Function (A)

fore, the effectiveness of HRD often suffers. One-person HRD programs are common in small- to medium-size organizations.

To further complicate things, many of the individuals responsible for HRD are neither professionally qualified nor passionate about their role as an HRD practitioner. In some cases, they fail to understand the true purpose of HRD. Many are former line managers, salespersons, customer service representatives, or office managers who have demonstrated they can work well with or train people. Such experience helps them understand the day-to-day operations of the organization, although it is inadequate preparation for improving organizational performance and effectiveness. Such a practice may harm the credibility of HRD, prevent its acceptance within the organization, or prevent it from evolving to the next phase.

Isolated Training.   In one-person HRD programs, the most common type of learning intervention is isolated training (Silber 1992). It is the simplest form of learning intervention and is used to fix an isolated performance problem such as time management, planning skills, scheduling skills, writing skills, and so on.

Strategy, Partnerships, HRD Practice, and Structure.   During this evolutionary phase, there is no definable organizational effectiveness strategy, nor are performance partnerships formed. In one-person HRD programs, practitioners are so busy trying to provide training that they have little time for any other activities. As you would imagine, the HRD practice is based on the experience of the HRD practitioner and is delivered informally, during meetings, or on the job.

Sometimes formal training sessions are conducted that are informational in nature. Because of limited focus, most training sessions are not useful in changing performance, improving quality, or enhancing organizational competitiveness. Patrick Combs, vice president of marketing for Waitt Radio in Omaha, Nebraska, said this phase of HRD is at best "a starting point for organizational improvement but fails to capture the energies of the organization or help develop people or the organization."

The HRD program is often housed as a part of a small human resource department generally staffed by one or more HR specialists. Since this is a one-person operation, the structure of the HRD department is simply defined by the placement of the person responsible. The HRD program is not taken very seriously nor is it considered an intricate part of the strategic focus of the organization. A full-time trainer is usually assigned to fulfill all the duties and responsibilities of the program while balancing other assignments.

Phase 3: Vendor-Driven HRD (VD-HRD)

As the HRD program grows stronger, it begins to penetrate the organization (Figure 1.1). Over time it develops a firm grip on the organization but is still perceived as outside the mainstream. The HRD program is still very weak and cannot sustain itself without organizational support. Management can easily eliminate the HRD program by cutting its budget, and often does. If the HRD program survives this period, it often completely penetrates the organization and becomes a full-fledged department within the firm. During this evolutionary phase training for training's sake is an HRD practitioner's philosophy.

We call this phase vendor-driven HRD because most HRD practitioners believe that their primary responsibility is to identify, evaluate, and select training programs from a myriad of outside training houses. HRD practitioners who operate in such a manner are brokers of training programs. Furthermore, most HRD practitioners do not have the time to design and develop the training programs that they need because the HRD program is still relatively small and they lack the necessary expertise to do so. Therefore, they select training programs from a variety of training vendors (such as Wilson Learning, DDI, AchieveGlobal) that offer complete and comprehensive programs.

Tremendous training activity is characteristic of VD-HRD, although organizational performance seldom improves. In VD-HRD programs, little attention is paid to why employees participate in training as long as they attend some training class each year. Moreover, training is sometimes viewed as a reward for a job well done, which reinforces the "activity philosophy" of HRD.

Vendor-driven HRD programs have healthy budgets and practitioners who are busy selecting and delivering training programs. They are one of management's favorite forms of HRD owing to its ease of administration and management. Through its activity, the HRD program often provides isolated value to the organization, thus enabling HRD to become more important.

Consequently, the VD-HRD program picks up important sponsors and advocates who help improve its image within the organization. This is a highly critical time for the HRD program. Its budget can still be eliminated because it has yet to become an essential tool used to improve organization performance and effectiveness. Unfortunately, the HRD program is still not viewed by senior management as a critical partner in helping them achieve organizational business goals and objectives.

Fortunately, VD-HRD practitioners ask a more sophisticated and critical question than practitioners in one-person HRD programs, which is "What skills or knowledge are preventing optimal performance?" However, HRD practitioners have not yet addressed the most important question, which is "How can HRD help the organization accomplish its strategic business goals and objectives?" Vendor-driven HRD is, however, a move along the continuum in the right direction.

Unfortunately, many HRD practitioners believe that training programs provided by vendors are better than the ones designed internally, and since their job is to provide as much training as possible it appears to be the most efficient way of achieving this goal. We however, believe that this clearinghouse approach is primarily what is wrong with the HRD profession because it allows training activity to become the focus of HRD, which produces long-term damage to the image and credibility of HRD.

Isolated Performance.   Common during this evolutionary phase of HRD is a more sophisticated type of intervention known as isolated performance. This type of training requires minor environmental redesign, incentive and motivation system changes, and job aids to fix isolated performance problems (Silber 1992). The effects of most isolated performance interventions are short-lived because the system has not really changed enough for real performance improvement to occur. Examples of isolated performance interventions include training in supervisory skills, time management, meeting management, and interpersonal skills. These are most common during the vendor-driven HRD phase.

Strategy, Partnerships, HRD Practice, and Structure.   During this phase, an HRD practitioner's organizational effectiveness strategy is isolated to improve individual employee performance. Little attention is given to how training enhances organizational performance, competitiveness, or efficiency. In other words, vendor-driven HRD is focused on improving employees' skills and knowledge in hopes that such development can and will help maximize organizational effectiveness and performance.

During this phase, VD-HRD practitioners are beginning to develop performance partnerships. These occur because HRD practitioners are providing as much training to as many departments and divisions as possible. As a result, VD-HRD practitioners are becoming more customer oriented. Natural outcomes of this approach include better customer relationships and improved organizational awareness of HRD, its interventions, and services. It is important to understand that developing formal performance partnerships is not a VD-HRD practitioner's primary objective but a natural by-product of increasing training activity.

HRD practice becomes more formalized during this phase. Vendor-driven HRD practitioners are conducting more needs assessment activities designed to uncover skills and knowledge deficits as well as identifying areas of training interest. Needs assessment activities are still not seen as a way of developing performance partnerships or as a way of providing direction for the HRD program. They are viewed merely as ways of identifying the next series of training activities that organizational leaders perceive to be of value.

Providing formal training activities is the only objective of VD-HRD programs. Naturally, this becomes the principal focus of HRD practice. In order to keep up with ever-increasing training demand, organizations begin to hire more and more trainers whose primary job responsibility is to provide training. During this phase, HRD practitioners are making little if any effort to ensure that employees are transferring learning to the job. In fact, managers and executives often refer to training as "something that those trainers do" and do not see employee development as their responsibility. This attitude becomes the Achilles' heel of VD-HRD programs. Finally, identifying employees' reactions to training is the only type of formal evaluation being conducted during this phase.

During the VD-HRD phase, the HRD program begins to separate itself from the HR department and to establish its own structure. Sometimes the HRD program remains in the HR department but is a separate operating unit with a coordinator (broker of training) and a few full- and part-time trainers assigned. As we said previously, the program is only loosely attached to the organization (Figure 1.1) and can be eliminated at any time. It is, however, emerging and beginning to be recognized as a potential source for improving employees' knowledge and skills.

Phase 4: Vendor-Customized HRD (VC-HRD)

The next evolutionary phase of HRD is similar to the vendor-driven phase. The principal difference is that HRD practitioners are customizing training programs to align with the organization's environment and culture (Gilley and Coffern 1994). Formal instructional design activities emerge during this phase. Consequently, HRD practitioners become responsible for redesigning and redeveloping training programs as a way of customizing them to fit the organization. This evolutionary phase is vendor-customized HRD.

Again, HRD practitioners are asking more sophisticated questions in their effort to address the critical issues facing the organization, the most essential of which is "How can training become more organizationally focused?" The answer to this question motivates VC-HRD practitioners to customize vendors' programs so that they complement and match their organizational culture. Gloria Regalbuto, former president of SeaFirst University, a division of SeaFirst Bank in Seattle, said, "HRD programs which are in the vendor-customized HRD phase are beginning to examine the critical issues facing the organization. Once determined, HRD practitioners can begin customizing training programs in order for them to become organizationally focused."

The philosophy of HRD is the same during the vendor-customized phase as it was in the previous phase (VD-HRD), except that the "training house" approach is brought inside the organization. This slight philosophical shift allows the instructional design role of HRD to become paramount. HRD practitioners begin spending a majority of their time as instructional designers rather than taking the opportunity to help executives change the organization or improve its performance.

During this phase of evolution, the HRD program has developed to full departmental status within the organization. The VC-HRD program has a comprehensive and complete budget, a mission statement describing its purpose, a manager responsible for overseeing its internal affairs and providing direction within the organization, a complete staff including trainers and institutional designers, and a formal reporting relationship and position on the organizational chart. In other words, the HRD program has finally arrived and is considered a viable and productive department within the organization.

Total Training.   Total training requires HRD practitioners to take a broader view of performance problems. Rather than looking at a single skill to be changed, the performance problem is addressed holistically. Consequently, employees may attend training programs that address a set of skills that contribute to their performance. Isolated training programs address sets of skills including time management, planning, scheduling, and writing. Total training blends each of these skill areas into a single performance activity. For example, managing projects requires employees to develop time management, planning, scheduling, and writing skills. Therefore, employees receive total training in project management instead of attending four separate training programs that on the surface may appear to be unrelated. However, "total training is limited in the solution set it considers: it is still only using training as a vehicle for change" (Silber 1992).

Total training is common during the early part of the VC-HRD phase because HRD practitioners recognize potential to improve the organization; however, they often fail to focus on transfer of learning, and managers often fail to properly conduct performance appraisals and provide feedback. Learning, then, is rarely applied to the job. Consequently, the total training approach seldom improves organizational performance. The primary limitation to this approach is the heavy reliance on comprehensive training activity as the solution to complex performance problems. Employees return from training and most likely fail in integrating what they have learned on the job because the organizational system has not been altered to support the new learning.

Strategy, Partnerships, HRD Practice, and Structure. As VC-HRD practitioners begin providing more and more total training activities, their organizational effectiveness strategy matures. The strategy becomes more performance focused and begins to incorporate organizational issues such as culture, work climate, structure, mission and strategy, leadership, policies and procedures, and management practices. The process of customizing training programs also focuses VC-HRD practitioners on these issues. Consequently, they begin to develop an awareness of both the organizational system and the performance management system approaches that enhance performance and organizational development (see Chapters 8 and 9). Such knowledge will be important if the program is to evolve to the results-driven phases of HRD.

Because VC-HRD practitioners are required to customize training programs to fit the organization, they must further develop relationships with their internal clients. These relationships are more formalized than in the previous phase because clients are expected to help HRD practitioners customize training programs.

It could be said that the most important part of the VC-HRD phase is that practitioners are being forced outside of their isolated departments and required to work directly with the people they are trying to serve. Because of this opportunity, VC-HRD practitioners develop an understanding of the organization and its business. Over time, interaction with clients help them understand that their real purpose is to help the organization achieve its business goals and objectives through a variety of performance improvement interventions and change initiatives.

One of the biggest changes in HRD practice occurs during this evolutionary phase as practitioners become instructional designers responsible for customizing training programs. Organizations such as Motorola, Waste Management, and AT&T employ entire departments of instructional designers. Such a shift is critical to the future evolution of HRD because designing performance improvement interventions and change initiatives will be essential to maximizing organizational performance and will continue to be a useful service during the next two evolutionary phases.

Unfortunately, training activity remains the central focus of VC-HRD programs. As such, training conducted by full-time trainers continues to be viewed as an important activity. During this phase, managers and supervisors are rarely used to provide training. The HRD manager's role emerges as critical here because increasing training activity drives increases in the HRD budget, which becomes one of the most important battles fought during the VC-HRD phase and the HRD manager's primary responsibility.

Another major evolutionary change involves the structure of HRD programs. During the VC-HRD phase, HRD programs are separate operating departments with a complete staff and budget. Departmental players include an HRD manager, trainers, instructional designers, and one or two quasi-internal consultants—generally senior trainers responsible for client relationships or needs analysis activities. Typically, HRD departments are centralized in the organization's head office or headquarters as a way of improving "training coordination and design and development activities" (Gilley and Coffern 1994). In many organizations, VC-HRD programs are separate from the HR departments but generally report to the same person within the organization (such as the vice president or the director of human resources).

The ever-increasing complexity of organizations requires HRD practitioners to continuously examine their roles, responsibilities, and activities. Such analysis helps determine which roles have the greatest influence and impact on achieving the organization's strategic business goals and objectives. Additionally, it helps HRD practitioners to establish a plan of action for enhancing their credibility within their organization.

Conclusion

Activity-based HRD programs are commonly found in three of the first four phases of the evolution of HRD. It could be argued that such programs have failed to improve the effectiveness, efficiency, and competitiveness of most of today's organizations. Moreover, the nature of the worldwide business environment is forcing organizations to look for new solutions to old problems. As a result, the centralized and slow-moving activity-based HRD program is being replaced by a streamlined, efficient, fast-moving, and effective HRD function designed to improve organizational performance and effectiveness—one that is results-driven, relying on a new type of HRD practitioner. This type of organization is the subject of the last two phases of the evolution of HRD, which will be addressed in Chapter 2.

Results–Driven HRD

The first four phases of the evolution of HRD are based on an activity-based philosophy (see Figure 2.1). As a result, HRD practitioners operate as though training by itself improves organizational performance and effectiveness. Little thought is given to training's impact or achievement of the organization's strategic business goals. The last two phases in the evolution of HRD are based on a results-driven philosophy, which include operationally integrated HRD and strategically integrated HRD.

Crossing the Line of Demarcation

Moving from vendor-customized HRD toward strategically integrated HRD is the most difficult part of the evolution process. In order to evolve to the highest level, HRD professionals must begin to think strategically about how HRD interventions can and will positively impact the organization. They must determine which interventions add value to the organization and which do not, always striving to improve organizational performance in everything they do. HRD professionals must understand that organizational decisionmakers are not interested in "training" but in what training can do for them. Such an understanding forces HRD professionals to change their practice. They should be cautious. It is easy to generate a lot of training activity and claim that it makes a difference; it is much harder to identify the organizational results needed and determine whether they have been accomplished. When HRD professionals begin providing interventions that help the organization accomplish its strategic business goals, then HRD has crossed over the line of demarcation from the activity zone into the results-driven zone.

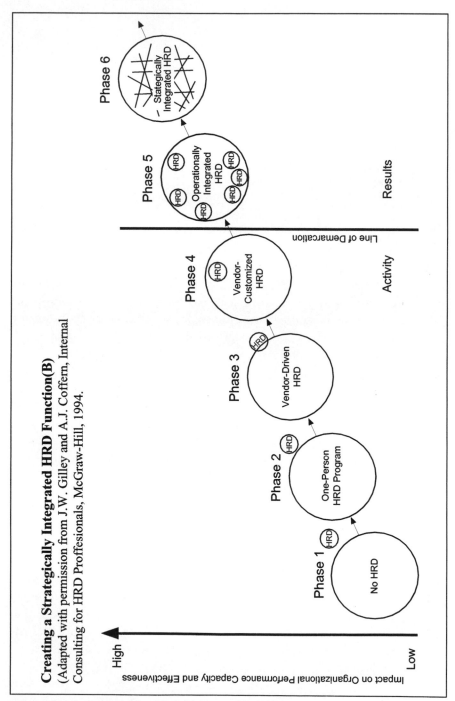

FIGURE 2.1   Creating a Strategically Integrated HRD Function (B)

Two Phases of Results-Driven HRD

The remaining two phases in the evolution of HRD are both results-driven: operationally integrated HRD and strategically integrated HRD.

Phase 5: Operationally Integrated HRD (OI-HRD)

As HRD professionals customize their training programs, they direct their attention toward a critical question, one that changes the entire focus of HRD. This question, when asked and answered, demonstrates that the HRD program has moved into the next evolutionary phase of HRD. The question is "How can HRD maximize organizational performance and improve the effectiveness of the organization?" In other words, how HRD can make a difference in the organization becomes an HRD professional's overriding passion, the philosophy of HRD, during this phase. This important question forces you to consider the issue of employee performance improvement and its impact on the organization; it helps you move from an activity-driven to a results-driven HRD approach.

In order to evolve into the operationally integrated phase, you will have to make an important strategic decision. To move forward, you must have the courage to make some fundamental changes, to question the organizational mission and its impact on the firm, and to abandon the traditional approach of HRD. You must be willing to be integrated into an operational department and focus on helping it improve its performance, efficiency, and quality, thus allowing HRD to become strategically placed throughout the organization rather than centrally located. Then several smaller operationally focused HRD units will be in place.

Operationally integrated HRD requires a much different HRD effort. Gone are the days of delivering training as an activity and relying on employees' reactions to training to validate the value and importance of HRD to the organization. Gone are the days of HRD practitioners with little operational experience. In their place is an HRD program with operationally proficient professionals focused on improving organizational performance and effectiveness through learning, performance management, and change.

During this period, performance measurement becomes a strategic weapon used to help determine whether HRD interventions improve employee performance and have a positive impact on organizational effectiveness. Interventions that produce the desired results are continued whereas others are not. HRD professionals are also building collaborative relationships with management to help improve learning transfer and on-the-job performance. Such relationships make it easier for management to share critical information about the organization, including changes in management, new product developments, modifications in the compensation and incentive system, and strategic decisions affecting the direction of the organization. This type of information exchange is essential for improving organizational performance and effectiveness.

Total Performance.   When you use total performance interventions, all aspects of a performance problem are examined before arriving at a solution (Silber 1992). Issues under consideration include the compensation and rewards system, managers' and supervisors' skills and techniques, barriers to performance improvement, transfer of learning issues, environment and work design, motivations and feedback systems, organizational structure and design, and job processes. These types of factors are examined to determine the exact cause of the performance breakdown. A systematic approach enables the design and implementation of a more comprehensive and complete performance intervention.

With total performance interventions, you examine the cost effectiveness and return on investment for the solutions implemented. In other words, the evaluation process is no longer simply an employee's reaction to training but is used to determine whether HRD is adding value to the organization, and if so, where and how much.

Total performance interventions, by their very nature, are results-driven, and are most commonly found during the last two phases of HRD. In fact, this type of intervention separates activity-based HRD programs from results-driven ones.

Burning the Mothership: An Operational Reality.   During the early stages of an operationally integrated HRD program it may be necessary to maintain a small group of HRD professionals who are responsible for instructional design, training managers as trainers, and coordinating organizationwide projects. Traditional training activities may even continue as you make the transition from trainers to transformational professionals and as managers begin to shoulder more and more training responsibility. As you make the successful transition into other operational units, the centralized HRD department disappears as it is reduced to a support unit responsible for intervention design and development.

Willingness to leave the mothership and venture into uncharted lands enables HRD programs to become results-driven. Much like Cortez, the Spanish explorer, you must burn the mothership (centralized HRD department) and venture into uncharted lands in search of better ways of helping organizations improve their effectiveness and performance capacity. This requires you to be permanently assigned to business units and to become responsible for improving their productivity and performance. In other words, you become members of an operational group rather than part of a centralized HRD department. A departure of this sort proves quite difficult because you must become accountable for results, no longer able to hide behind an avalanche of training activity.

Effective HRD professionals are willing to embrace rapid change by becoming part of their organizations' operational units, rather than retreating to the safety of their centralized department (the mothership). Finally, you may have a difficult time achieving your new operational mission when the old centralized HRD department still exists. This is because their philosophies are polar opposites.

Centralized HRD adheres to the training for training's sake philosophy so common in activity-based programs, whereas OI-HRD's philosophy is one of improving results at the operational level.

When operationally integrated and centralized HRD programs coexist, their two completely incompatible philosophies are in a constant struggle for control. This creates a psychotic atmosphere within the organization resulting in confusion and frustration on the part of decisionmakers. Consequently, you must choose. Either return to the mothership and sail back across the line of demarcation to produce training activity or go forward and help the organization achieve its strategic business goals by applying an organizational effectiveness strategy, creating and implementing performance partnerships, and unleashing HRD practice at the operations level.

The movement from a centralized department to an operationally integrated unit requires a shift in thinking. Accordingly, you need to think like your clients instead of like an HRD practitioner. As a businessperson, you must understand the revenue and cost implications of recommendations, and filter suggestions through the prism of practical reality and operational priorities. Also, you need to think strategically about the long-term implications of change prior to implementing interventions. In short, you must become a strategic business partner. For some, the transition is easy because they have always operated from this perspective or were part of an operational group prior to joining HRD. For others, the journey is a road less traveled, full of uncertainty and insecurity. As always, you must establish credibility by demonstrating professional competence, integrity, and sincerity.

Organizational Effectiveness Strategy. During the OI-HRD phase, your organizational effectiveness strategy involves serving as an organizational architect (see Chapter 6) and maximizing organizational performance through performance management systems (see Chapter 8) rather than improving individual employee skills and knowledge through training. Although this approach embraces most of the transformational responsibilities (organizational development occurs during phase six—strategically integrated HRD—when you are able to serve in a professional or leadership capacity responsible for organizational enhancement [see Chapters 6–10]). Better business results and organizational performance are achieved under OI-HRD than within the activity strategy–based VC-HRD and VD-HRD programs. Consequently, improving organizational performance capacity through such systems and activities is the preferred strategy.

Performance Partnerships. Although performance partnerships emerged during the last phase, they now become formal alliances. Operationally integrated HRD programs require working relationships with business units. In fact, the operationally integrated HRD approach cannot succeed unless performance partnerships are formed and are functioning effectively.

During this evolutionary phase, you accept the transformational roles of relationship builder (see Chapter 5) to foster partnerships within your operational unit. Creating long-lasting partnerships is important during this phase because they help you develop the relationships needed to improve organizational performance.

HRD Practice. During this phase, you begin to relinquish your training responsibility to managers and supervisors who are ultimately responsible for improving employee performance and organizational productivity. By doing so, organizations allow the only organizational players accountable for performance appraisal and employee development to become the champions of HRD, rather than its gatekeepers.

HRD practice makes a serious shift during this phase, which allows for the birth of the performance engineer (see Chapter 8). As a performance engineer, you are responsible for implementing performance management systems that maximize organizational performance. This includes improving work design, motivation and feedback systems, management action, environmental conditions, resource allocation, and compensation and reward systems. Accordingly, you are responsible for helping managers make the transition to performance coaching and for implementing performance appraisals that bring about lasting change.

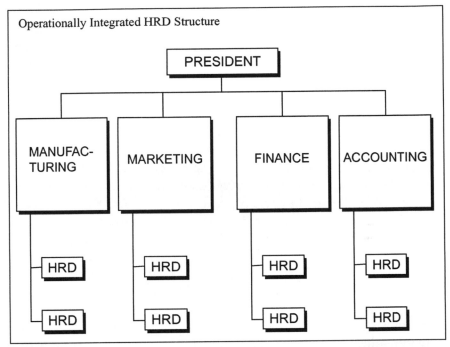

FIGURE 2.2   Operationally Integrated HRD Structure

HRD interventions also begin to change during this phase. Instead of simply designing performance improvement programs as a way of improving employees' skills and knowledge, you begin to develop interventions focused on improving the performance capacity and effectiveness of organizations. Although these interventions are more common during phase six, they become more familiar during the operationally integrated phase.

HRD Structure.   During this phase the walls of the HRD program begin to come down. You realize that, to be effective, HRD must be integrated into the organization. As a result, operationally integrated HRD programs are often assigned to operational units within the organization (Figure 2.2). You are now held accountable for improving the results of the operational units rather than generating organizationwide activity.

Professional identity during the OI-HRD phase begins to change. You are no longer a trainer type but are a full-fledged operational partner responsible for performance management within an operational unit. Reporting relationships also change since you are not a member of a centralized HRD department. Consequently, you report to the vice president or director of the unit. Finally, you work cooperatively across operational units to maximize organizational performance (see relationship mapping, Chapter 6). Accordingly, the hierarchy that existed during previous phases has been replaced by a collaborative team approach. Such an approach is project based and requires the creation of shared partnerships with others (see Chapter 9).

During the OI-HRD phase, the centralized HRD budget shifts to the operational unit where the HRD program is now housed. This helps the organization and HRD in two ways. First, operationally integrated HRD programs demonstrate their ability to help their units accomplish business objectives since they no longer hide among myriad activities commonly found in centralized HRD departments. You become an operational partner within the units, and therefore produce results. Second, organizations are compelled to view HRD as an investment rather than as a cost. For example, operational budgets are established to produce results that managers are held accountable for achieving. Staff budgets—those used to support non-revenue-producing units such as public relations, human resources, and HRD—are established to provide services for the organization. Traditionally, managers of these departments were held accountable for producing service activity, not organizational results. Thus, HRD was viewed as a cost to the organization (to provide activity) rather than as an investment (to produce results). Decentralizing HRD and shifting its budget to the operational level makes HRD programs accountable for producing results; thus, they will be viewed in the same way as other operational units.

Phase 6: Strategically Integrated HRD (SI-HRD)

The future of many organizations depends on developing a human resource strategy that enables them to remain competitive in a global economy. Therefore, organizations are in search of new ways to develop human resources. To accomplish this, organizations must be willing to adopt an innovative approach to HRD practice, one that allows HRD to be within the mainstream of the organization and enables HRD professionals to enhance organizational performance and effectiveness. In other words, HRD programs must become strategically integrated into every aspect of the organization, which is the second results-oriented phase of HRD.

HRD programs must be the responsibility of every manager, supervisor, executive, and employee. Quite simply, an HRD program cannot be a department, it must be a philosophy of operation that is the cornerstone of organizational transformation and development.

Strategically integrated HRD is a results-driven philosophy that describes what HRD professionals believe to be true about the field of HRD. It defines

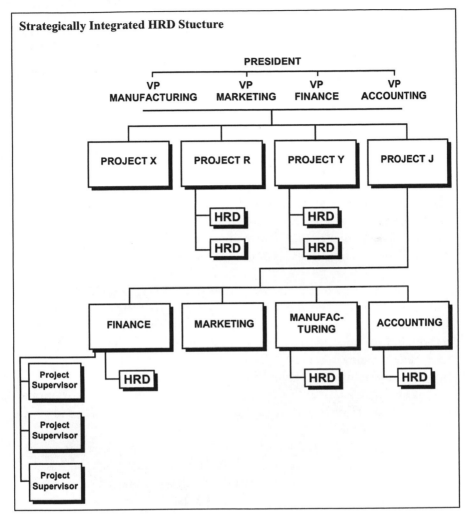

FIGURE 2.3   Strategically Integrated HRD Structure

their fundamental beliefs about HRD and helps them conceptualize and translate practice into action. Strategically integrated HRD embodies a system of values and guiding principles by which HRD professionals operate—a set of operational guidelines used in improving organizational effectiveness. In short, strategically integrated HRD epitomizes one's basic theory or viewpoint of HRD.

HRD Structure.   When HRD programs begin to be blended into the fabric of the organization they are becoming strategically integrated. HRD is no longer an individual department but a function within the firm containing several crossover points (Figure 2.1). You must now work collaboratively with management at all levels to improve organizational performance. When this happens, the final phase of the evolution of HRD has begun.

Because SI-HRD programs blend into the fabric of the organization, some believe there is no structural framework. Consequently, they assert that HRD does not really exist any more since a departmental structure cannot be found. To the contrary, SI-HRD programs are organized much like management consulting and professional service firms, which become an integral part of an organization during major organizational development projects. During these projects, senior management consultants reside within an organization, working alongside executives and managers, analyzing organizational and performance needs, providing recommendations, selecting and implementing change interventions, and evaluating the impact of change (Figure 2.3).

When such a structure is in place, strategically integrated HRD programs operate on a project-by-project basis, assigning you to one or more projects at a time. This operational approach challenges you with three development responsibilities: building performance partnerships throughout the organization while bringing about organizational change, enhancing business operations by improving the organizational performance management systems, and as an organizational leader responsible for facilitating organizational change, which improves the organization's performance capacity and effectiveness (see Chapter 9).

It is no longer enough for HRD programs to improve performance, they must also improve the overall effectiveness of their organization. In other words, HRD must help the organization achieve its strategic business goals. Therefore, you must create interventions that help the organization change. This shift requires you to change your philosophy to one dedicated to improving organizational effectiveness, rather than remaining the deliverers of training events. In short, you must become results-driven.

Total Cultural. Total cultural interventions incorporate an examination of problems and solutions in a context that addresses the organization's values and corporate culture (Silber 1992). During this intervention, use techniques that determine the influence of organizational policies, procedures, and culture that may impede performance and prevent the implementation of organizational change. This type of intervention can have the most positive impact on organizational performance and effectiveness. Only HRD programs that have created HRD/business partnerships can successfully implement total cultural interventions; this type of partnership is only found during the last evolutionary phase.

Organizational Effectiveness Strategy.   Strategically integrated HRD programs are no longer merely training houses within organizations. Instead, they help organizations manage change and improve their competitiveness. Several core strategies are commonly used during this phase, including:

- Establishing a developmental culture: Helping senior management embrace the importance and value of a developmental culture, which enhances organizational performance and effectiveness.
- Assessing organizational effectiveness: Helping clients determine what their needs are and which services will have the highest organizational impact (see Chapter 9).
- Implementing performance management systems: Helping clients improve performance through the use of appropriate development and feedback strategies linked to the compensation and rewards systems. This includes identifying competency maps for all job classifications, performance standards, and evaluation methods that enhance employee and organizational performance (see Chapter 8).
- Setting strategic direction: Helping business units set long-range strategic goals and develop tactical plans in support of those goals (see Chapters 7 and 9).
- Leadership development: Helping clients ensure that current leaders have appropriate performance coaching skills to produce organizational results (see Chapters 8–10).
- Managing change: Helping clients develop effective strategic plans for implementing change and understanding the human implications of change (see Chapter 9).

Another characteristic of this period is the movement from improving employee performance to improving organizational performance and effectiveness. This shift appears subtle, although HRD interventions are now targeted at improving overall performance problems rather than fixing isolated ones. Discussions about installing performance management systems are now commonplace events with senior management.

Performance Partnerships.   Bellman (1998, 39) suggests that partnerships are essential to the success of any organization. He believes that a partner is a person who takes part with others, and partnerships involve the parts we each play in our work. We believe that a partnership is a mutually beneficial relationship created to help the organization better achieve its goals and objectives. These intraorganizational alliances are formed to ensure successful completion of the organization's overall strategic plan. They are mutually beneficial and long-term oriented in their quest to help an organization succeed.

Bellman (1998) asserts that the two primary elements of partnerships are purpose and partnering. No partnership exists without a purpose, which brings you and your stakeholders together. Purpose can be both explicit or implicit. The former is quite clear and typically imposed by a client. The latter results due to a mutual exploration of a purpose about to be defined. Partnering occurs when you and your stakeholders pursue a common purpose together. By examining the visible and invisible dynamics between you, stakeholders, and purpose, you can better clarify roles and purpose. Additionally, partnering helps you surface underlying assumptions, trust and risk, shared values, and expectations. Bellman (1998) suggests that much that is key to partnering often goes unexpressed, and some may not be rational.

Demonstrating your willingness to create partnerships involves developing a responsive, customer service orientation that better surfaces, anticipates, and articulates stakeholder needs. The principal benefit for stakeholders is need satisfaction (for example, improved performance), and you enjoy increased credibility within the organization.

We believe that creating partnerships is one of the most important activities in which you may engage. Partnerships are long-term oriented and interdependent, allowing for better understanding and anticipation of your clients' needs. These partnerships help you develop a responsive attitude, which is necessary to improve your customer service orientation.

As a partner, you break down the walls between yourself and your stakeholders. Partnerships give you the opportunity to develop personal relationships with stakeholders. Alliances allow you and your stakeholders to create trust and develop a shared vision of the future through a free exchange of ideas, information, and perceptions. According to Wilson (1987), partnerships also promote establishment of working relationships based on shared values, aligned purpose and vision, and mutual support. As a result, lasting commitments are forged and investments are made in learning, performance, and change efforts (see Chapter 3). Partnerships encourage you to fully understand your clients' contributions and the values they bring to an interaction. Consequently, you become immersed with your stakeholders' performance problems, needs, concerns, and expectations.

Bellman (1998, 41) believes that the client's role may entail

- products and outcomes
- accountability for results
- clarity of vision and values
- managing resources (time, energy, money, human talent, materials, equipment, environment); creating structure and systems
- strategic decisionmaking.

Your role exudes competence combined with adaptability in its focus on stakeholder needs. This role encompasses "clarity regarding one's contributions, awareness of the organization's needs, developing alternatives, revealing new perspectives, modeling risk-taking, and knowledge of the consulting process-all while honoring one's personal purpose, vision, values, and core beliefs" (Gilley and Maycunich 2000a, 93).

Partnerships may form at three levels. First, you must be willing to become a strategic business partner with stakeholders from different business units, divisions, and departments to provide them with better service. Partnerships require you to become responsible for providing customer service, help clients make performance improvement and organizational development decisions, and identify demands facing clients along with potential responses.

Second, management development partnerships improve organizational performance. Alliances with managers and supervisors develop their performance coaching skills and managerial expertise. In this way, managers and supervisors become responsible for the lion's share of training and mentoring for their employees, which enables you to focus on developing transformational roles in the organization (see Chapters 5–10). This type of partnership is referred to as a micro approach, where performance improvement occurs one manager and one employee at a time.

A final type of partnership, known as the macro approach, occurs when you focus your attention on improving organizational effectiveness by altering the organizational and performance management systems (see Chapters 6 and 8). This type of partnership with organizational leaders and decision-makers includes engaging in strategic planning activities and organizational development initiatives (see Chapters 7 and 9) that directly maximize organizational performance.

Unleashing HRD Practice.   Results-driven professionals adopt a new approach to maximizing organizational performance—one that addresses the real problems of an organization and enables it to achieve needed results. HRD professionals need to develop an approach that helps them connect performance improvement and change interventions to the organization's strategic business goals. Such an approach focuses on learning transfer strategies rather than on training activity. In short, you must redesign the performance improvement and organizational change process in order to develop a strategically integrated HRD program. The process consists of four phases:

- identifying organizational and performance needs
- designing and developing performance improvement and change interventions
- facilitating learning acquisition and learning transfer
- measuring performance improvement and organizational results.

Identifying Organizational and Performance Needs

The first step in the needs analysis process involves clearly identifying opportunities for performance improvement and organizational development. This requires you to examine, analyze, and evaluate possible sources of opportunity. Managers' and supervisors' expectations regarding employee performance can help you identify organizational and performance needs. The strategic direction of the organization also identifies critical organizational and performance needs. Customers who use the organization's products and services may provide feedback about their quality, performance, and effectiveness, further helping identify organizational and performance needs.

Designing and Developing Performance Improvement and Change Interventions

HRD professionals concerned with identifying learning objectives; choosing, arranging, and sequencing learning objectives; designing or selecting learning activities; writing participant manuals; selecting the location for learning to take place; identifying the target audience; and getting managers and supervisors involved are engaged in the design and development process. It is the foundation of all performance improvement and change interventions.

Facilitating Learning Acquisition and Transfer

During the performance improvement process, HRD professionals and managers do several things to ensure that employees acquire and retain learning. These include managing learning activities, providing feedback to participants during learning activities, monitoring learning acquisition, and providing a supportive and positive learning environment. Each of these is essential in producing learning that brings about skill development, increased knowledge, and changed attitudes.

You can foster learning acquisition and transfer by providing practice opportunities both during and after training. In addition, you can design peer coaching materials to reinforce on-the-job application and integration. Providing individualized feedback, job performance aids, realistic work-related tasks, opportunities for support groups, follow-up support, timely feedback, and problem-solving sessions are other ways to enhance learning acquisition and learning transfer.

Before learning can be translated into value for an organization, it must be applied to the job. Therefore, no other step in the performance improvement and change process is more important than this one. Unfortunately, too many learners are on their own immediately after a training event, struggling to integrate new skills or knowledge on the job. Confused and frustrated, employees often fail to confidently and accurately transfer learned principles to their work. Consequently, much of what is learned during training is lost, never to be applied or used.

Measuring Performance Improvement and Organizational Results

The outcomes of the performance improvement process are ultimately assessed through evaluation. The most common forms of performance evaluation are formative and summative. Formative evaluation provides feedback for program improvement and facilitates choosing among possible modifications. It should be used as the basis for constructively modifying the HRD effort in the future, not simply as a basis for keeping it alive or alternatively completing the process. Summative evaluation, on the other hand, assesses the overall outcomes of the performance improvement process and leads to a decision to continue or terminate the process.

One of the reasons HRD professionals do not conduct impact evaluations of their programs is that they do not know how. Although they are experts at designing, developing, and implementing training, when it comes to evaluating the results of training many HRD professionals are lost. They do not know the strategic and diagnostic questions to ask when evaluating results from training. This lack of knowledge prevents the discovery of training outcomes. Therefore, they cannot with any degree of certainty defend HRD's contribution to organizational improvement.

Impact evaluations are very difficult to perform, because they do not provide immediate feedback regarding the effects of training. Therefore, HRD professionals put them off or never get around to conducting them. In other words, they are not a priority of most HRD professionals.

One of the questions that perplexes HRD professionals about impact evaluations is "When is the proper time to evaluate the impact or return on investment (ROI) of training—is it an activity to be conducted several months after training, as part of front-end analysis, or both?" The answer to this question gives HRD professionals direction when using impact evaluations.

Overcoming the Fear of Letting Go

During this phase of evolution, HRD programs seemingly disappear altogether. For some HRD professionals this is an unsettling time, as they believe they have been stripped of their organizational identity and influence. This is not true; in fact, their influence is at its zenith for two reasons. First, organizational transformation is an everyday reality, and for the first time in the history of the firm, human resource development is everyone's responsibility. Only under these circumstances can organizations maximize their performance or implement lasting change. Second, people support what they create. In other words, when executives, managers, supervisors, and employees accept that human resource development is part of their everyday responsibilities, they will support learning and change as a naturally occurring event, rather than resisting it. Gone are the days of trying to convince the organization of the importance and value of HRD interventions. Gone are the days of struggling to implement organizational change and learning transfer. As a result, you become a facilitator of learning and change by executing an organizational effectiveness strategy, creating performance partnerships, and unleashing HRD practice.

SI-HRD: Theory or Practice?

Some may argue that the strategically integrated HRD phase is merely a theory and cannot become a reality. They ask for real examples of its existence and application. Like every evolutionary process, it is difficult to determine exactly where one is at any period in time. It is only when an evolutionary phase has been completed that we can provide definitive evidence that we passed through it.

In the case of the vendor-driven or vendor-customized phases of HRD, we can provide evidence of their existence. These periods are real transformation phases in the life of HRD and are important steps toward a more progressive, responsive, and responsible HRD program. We can even provide real evidence that supports the existence of IO-HRD programs (Kellogg Corporation, Foremost Insurance, Principal Financial, Pioneer Hi-Bred Incorporated). However, the evidence to support the existence of strategically integrated HRD is found only in small bits and pieces within many organizations. Such evidence can be uncovered when organizations like Steelcase, Mercer Human Resource Consulting, Interstate Engineering, Kaiser Permanente, Henry Ford Medical Group, and Sonic Software embrace the principles and techniques of SI-HRD and reorganize their operations accordingly. Another example of SI-HRD is the formation of organizational development "SWAT teams" responsible for the continuous improvement of the organization. In fact, most experimental HRD activities are attempts to develop better ways of helping the organization achieve its goals. Many are consistent with the principles and techniques outlined in this book, but are not commonly referred to as strategically integrated HRD approaches. These examples, though, are evidence of the emerging existence of SI-HRD.

Thousands of HRD professionals in every type of organization are making an effort to change from activity-oriented to results-driven HRD. To do so, they must first evolve through phases four and five on their way to phase six, since it is virtually impossible to skip a phase. An evolutionary process implies a slow, continuous progression. Therefore, HRD programs must progress through every evolutionary phase, though the amount of time spent on any one phase differs from organization to organization. Unfortunately, some HRD programs never progress beyond vendor-driven HRD and the organization suffers accordingly.

The real growth and development of any person or organization is in the journey toward a "perceived end." In other words, learning is a process of becoming and therein lies its benefit. We realize that the strategically integrated phase is not the absolute final evolutionary phase of HRD. Once this phase has been closely achieved another, yet unknown, phase will emerge. This is the exciting part of being in a dynamic and ever-changing field.

Barriers to Strategically Integrated HRD

One of the most difficult questions to answer about the evolution of HRD is "Why do HRD professionals have such a difficult time embracing the obvious advantages of strategically integrated HRD?" HRD professionals resist for several reasons. First, organizations place extreme pressure on HRD professionals to solve performance problems. As a consequence, they react by providing a simple solution (training) to a set of complex problems. In some rare cases, training is the answer and HRD professionals are rewarded for their immediate and responsive behavior. Thus, they are convinced that training is the answer to all performance problems.

Second, many HRD professionals have a difficult time saying "no" to management when a training solution is requested. Many find it hard to question the authority and wisdom of management and give in to management's demands for training. It requires courage to suggest another alternative—courage that many HRD practitioners lack.

Third, some HRD professionals are afraid to take chances. The strategically integrated HRD approach places HRD professionals on unfamiliar turf. No longer in their familiar, comfortable classroom, they feel overwhelmed by the complexities of the problems they must solve. There is a tendency to retreat to the classroom (avoidance) or to bring an easy classroom solution to difficult problems (simplification) (Gilley and Coffern 1994).

Either as trainers or instructional designers, HRD professionals have time to plan, design, and adjust. As a strategic planner, performance engineer, or change champion, however, you are often asked to make decisions in seconds. People may not respond or behave exactly the way textbook models predict.

Fourth, many HRD practitioners see training as an end in itself. Having entered the field of HRD to be trainers, they believe training will add value to the organization. They are good at delivering training and want to continue, regardless of the organization or type of industry in which they perform.

Fifth, training has a beginning and an end. It begins when the class starts and ends with employees' reactions to the training event. Training is clean and manageable, with no uncertainty or ambiguity to deal with or overcome. HRD practitioners can feel in charge and secure. They strongly resist using a consulting process to identify the causes of poor performance, which is required in strategically integrated HRD.

Sixth, many HRD practitioners assume that performance improves if learning takes place; therefore, the emphasis is on classroom activity. The strategically integrated approach, however, requires HRD practitioners to consider other factors as well, both before and after training. In fact, HRD professionals who embrace the strategically integrated approach believe that the majority of performance improvement occurs on the job as employees struggle to apply what they have learned, with managers providing performance coaching to encourage success. For many HRD practitioners, however, this is just too difficult a proposition to consider.

Seventh, some HRD professionals simply cannot let go of their fear of losing their safe and secure training positions. They are afraid of venturing into the unknown regardless of the positive impact it may have on the organization. These HRD professionals would rather complain about the lack of respect and credibility afforded them by the organization than embrace new ideas and better ways of achieving results.

Eighth, a real and serious problem facing HRD is the lack of qualified and capable HRD professionals willing to make the transition from trainer to organizational development consultant, which is required of SI-HRD programs. To compound this problem, many qualified HRD professionals elect to serve as outside consultants because internal opportunities have been limited. Large management consulting and professional service firms house a majority of the available candidates and are reluctant to give them up.

Finally, some HRD practitioners have spent a lifetime building an HRD "kingdom" within their organization, complete with a large budget, many employees, and perceived organizational respect. Operating like a large university disseminating knowledge, HRD programs charge tuition to operational units and tell others of the value that their department brings the organization. Activity abounds, fostering the belief that HRD is a valuable part of the organizational framework. Changing to a strategically integrated HRD approach would require practitioners (vendor-driven) to give up their kingdoms—a proposition many simply do not want to consider.

Like all great kings and kingdoms, the day of destruction is coming. HRD will be and is being eliminated in many organizations. HRD professionals are losing their kingdoms. Practitioners will wonder "What happened?" "What could we have done to prevent this?" The answer is to be found in strategically integrated HRD.

Preparing for the Journey to Results-Driven HRD

Now that we have examined the six phases of the evolution of HRD, it is time to direct our attention to the essential keys to developing results-driven HRD programs.

Reexamining Your HRD Philosophy

Making the transition from activity-based to results-driven requires a reexamination of your philosophy of HRD. For some, a minor revision proves sufficient, whereas others require a major shift in thinking. To examine your philosophy, answer several of the following reflective questions:

- How do my efforts align with my organization's strategic goals and objectives?

- Why is training needed?
- What skills and knowledge are you trying to improve?
- What business problem are you trying to resolve?
- How will you know whether training was applied to the job?
- Who should receive the training intervention?
- What kind of training interventions fit the business strategy?
- How will the impact of training be evaluated?
- When should training be delivered?
- Who should be involved in delivering training?
- What other factors must be considered for training to be successful (motivation system, management action, reinforcement schedule)?

Engaging in five activities will help frame your HRD philosophy: identifying assumptions, analyzing choices, making commitments, selecting appropriate actions, and engaging in critical reflective activities (Figure 2.4).

Identifying Assumptions.   First, identify your assumptions regarding HRD. Brookfield (1992, 13) tells us that assumptions are "taken for granted" beliefs about reality, rules of thumb that guide your actions, or a common set of beliefs and conventional wisdom invoked when asked why you did something or why you think or believe what you do. Schwinn (1996) adds that assumptions are an explicit set of conditions, principles, ethics, and expectations considered true regarding the basis for choosing actions and studying their consequences. Quite simply, assumptions are the anchors to which most decisions are tied. As a result, identifying your assumptions about HRD prior to engaging in change activities proves critically important. Unless assumptions are isolated and understood, you may have difficulty accepting a new philosophy of HRD. This is particularly true when such a philosophy requires adopting a radical perspective regarding your role in your organization.

Exercise 1: Briefly describe your philosophy of HRD. Identify as many assumptions as you can that reinforce this belief. For example, people are inherently good; people are lazy; HRD should serve the needs of societies. Once this is done continue reading this section.

Engaging in Critical Reflective Activities.   Next, engage in a critical reflective activity that allows you to better plan and sculpt change opportunities. Critical reflection enables you to truly understand and embrace possibilities.

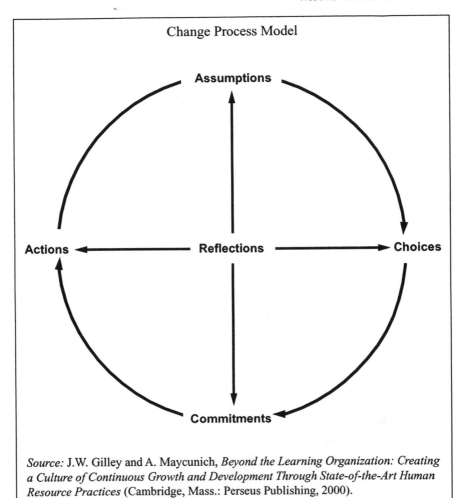

FIGURE 2.4   Change Process Model

Critical reflection has been described as the "practice of analyzing one's own assumptions, actions, decisions, or products by focusing on the processes involved" (Killion and Todnem 1991, 14). We believe that critical reflection allows you to develop a greater level of self-awareness of the nature and impact of your decisions and beliefs, which provides additional opportunities for professional growth and development (Preskill 1996). Thus, critical reflection enhances awareness of why you act and behave the way you do.

Reflection allows you to consider, examine, analyze, critique, or contemplate your past, to ask "what if" questions, and to consider possibilities. As a result, you piece together the fragmented parts of your life. Reflection allows you to better understand yourself by examining your beliefs and assumptions. It provides insight into your mistakes, your successes, failures, and difficulties, and thereby help understand how you evolve.

Schwinn (1996) tells us that reflection is a process by which you comprehend the existence or meaning of what was previously unknown or unrecognized, and then act on the differences between prior and current expectations. Not only is reflection the window to an understanding of your past, it is also the door to our future. Reflection is the key to change, allowing you to challenge your assumptions and beliefs, which enables you to change your philosophy of life. Ultimately, you begin to change your personal philosophy, life strategy, and personal and professional practice. As a result, you become a different person.

Reflection is critical in your personal and professional lives. As an HRD professional, you may struggle with how you have evolved within your career and the arena of HRD. Perhaps your philosophy of HRD, the organizational effectiveness strategies you embrace, the partnerships you develop, and your HRD role and practice have changed dramatically over the years. The interaction of these four elements holds the key to success in HRD (see Figure 2.4). Critical reflection may begin in any one of these four places. Further, the changes made as a result of your reflection in one area impact the three other areas.

For example, by implementing a performance management system (organizational strategy) within an organization, employees receive specific, timely, meaningful, and positive performance feedback. Consequently, their productivity increases. From this positive experience, you begin thinking differently about the purpose of HRD (philosophy). As a result, you may begin to believe that the purpose of HRD is more than simply providing training programs. Thus, you begin changing your HRD practice, which might mean developing a performance partnership with a new department in the organization. This partnership might affect the "You" strategy, HRD philosophy, or practice. Thus, the cycle continues.

The same cycle occurs when you reflect on your role as a change champion (Chapter 9) within the organization. Let's say that you believe that you need to initiate significant change in the organization (organizational development partnership). Therefore, you actively look for opportunities to help senior executives and managers in decisionmaking or problem-solving efforts. As a result, you consider how you can help the organization achieve its strategic mission. Such thinking begins to impact and change their beliefs regarding HRD (philosophy). As they rethink your philosophy of HRD, they begin to realize the importance of facilitating a strategic planning activity (see Chapter 7) within the firm, which reinforces your leadership role in the organization.

Reflecting on your philosophy of HRD can impact your organizational effectiveness strategy, performance partnerships, and HRD practice individually or simultaneously. For example, several years ago, three senior HRD professionals at Mercer Human Resource Consulting were in a heated and serious discussion regarding the purpose of HRD (philosophy) in their organization. They were concerned about how to reverse the organization's perception of HRD. In the past the HRD department was perceived as an activity-based training house rather than as a program that could transform the organization. As a result of their discussion, they adopted a new philosophy of HRD, one that focused on improving organizational learning, performance, and change (see Chapter 3) through a variety of interventions, initiatives, and strategies. Over time, Mercer's HRD practice began changing in the organization. They developed performance partnerships, which reinforced the change in their HRD philosophy. They conducted high-level performance and organizational needs assessments, designed performance appraisal systems, examined the work climate and culture of the organization, and coached executives on performance issues. In other words, a change in their HRD philosophy dramatically changed their entire HRD practice, partnerships, and strategic approach.

Exercise 2: Reflect on your HRD roles, practice, philosophy, performance partnerships, and organizational effectiveness strategies. Write down your awarenesses. This is the current state of HRD in your organization and your respective role. Next, compare the assumptions that you previously identified with your descriptions of the above. Are they congruent? If not, why aren't they? Is so, are you satisfied with the current state of HRD in your organization? If yes, go to Chapter 4 for some suggestions on improving results-driven HRD programs. If not, identify the desired state of HRD in your organization and continue reading this section.

Analyzing Choices. The next step in the change process is analyzing your possible choices (Figure 2.4). Doing so allows you to carefully construct a rationale for decisionmaking. Although apparently a simple, straight-forward activity, the benefits of understanding the conclusions you draw are invaluable. The process of analyzing choices includes examining

- *how* decisions are made in your HRD function
- *who* participates in the decisionmaking process

- *what* criteria will be used to determine the correct course of action
- *what* consequences will follow the choice(s) made.

Once this process has been completed, you are in a better position to determine whether you can make decisions that will help bring about desired change.

Exercise 3: Return to the description of the desired state of HRD and apply the four criteria of analyzing choices. These will help you determine how to proceed in transforming your HRD program.

Making Commitments.   Once you have isolated your assumptions regarding HRD, participated in a critical reflection activity, and created criteria for your future choices, you can make commitments that bring about real, lasting change. Making commitments may require you to choose between two desirable outcomes. When confronted with such a situation, determine which of the positive outcomes you desire most and to which you are willing to allocate important resources over a long period of time.

Occasionally, you are confronted with a decision between a positive and a negative outcome, which is often the easiest commitment to make. Regrettably, some situations require you to commit to one of two negatives, each possessing little or no perceived value. Under these conditions, minimize your risk and commit to a choice you can live with, both in the short and long term.

Exercise 4: Identify the commitments that you are willing to make to transform your HRD program from activity-based to results-driven. What possible obstacles might you encounter? What alternatives are you willing to adopt? What are your contingency plans?

Selecting Appropriate Actions.   Taking action to satisfy your assumptions, choices, and commitments may include

- allocating financial and human resources needed to transform the HRD program
- restructuring your HRD department
- identifying developmental strategies for yourself and others
- proactively creating partnerships

- identifying ways of influencing organizational leaders regarding the new mission of HRD
- demonstrating leadership capacity in the organization.

Each of these will be required as your HRD program makes a transition from activity-based to results-driven.

Exercise 5: Read the remainder of this book and make applications of its suggestions, ideas, principles, and recommendations. We are confident that these will help you make the transition to results-driven HRD.

Conclusion

The activity era has definitely passed. Today, the success of HRD is based on whether performance improvement and change interventions enhance organizational effectiveness and performance. In other words, does HRD add value to the organization? The HRD function must produce specific outcomes that the organization needs to accomplish its strategic business goals. Otherwise, organizational decisionmakers will not need HRD.

The journey from vendor-driven HRD to strategically integrated HRD begins when you become dedicated to helping the organization achieve its business goals. Each and every HRD professional must accept responsibility for changing the way the HRD community does business. They must become responsible for maximizing organizational performance and change. In short, you must accept the challenge of transforming HRD in your organizations and become dedicated to making a difference in the field.

Finally, you can choose an activity strategy where training is the cornerstone or a results-driven strategy that is performance-centered and organizationally focused. These strategies differ in their outcomes and in their contribution to an organization. The former leads to training for training's sake whereas the latter helps organizations achieve their strategic business goals and objectives. HRD is at a crossroads and you must choose which path you wish to follow.

PART B

Creating Credibility by Redesigning and Repositioning HRD

Before engaging in the radical alteration of your HRD program, answer two simple questions. Why are you considering transforming your HRD program? What will be the advantages and benefits of doing so? Answers to the first question should include things like: improving the linkage between HRD interventions and initiatives and the organization's strategic goals and objectives; increasing organizational effectiveness, competitive readiness, or organizational renewal; or enhancing learning transfer and improving performance. The answer to the second question involves improving the credibility of HRD and its professionals. This can be accomplished by enhancing partnerships (Chapter 5), implementing professional roles (Chapters 6–8), or providing leadership (Chapters 9–10) within the organization. In short, adding value to the organization enhances credibility.

Strategies for Improving Credibility

Improving credibility occurs when you demonstrate your professional expertise as well as your understanding of the organization's operations and culture. In this way, you communicate your potential to provide real value to the organization. In other words, creating credibility means that you are believable and reliable. Several behaviors demonstrate and enhance your credibility:

- Be accurate in all HRD practices, which includes analysis activities (performance, needs, causal, organizational), design of interventions and initiatives, performance and organizational development consulting activities, and evaluation.
- Be predictable and consistent—dependable and reliable so that decisionmakers have confidence in your actions and recommendations.
- Meet your commitments in a timely and efficient manner.
- Establish collaborative client relationships built on trust and honesty.
- Express your opinions, ideas, strategies, and activities in an understandable and clear manner, and at the most appropriate times.
- Behave in an ethical manner that demonstrates integrity.
- Demonstrate creativity and innovation.
- Maintain confidentiality.
- Listen to and focus on executive problems in a manner that brings about mutual respect (Ulrich 1997, 253–254).

Earning Credibility

Professional credibility can be earned in one of three ways. First, by demonstrating the ability to solve complex and complicated problems. Quite simply, you must have the ability to satisfy clients' needs and expectations. Various activities such as conducting needs assessments, developing performance management systems, and implementing and managing change can provide you the opportunity to demonstrate this ability.

Another way of earning credibility is by attempting to identify with clients. This can include simple things like dress, manners, speech, and language, or complex actions like identifying their interests and expectations. HRD professionals must be willing to communicate with clients on their level and in ways that clients value, such as communicating how HRD can improve the organization's profitability or how a performance improvement intervention or change initiative improves the quality and efficiency of the organization. This type of effort lets you demonstrate your awareness of organizational issues and concerns.

Earning credibility may also require you to search out common interests, histories, ideas, and experiences among clients. Such commonality provides a starting point for you and your clients and allows for mutual sharing, which often proves very valuable early in a relationship.

Transferring Credibility

Credibility can be transferred, most commonly through third-party references, who are often referred to as a network. A network is a collection of individuals who can introduce you to key organizational decisionmakers as well as keep them informed. In fact, you can gain instant access and establish immediate credibility with the right contacts.

Developing Credibility Through Reputation

Credibility can be developed through reputation. This includes having a record of delivering results, experience in the business, technical expertise, educational and professional background, professionalism, demeanor, and client contacts. Share your professional accomplishments, knowledge of the client's situation, and identify possible problems with potential clients to communicate your understanding of the client's difficulties. It is also a way of communicating your insight so that your clients understand the level of professional expertise available.

Additional Techniques for Establishing Credibility

Credibility can also be established by demonstrating the ability to solve complex problems, satisfying client developmental needs and expectations, exhibiting an understanding of organizational operations and culture, demonstrating integrity by delivering results on time, within budget, and at quality standards, and networking with organizational decisionmakers. Seven additional techniques for establishing credibility have been identified:

- Demonstrate understanding of business strategies, goals, tactics, and financial performance, and connect that knowledge to the skills, competencies, practices, and people who are available to execute the business strategy.

- Establish performance goals that relate directly to business strategies.
- Provide credible follow-up to management on HRD's effectiveness in supporting the business strategy.
- Know the value of the HRD skills, competencies, practices, and business knowledge available to execute business strategies.
- Market competencies to management because, in too many cases, they are not aware of what HRD can do to support them.
- Provide management with value-added service.
- Provide efficient and effective service (Anderson 1997, 148–149).

Enhancing Credibility by Redesigning and Repositioning HRD

In addition to the strategies previously identified, you can enhance credibility by redesigning and repositioning HRD within the organization. Such an approach enables you to incorporate most if not all of the previous strategies. Further, you will create a more functional HRD program, one in concert with the organization and its overall strategy and operation.

To achieve this end, you need to determine what you are going to build your HRD program upon and how you are going to make the transition from an activity-based to a result-driven approach. In Figure B.1, we provide a model that illustrates our approach to addressing these two questions. Moreover, we will discuss the foundations of our redesign and reposition strategy (Chapter 3) as well as provide a seven-step process for successfully transforming HRD (Chapter 4).

We believe that the new HRD philosophy must be "organizational learning, performance, and change for maximum organizational results and impact." Such a strategy communicates the intention of an HRD program and what it is really trying to accomplish. In other words, HRD is about achieving organizational results rather than training. A total shift in emphasis is required to accomplish this strategy. As a result, interventions and initiatives must produce specific outcomes upon which the organization can rely in order to achieve its strategic business goals.

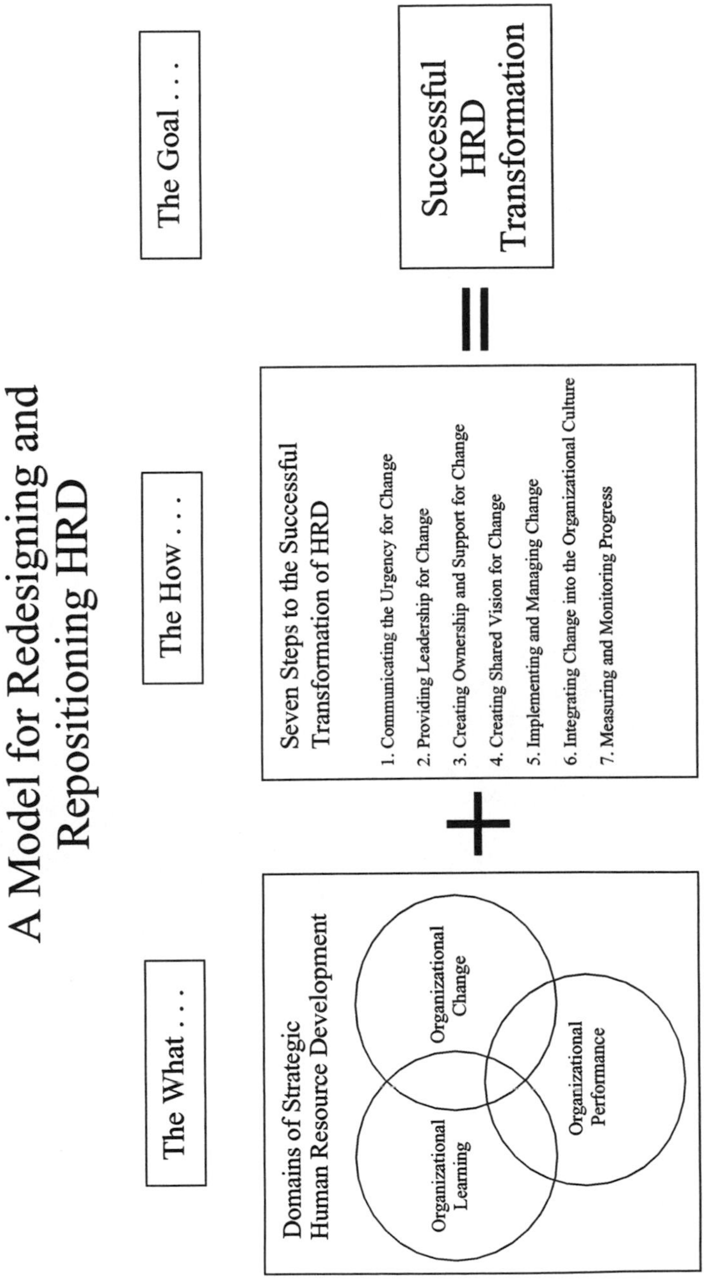

A Model for Redesigning and Repositioning HRD

The What . . .

The How . . .

The Goal . . .

Domains of Strategic Human Resource Development

- Organizational Change
- Organizational Learning
- Organizational Performance

Seven Steps to the Successful Transformation of HRD

1. Communicating the Urgency for Change
2. Providing Leadership for Change
3. Creating Ownership and Support for Change
4. Creating Shared Vision for Change
5. Implementing and Managing Change
6. Integrating Change into the Organizational Culture
7. Measuring and Monitoring Progress

Successful HRD Transformation

+ =

FIGURE B.1   A Model for Redesigning and Repositioning HRD

3

Domains of Strategic HRD: Organizational Learning, Performance, and Change

Redesigning and repositioning HRD begins by understanding the core domains of results-driven HRD: organizational learning, organizational performance, and organizational change (Figure 3.1). These serve as the first of two major components in the transformation of HRD equation. The other component is a seven-step process used to transform HRD programs from activity-based to results-driven (Chapter 4).

Results-driven HRD professionals are aligned to one of these three philosophical orientations that affect their decisions and actions. Their choices are based on the assumptions that HRD professionals hold when addressing performance issues and change initiatives. We believe that all three of the domains are essential to the transformation to results-driven HRD because all are fundamental to serving as transformational HRD professionals (Chapters 5–10). Failure to embrace one of the domains severely limits your ability to respond to various organizational contingencies, problems, or breakdowns.

The complexity of each domain serves as a testament to the advanced knowledge required of results-driven HRD professionals. Crossing the line of demarcation begins an exciting journey. As it was once stated, "Toto, we aren't in Kansas any more." Let's examine each results-driven domain of HRD.

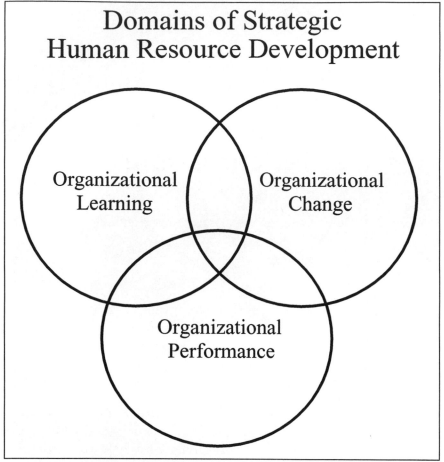

FIGURE 3.1   Domains of Strategic HRD

Organizational Learning

Professionals who believe that employee learning and development represents the primary purpose of HRD embrace the organizational learning domain. They contend that learning is the key to organizational development and change, and embrace the principles and practices of the learning organization (Senge 1990), critical reflection (Argyris and Schon 1996), transformative learning (Mezirow 1991), and their application within organizations. These HRD professionals are primarily responsible for creating learning cultures that foster continuous employee learning.

When a performance problem surfaces within an organization, learning-oriented HRD professionals typically rely on learning or development solutions to address the issue. The perception that learning is essential to performance improvement drives their belief that learning is appropriate when dealing with most organizational problems. They typically encourage the use of formal learning interventions and career development programs, seeing them as critical when addressing performance breakdowns. With the understanding that learning is not of any value unless it is applied on the job (Broad and Newstrom 1992), more experienced learning-oriented professionals encourage the use of learning transfer activities. These individuals place great value on group learning as a way of bringing about organizational change (Marquardt 1999; Watkins and Marsick 1993). Accordingly, they are responsible for integrating action learning (Marquardt 1999) and self-directed learning activities (Knowles 1975) in daily practice. Finally, they contend that creating a developmental culture is essential in fostering continuous employee learning and in creating a responsive organization, one capable of enhancing its renewal capacity and competitive readiness (Redding 1994; Senge 1990).

Bierema (2000, 292) nicely framed the philosophical orientation of an organizational learning professional when she stated:

> HRD is about *development*, not profit, and HRD practitioners need to carefully consider how their work impacts human growth, not just the corporate wallet. It has also been argued that focusing on individual development has long term benefits for the individual, organization, and society . . . there are long term costs associated with failure to provide the resources and infrastructure to support whole person learning such as turnover, mistakes and employees leaving to work of the competition. There are also social costs of such neglect that will impact lives, communities, and the environment.

Organizational learning can be defined as how learning occurs on an organization-wide basis. In contrast, the term *learning organization* is defined as "the systems, principles, and characteristics of organizations that learn as a collective entity" (Marquardt 1996, 230). Organizational learning occurs at three levels:

1. It occurs through the shared insights, knowledge, and mental models of members of the organization.
2. It builds on past knowledge and experience—that is, on organizational memory, which depends on institutional mechanisms (for example, policies, strategies, and explicit models) to retain knowledge.

3. It represents the enhanced intellectual and productive capability gained through corporatewide commitment to continuous improvement (Marquardt 1996).

The majority of organizational learning models focus on learning as a change process in that they seek to involve all of its employees in an effort to harness their intellectual capacity and knowledge capital for the purpose of individual, team, and organizational learning (Preskill and Torres 1999). They are also grounded in a social constructivist theory of learning, which suggests that learning takes place through the collective creation of meaning, employee action, the development of new knowledge, and an improvement in systemic processes (49).

Organizational learning is a "continuous process of organizational growth and improvement that is integrated with work activities, invokes the alignment of values, attitudes, and perceptions among organizational members, and uses information or feedback about both processes and outcomes to make changes" (Torres, Preskill, and Piontek 1996, 2). Moreover, organization learning represents the "enhanced intellectual and productive capability gained through corporate-wide commitment and opportunity for continuous improvement. It occurs through the shared insights, knowledge, and mental models of members of the organization . . . and builds on past knowledge and experience—that is, on organizational memory which depends on institutional mechanisms (e.g., policies, strategies, and explicit models) used to retain knowledge" (Marquardt 1999, 21–22).

Organizational learning encourages individuals at every level to be self-directed. This is accomplished through learning through failure, which is essential to development that enhances future business growth. To achieve this goal, organizations need to create an environment that is supportive of continuous growth and development, and embrace the belief that ideas can be developed best through dialogue and discussion (Kline and Saunders 1998, 16–18). Thus, organizations need to:

- rework organizational systems and structures to account for and encourage organizational learning
- celebrate the learning process for its own sake, not just its end product, and celebrate all learners equally
- transfer as much knowledge and power from person to person as possible
- encourage and teach employees to structure their own learning, rather than structuring it for them

- facilitate the process of self-evaluation, and recognize and accept as a goal the complete liberation of all human intelligence everywhere
- encourage employees to discover their own learning and thinking styles, and make them accessible to others
- recognize that different learning preferences are alternate tools for approaching and accomplishing learning
- cultivate each employee's abilities in all fields of knowledge, and spread the idea that nothing is forever inaccessible to people
- recognize that, in order to learn something so it is easy to use, it must be logical, moral, and fun, and that everything is subject to reexamination and investigation.

When senior management and executives embrace these actions, they affect employees' beliefs regarding learning, which over time become evident in the organizational culture and structure.

Learning Organizations and Action Learning

Two critical subcomponents of organizational learning are the learning organization and action learning.

Learning Organization. Senge (1990), often considered the father of the learning organization, identified five disciplines of learning organizations:

1. *Personal mastery* results from the acquisition of individual expertise and proficiency through education, formal learning activities, and work experience.
2. *Mental models* encompass values, beliefs, attitudes, and assumptions, forming one's fundamental worldview.
3. *Shared vision* represents the collective perspectives of employees and evolves from their understanding of the firm's mission and goals.
4. *Team learning* encourages communication and cooperation, leading to synergy and respect among members.
5. *System thinking* involves examination of and reflection upon all aspects of organizational life, such as mission and strategy, structure, culture, and managerial practices.

These serve as the foundation for learning organizations.

Learning organizations are institutions that learn powerfully and collectively, continually transforming themselves to better manage and use knowledge for corporate success; empowering people within and outside to learn as they work, and use technology to maximize learning and production (Marquardt 1996, 229). To make the transition from the traditional to the learning organization, firms must:

- alter the environment to support and encourage learning
- link learning to business operations
- communicate the importance of the learning organization
- demonstrate their commitment to learning
- transform the organizational culture to one of continuous learning and improvement
- establish organizationwide strategies for learning
- eliminate organizational bureaucracy
- encourage employee involvement
- embrace continuous, adaptive, improvement-oriented learning approaches throughout the organization (Marquardt 1996, 180–191).

Accordingly, organizational priorities must focus on improving learning capacity as well as encouraging self-directed learning behavior on the part of all employees. Learning organizations are as concerned about market share, productivity, and profitability as the traditional organization. The principal difference is that learning organizations understand that learning is the key to acquiring greater business results.

"Learning has very little to do with taking in information. Learning, instead, is a process that is about enhancing capacity. Learning is about building the capabilities to create that which you previously could not create. It ultimately relates to action, which information is not" (Senge 1990, 191). The primary assumption of learning organizations, therefore, is that as an employee's learning capacity improves, his or her performance capabilities also improve. Consequently, learning takes on several specific characteristics (see Table 3.1).

Action Learning. "One of the most valuable tools for organizational learning is *action learning*" (Marquardt 1996, 39). Action learning is "both a process and a powerful program that involves a small group of people solving real problems while at the same time focusing on what they are learning and how their learning can benefit each group member and the organization as a whole" (Marquardt 1999, 4). Revans (1994), often considered the pioneer of

---

Characteristics of Learning Organizations

Marquardt (1996, 19–20) identified a number of important characteristics of the learning organization. They are helpful when transforming a traditional activity-based program into one based on the principles of the learning organization. The characteristics include:

- Learning is accomplished by organizational systems as a whole, almost as if the organization were a brain.
- Organizational members recognize the critical importance of ongoing organization-wide learning for the organization's current and future success.
- Learning is a continuous, strategically used process—integrated with and running parallel to work.
- The focus is on creativity and generative learning.
- System thinking is fundamental.
- People have continuous access to information and data resources that are important to the company's success.
- The corporate climate encourages, rewards, and accelerates individual and group learning.
- Workers network in an innovative, community-like manner inside and outside the organization.
- Change is embraced, whereas unexpected surprises and even failure are viewed as opportunities to learn.
- It is agile and flexible.
- Everyone is driven by a desire for quality and continuous improvement.
- Activities are characterized by aspiration, reflection, and conceptualization.
- There are well-developed core competencies that serve as taking-off points for new products and services.
- It possesses the ability to continuously adapt, renew, and revitalize itself in response to the changing environment.

TABLE 3.1   Characteristics of Learning Organizations

action learning and learning organizations, believes that "There is no learning without action and no action without learning." Thus, he believes that the learning equation is: Learning = Programmed instruction (for example, knowledge in current use) + Questioning (fresh insights into what is not yet known), or L = P + Q. "Action learning builds upon the experience and knowledge of an individual or group and the skilled, fresh questioning that results in creative, new knowledge" (Marquardt 1996, 40).

The following proven principles of adult learning are demonstrated and practiced as people participate in action learning.

- Learning is increased when people reflect on what they experience.
- People become immobilized and neglect to seek their own solutions when they rely solely on experts.
- People learn critical thinking skills when they are able to question the assumptions on which actions are based.
- People learn best when they receive accurate feedback from others.
- The results of one's problem-solving actions provides constructive insight.
- The greatest learning occurs when people work on unfamiliar problems in unfamiliar settings.
- People are better able to gain new perspectives and, therefore, new learning when nonhierarchical groups from across organizational departments and functions are assembled.
- Action learning is most effective when the learners are examining the organizational system as a whole (Marquardt 1996, 40).

Learners gain several key organizational learning skills through the action learning process. Action learning enables employees to develop self-understanding from the feedback of others. Action learning helps employees develop critical reflection and retraining skills, and provides employees new ways of thinking about the organization by addressing unfamiliar problems (Marquardt 1996, 41). Furthermore, skills and insights can help employees test assumptions that may be preventing them from acting in new and more effective ways. As a result of their participation in problem-solving teams, action learning helps employees acquire teamwork skills (see Table 3.2).

Establishing a Learning and Development Culture in Organizations

One of the most important outcomes realized when the organizational learning domain is appropriately applied is the establishment of a learning and development culture within a firm. Such cultures are a result of a collaborative effort between executives, senior management, managers, employees, and results-driven (learning-oriented) HRD professionals. The purposes of such a culture are to encourage continuous learning and development, maximize learning opportunities, and reinforce and reward learning and development activities.

We (2000b) recently identified the benefits of a learning and development culture, which are provided in Table 3.3.

Characteristics of Action Learning

Marquardt and Reynolds (1994, 23) identified characteristics of action learning. These characteristics are helpful in enhancing organizational learning and moving your program from activity to results-driven status. Action learning:

- Is outcome-oriented
- Is designed to systematically transfer knowledge throughout the organization
- Enables people to learn by doing
- Helps develop learning-how-to-learn skills
- Encourages continual learning
- Creates a culture in which learning becomes a way of life
- Is an active rather than a passive approach
- Is done mainly on the job rather than off the job
- Allows for mistakes and experimentation
- Develops skills of critical reflection and reframing
- Is a mechanism for developing learning skills and behavior
- Demonstrates the benefits of organizational learning
- Models working and learning simultaneously
- Is problem-focused rather than hierarchically bound
- Provides a network for sharing, supporting, giving feedback, and challenging assumptions
- Develops the ability to generate information
- Breaks down barriers between people and across traditional organizational boundaries
- Helps an organization move from a culture of training (in which someone else determines and provides the tools for others' development) to a culture of learning (in which everyone is responsible for his or her own continuous learning)
- Is systems-based
- Applies learning to other parts of the organization as appropriate.

TABLE 3.2   Characteristics of Action Learning

HRD professionals who are learning and development oriented strive to create organizational cultures that exemplify these benefits. They are creating conditions that support redesigning and repositioning HRD from activity-based to results-driven.

Organizational and Employee Benefits of a Learning and Development Culture	
Organizational Benefits	**Employee Benefits**
Dynamic, pro-active environment	Dynamic, pro-active environment
Qualified employees	Personal and professional growth / lifelong learning
Inspired employee commitment	
Synergy	High satisfaction
Achieves goals and objectives	Greater involvement / participation
Increased employee productivity	Equality of opportunity
Championship performance	Improved self-esteem
Continuous and rapid growth	Greater compensation and rewards
Improved succession planning and career pathing	Broadened entrepreneurial spirit and environment
Enhanced organizational capability	
Organizational renewal and competitive readiness	
Developmental readiness	
Overcoming employee depression	

TABLE 3.3   Organizational and Employee Benefits of a Learning and Development Culture

Organizational Performance

The organizational performance domain houses professionals who believe that performance improvement and management are the essential components of HRD (Rummler and Brache 1995). HRD professionals must first analyze performance to isolate the cause of performance breakdowns before recommending or designing an intervention (Gilbert 1978; Harless 1974; Mager 1975). Therefore, they believe that training is not appropriate in most performance improvement situations (Silber 1992). Rather, they believe that management action (for example, removing performance barriers, providing resources, redesigning jobs, establishing appropriate compensation and reward systems) is essential to improving organizational performance (Stolovitch and Keeps 1999).

Organizational performance professionals use system theory, behavioral psychology, and knowledge management when examining performance shortfalls (Brethower 1999). They believe that their primary responsibility is to use the human performance system to improve organizational effectiveness (Fuller and Farrington 1999; Rosenberg 1996). Typically, these professionals have a behaviorist approach to solving performance problems and use reinforcement schedules to bring about changes in performance and behavior (Brethower 1999). They contend that compensation and reward systems, organizational structure and culture, job design, and motivational factors should reinforce performance change and improvement (Gilbert 1978; Rummler and Brache 1995). These practitioners advocate the principles and practices of human performance technology (Jacobs 1987), performance consulting (Robinson and Robinson 1996), and performance engineering (Dean 1999). They even advocate creating separate performance improvement departments (Robinson and Robinson 1996) dedicated to performance analysis (Rossett 1999b) and evaluation (Robb 1998). Finally, organizational performance professionals believe that their credibility is improved when the organization improves its overall performance.

Initiate Innovative HRD Practices

Organizational performance professionals believe that organizations need to employ several state-of-the-art human resource practices to transform the program to results-driven status. These include establishing a targeted human resource acquisition strategy, designing jobs to improve organizational performance, and establishing compensation and reward systems that improve performance. HRD professionals may need to establish partnerships and alliances to accomplish these strategies since they may not be directly responsible for them within the organization.

Organizational performance professionals believe that a fundamental shift is needed for HRD programs to become results-driven. Four approaches are needed to facilitate this change:

- Communicating to all employees that performance improvement and change are critical to business success;
- Defining the deliverables of HRD professionals and holding them accountable for results;
- Investing in innovative HRD practices and using new technologies and practices to transform the organization through performance management;
- Insisting on increased professionalism of their practitioners (Ulrich 1998, 133–134).

In short, organizations need HRD professionals who know the business, understand the theory and practice of HRD, and are able to coordinate performance management activities.

Establish a Targeted Human Resource Acquisition Strategy

Three processes make up an organization's human resource acquisition strategy: human resource planning, recruiting, and selection. These processes are primary tools by which organizations obtain the necessary human resources to accomplish its business objectives and gain competitive advantage.

An organizational performance professional believes that an organization's long-term success depends on its employees' capabilities, which can be developed internally or acquired on the open market. Thus, human resource planning can be defined as an effort to anticipate future business and environmental demands on an organization, and provide qualified people to fulfill business needs and satisfy demands (Cascio 1997). It proves a complex activity that requires careful analysis, forecasting skill, and input by organizational leaders, managers, and employees.

We (2000b) believe that human resource planning is a process of systematically organizing the future and planning to address future performance and quality requirements. As such, human resource planning focuses on identifying an organization's human resource needs under changing conditions and developing the strategies to address those needs. It should be integrated with organizationwide strategic planning and implementation, as well as performance management activities. Absent this integrative approach, you cannot adequately identify the type and quality of employees needed to ensure effective organizational renewal and competitive readiness.

Recruiting and selection activities should be based on an agreed-upon set of competencies for each job within the organization. This is necessary to obtain the most talented, skilled employees. The process begins by profiling a job and identifying the respective competencies that are required in performing adequately. Next, the recruiting process involves developing a grand plan for communicating the opportunities to both internal and external labor markets. The purpose of this effort is to identify individuals who possess the skills, knowledge, and attitudes appropriate for the job. Remember, recruiting is more than institutional advertising; rather, it is a long-term strategy intended to attract and retain the type of individuals who will enhance an organization's competitive readiness and renewal capabilities.

The selection process is intended to choose the most qualified individual, the one who possesses the competencies necessary to perform at an exceptional level. More and more, character surfaces as an important criterion. Organizational performance professionals face one additional criterion—selecting individuals who are lifelong learners—ones who want to continuously grow and develop. We believe that you can determine a potential employee's predisposition for personal growth and development by identifying his or her coachability, which reflects one's receptivity to constructive criticism, suggestions for improvement, and willingness to learn, discover, or accept new ways of performing. Employees who resist new and better ways of performing, are contrary, or ignore suggestions for improvement possess low coachability. Commonly, such employees are unwilling to listen to another's point of view, perspectives, or opinions. They typically exhibit a know-it-all attitude, are unwilling to try new ways of performing tasks, using technology, or implementing new approaches, are often critical of others' success, and may resist engaging in personal growth and development planning and activities.

On the other hand, high coachability is characterized by enthusiasm for learning and development, heightened interest in new and better ways of performing, desire to compare oneself with high achievers, impatient enthusiasm to be the best one can be, willingness to solicit and receive performance feedback, career-focused ambitions, and developed reflective and critical thinking skills. Seeking out these types of employees enables you to establish a strategy for long-term success.

Organizational Change

Today's organizations are experiencing a period of unprecedented change known as permanent white water (Vaile 1996). Permanent white water means that organizational life will be full of surprises; increasingly complex; poorly organized, structured, and ambiguous; quite costly; and brimming with problems. Preskill and Torres (1999, 3) point out that "what has become crystal clear is that organizations and institutions will never again be stable and predictable. No longer do organizations and institutions offer one product or service for 20 or more years with a homogeneous workforce that experiences little movement."

According to several authors, organizational change can take several forms (Burke 1992; Nadler 1998; Ulrich 1998). Most change deals with routines, activities, problems, issues, and circumstances, and occurs naturally as organizations grow and develop, which is sometimes referred to as first-order change (Mink, Esterhuysen, Mink, and Owen 1993). First-order changes are "minor improvements and adjustments that do not change the system's core" (Levy

1986, 10). There are two distinguishing types of first-order change, "those that enable things to look different while remaining basically the same . . . and those that occur as a natural expression of the developmental sequence [and are] embedded in the natural maturation process" (Smith 1982, 318–319). Under these circumstances, "first-order changes would not necessarily require organized intervention" (Mink, Esterhuysen, Mink, and Owen 1993, 209).

Another type of organizational change is known as second-order change, which requires a fundamental shift in the organization's culture (Burke 1992). This type of change is transformational, whereby leaders question their organization's basic assumptions and address new and unknown elements in their environment, structure, mission, and strategy (Ulrich 1998). Such change involves a comprehensive examination of an organization's culture, core processes (for example, communication, decisionmaking, performance management system), vision, values, and goals. Second-order changes are alterations designed to thoroughly transform an organization's basic nature, operational approach, or reason for existence.

Organizational change professionals adopt a systemic, strategic approach to organizational effectiveness. They embrace the principles and practices of organizational development, which is their primary orientation, and adopt the role of change agent within the organization (French, Bell, and Zawacki 1999). Organizational change is a full-time activity requiring an independent group of professionals responsible for its implementation and focused on permanently altering the organization's culture (Burke 1992; Nadler 1998). Accordingly, they work closely with management and employees to facilitate and manage change. They improve their credibility by bringing about change within the organization and managing its implementation (Ulrich 1998). These individuals function as change management consultants, whom we refer to as change champions in Chapter 9 (Burke 1992).

One of organizational change professionals' primary responsibilities is to help employees strengthen their adaptability to change, both personally and professionally. Such employees are referred to as resilient, and are "positive, focused, flexible, organized, and proactive" (Conner 1992, 238). Resilient employees demonstrate a special adaptability when responding to uncertainty, have a high tolerance for ambiguity, and require only a short time to recover from adversity or disappointment (Patterson 1997). Moreover, resilient employees are proactive in that they engage change rather than defend against it (Conner 1992, 240). These employees realize change is inevitable, necessary, or advantageous. Therefore, they use resources to creatively reframe a changing situation, improvise new approaches, or maneuver to gain a competitive

advantage. Resilient employees take "risks despite potentially negative consequences; draw important lessons from change-related experiences that are
then applied to similar situations; respond to disruption by investing energy
in problem solving and teamwork; and influence others to resolve conflicts"
(Conner 1992, 240).

Organizational change professionals' effectiveness depends on their ability
to tolerate ambiguity (Burke 1992, 177–178). We believe that these practitioners improve their organizational impact and influence by demonstrating
business understanding, political awareness, and organizational conscious-
ness. Accordingly, these individuals are in a unique position to serve as employee champions because they help employees identify legitimate work
demands and thus help workers set priorities (Ulrich 1997).

Levels of Change

Understanding change helps executives, managers, supervisors, and employees prepare for and integrate change (Conner 1992, 79). As such, change can
occur at three different levels:

- *Micro changes* are small, manageable, and common transitions, such
  as adopting a new performance technique or participating in a
  professional development activity.
- *Organizational changes* are large-scale transitions that affect
  interactions, reporting relationships, and responsibilities.
- *Macro changes* are massive transitions that alter one's life or change
  one's assumptions, values, or beliefs.

Micro change occurs when "you" change; organizational change is when
"we" change; macro change involves "everyone in a society." Macro change is
extensive and seldom occurs, but when it does it dramatically affects lives.
Macro change alters the way we think and behave forever, and is most often a
second-order or transformational change.

Organizational Culture and Change

Real organizational change transforms culture, which is referred to as the
normative approach of organizational change (Burke 1992). Adopting this
approach requires you to develop a better understanding of the effects that
change has on organizational culture. Accordingly, you will need to develop

an understanding of culture, the conditions for implementing change, and the change process.

Organizational Culture.   Organizational culture can be defined as the "interrelationship of shared beliefs, behaviors, and assumptions that are acquired over time by members of an institution" (Conner 1992, 164). Culture refers to norms of behavior and shared values among a group of people (Kotter 1996). Norms of behavior are common or pervasive ways of acting that are found in a group. They persist because group members tend to behave in ways that reinforce these practices in new members, rewarding those who fit in and sanctioning those who do not. Shared values are important constructs shared by most of the people in a group that tend to shape group behavior and that often persist over time, even when group membership changes.

Organizational culture provides cohesiveness among individuals throughout an organization and is developed over time. An institution's existing culture is the product of beliefs, behaviors, and assumptions that have in the past contributed to success. Schein (1992, 9) provides a compelling definition of organizational culture as "a pattern of basic assumptions invented, discovered, or developed by a given group as it learns to cope with the problems of external adaptation and internal integration that all works well enough to be considered valid and therefore to be taught to new members as the correct way to perceive, think, and feel in relation to those problems." Schein's definition stresses that culture involves assumptions, adaptations, perceptions, and learning. Quite simply, organizational culture is referred to as "the way we do things around here" (Burke 1992, 130). Organizational culture is a complex topic strongly influenced by history, customs, and practices. Moreover, it is what employees perceive to be the pattern of beliefs, values, and expectations that guide their behavior and practice within the firm. Accordingly, the culture of an organization dictates the type of institution it becomes.

Much has been learned in the last few years about culture change and your role in its accomplishment. Results-driven HRD professionals engage in five activities that bring about successful culture change, they:

- define and clarify the concept of culture change.
- articulate why culture change is critical to institutional success.
- define a process for assessing the current culture, the desired future culture, and the gap between the two.
- identify alternative approaches to creating culture change.

- build an action plan that integrates multiple approaches to culture change (Ulrich 1997, 169–170).

Conditions for Organizational Change

Several conditions must be present if organizational changes are to be successful. They include:

1. Management and all those involved must have high, visible commitment to the change.
2. Decisionmakers who are involved need to have advanced information to enable them to know what is to happen and why they are doing what they are doing.
3. The change effort must be connected to other parts of the organization.
4. The effort needs to be directed by managers and assisted by a change agent (transformational HRD professional, Chapter 9).
5. The change effort must be based on an effective diagnosis of the organization and must be consistent with conditions in the firm.
6. Management must remain committed to the change throughout all steps, from diagnosis through implementation and evaluation.
7. Evaluation is essential and must consist of quantitative as well as qualitative data.
8. Employees must clearly see the relationship between the change effort and the organization's mission, goals, and guiding principles.
9. The change agent (HRD professional) must be competent and credible within the organization.
10. Organizations must be at an optimal point of readiness for change in order for it to occur (Dyer 1989).

When these conditions are present within an organization, you will be more successful in implementing interventions that bring about or improve organizational effectiveness.

The Change Process

The procedures for the change process can be traced back to the original research conducted by Lewin (1951). Although many have attempted to create elaborate change models, the basic premises introduced by Lewin appear to be the most appropriate when initiating organizational change designed to improve effectiveness. He identified three steps in the change process, which are unfreezing, changing, and refreezing.

The unfreezing phase of the change process refers to conditioning organizations for change and establishing ownership within the firm. This effort creates momentum when decisionmakers, stakeholders, and influencers align in an effort to introduce change. Once organizational readiness for change has been achieved, HRD professionals identify possible interventions to help the organization maximize its developmental opportunities. This refers to taking action, which changes the organizational system from its original level of behavior and operations to its new desired level (Lewin 1951).

The movement component is often referred to as the transformation or intervention phase, whereby organizations are in the process of redefining and reinventing themselves as a way of achieving organizational goals and objectives.

The final phase of the change process is the period of establishing equilibrium within the organization. Once change has occurred, it is important for the organization to adjust, establish it as a norm within the firm, and perform accordingly. Your primary focus during this period is to help the organization reestablish its equilibrium or stasis so that it can perform at a higher level.

Myths and Assumptions About Organizational Change

Many HRD professionals proceed with the best of intentions in helping organizations and their employees adapt to change. Unfortunately, they often operate under a number of myths regarding organizational effectiveness, which results in the application of faulty strategies that can create a huge drain on organizational resilience. Nine myths can prove fatal during organizational change activities:

1. People act first in the best interest of the organization.
2. People want to understand the "what" and the "why" of organizational change.
3. People engage in change because of the merits of change.
4. People opt to be architects of the change affecting them.
5. Organizations are rationally functioning systems.
6. Organizations are wired to assimilate systematic change.
7. Organizations operate from a value-driven orientation.
8. Organizations can effect long-term systemic change with short-term leadership.

9. Organizations can achieve systemic change without creating conflict in the system (Patterson 1997, 7).

Each of these myths can lead to disaster if not appropriately addressed.

A number of harsh realities face organizations during times of change (Patterson 1997). In reality, most employees act in their own best interests, not in those of the organization. Second, most employees do not really want to know the "what" and the "why" of organizational change—they simply want to know what is in it for them. Third, most people engage in organizational change to avoid unnecessary difficulties or personal "pain," rather than to implement change based on its merits. Fourth, most employees view change with a great deal of skepticism and cynicism, even though they outwardly appear to be supportive. Fifth, most employees do not participate in a proactive manner when initiating change, preferring instead to be its victims. Sixth, most organizations operate irrationally and are wired to protect the status quo. Seventh, most organizations do not refer to their guiding principles and values when initiating change but rather are reacting to outside pressures such as the need for greater revenue, market share, or improved profitability. Eighth, most organizations are unrealistic about the amount of conflict that occurs as a result of change, and naively expect change to be accepted wholeheartedly by employees. Ninth, most organizations unfortunately implement long-term change with short-term leadership. Outside management teams are often brought in to the organization to initiate long-term change, instead of using the management team that must live with the ultimate decisions made.

As an organizational change professional, your primary responsibility in implementing change is to help organizations and employees increase their resilience. That is, the organization and its employees must be helped to increase their capacity and ability to adapt to change. Again, several suggestions can be used to accomplish this (Patterson 1997). First, ample time must be invested in trying to understand various group members' self-interests and in finding ways of satisfying those concerns while implementing change. Next, help members of the organization to see the connections between the particular change initiatives and the general direction in which the organization is headed. You must create a sense of urgency for major change by selling the change initiative to critical decisionmakers, stakeholders, and influencers. Trust must be established with this group prior to engaging in authentic and potentially redundant communications about the proposed change. Also, the connection between change and the organization's guiding principles must be shown. Establishing trust is accomplished by allowing employees to challenge, without fear of reprisal, the conduct and intentions of those initiating change (Patterson 1997, 46). Furthermore, help your employees understand that they do indeed have a choice between being a victim or an initiator of change, which includes helping employees approach change as an opportunity for advancement and improvement, rather than as an activity perceived as limiting.

The urgency of proposed change is underscored when employees realize that their future well-being is at risk if change is not achieved. Additionally, you are responsible for helping organizational leaders understand and accept the reality that organizational conflict is inevitable, that change will occur continuously, and that creating a safe environment that promotes constructive handling of conflict is the most appropriate action. This type of environment actively embraces conflict resolution and consensus building as accepted operational practices. Moreover, you can help the organization develop its long-term commitment to change by linking proposed changes to its guiding principles and core values. Finally, help organization leaders resist their natural tendency to deny the harsh realities of organizational change (Patterson 1997, 47). Instead, help them acknowledge these realities and apply strategies that enable the organization to become more adaptive to change.

Conclusion

Activity-based HRD programs are firmly established on the exchanges between the HRD program and their clients. Typically, these include training programs, needs assessment activities, and reaction evaluations. On the other hand, results-driven HRD is based on three domains of strategic HRD: organizational learning, performance, and change. These serve as both a filter and a foundation from which HRD professionals make decisions and execute practice. Redesigning and repositioning of HRD are based on these substantive domains. They are a rich reservoir from which to draw when implementing interventions and initiatives to enhance organizational effectiveness.

Seven Steps to Successful Transformation of HRD

Transforming HRD is more than reengineering or restructuring the HRD department to be more efficient or to remove inefficient steps in internal work processes. Although these are important steps in improving effectiveness, they often result is a temporary turnaround in the way HRD professionals conduct their daily activities or execute their responsibilities. A turnaround, however, is not transformation. Transformation results when internal stakeholders (executives, managers, supervisors, and employees) completely alter their perceptions of HRD (Ulrich 1997, 14). In other words, the transformation process changes the fundamental image of HRD as seen by its stakeholders. Real change is not an event used to temporarily fix something but rather a change in philosophy used to redesign HRD within an organization—including its operations, mission, roles, responsibilities, and activities.

To be successful, you must have the courage to see the transformation process through to the end. Consequently, you must be equipped with and willing to hold yourself and your colleagues accountable for the seven steps to successful transformation of HRD (Figure 4.1). Conceptually it may help you to associate the seven steps to Lewin's (1951) classic change model: the first three steps with unfreezing, the next two with changing, and the last two with refreezing (as illustrated in Figure 4.1). With this in mind, your overarching strategy for effective change management is clear—employ the seven steps to successful transformation of HRD to build momentum for the change effort, organize and implement the change plan, and provide performance accountability for your employees and the organization. If you fail to do so, the transformation effort will fail, which will negatively affect HRD, its professionals, and your personal credibility.

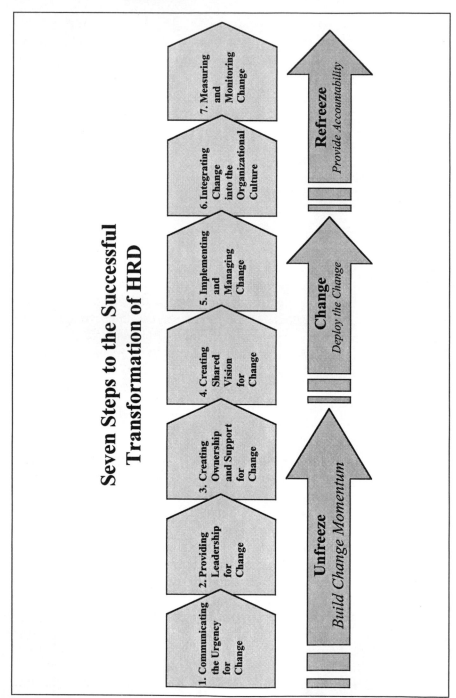

FIGURE 4.1   Seven Steps to the Successful Transformation of HRD

Although these seven keys to success may appear to be common sense, it is amazing how few HRD programs take the time to employ such a strategy. Once you begin to climb the slippery slopes of change, you must have the courage to clearly articulate these seven steps as nonnegotiable elements of the change initiative strategy as well as remain unswerving as you employ the steps. Further, you must continue to solicit your colleagues' ongoing support and commitment. Relying on practical strategies as you implement the seven steps is an essential part of keeping the courage you need to sustain you throughout the transformation process.

Step 1: Communicating the Urgency for Change

Your first step in the successful transformation of HRD is to communicate the urgency for change. Convince your colleagues that the sky is falling, this transformation is critical, and is needed now. They must realize that, absent their immediate action and support, HRD will never be perceived as vital to achieving the mission of the organization, and that it is simply a matter of time before the organization outsources or eliminates the HRD program. Kotter (1996) referred to this process as burning the platform to draw attention to the urgency for change.

Without communicating the urgency for change, the momentum for it never materializes. This is because far too many HRD professionals are content with providing training activity as a means of justifying their organizational value. As a result, they have become complacent. Under this condition, change usually goes nowhere because few if any HRD professionals are interested in working on transforming their HRD program. Consequently, it is difficult to cultivate support for a change vision.

Gilley and Boughton (1996, 10–11) refer to this period as organizational equilibrium, which is characterized by periods of low stress and adequate performance. HRD professionals are busy providing training on request and have yet to be held accountable for its lack of results. However, they warn that this period is where "the [HRD professionals] get too comfortable and fail to maintain [their] competitive spirit. If this period lasts too long, disaster can result. . . . Therefore, [HRD leaders] must be responsible for innovations and change during this period. They must recognize when apathy has taken root and take corrective action to eliminate it. Maintaining an attitude of continuous improvement is one of the best ways of combating apathy."

HRD professionals can find a thousand ingenious ways to withhold support for the transformation of HRD. Some sincerely think it is unnecessary; they are convinced that senior management perceives them positively, enabling them to perpetuate the daily rituals so common in an activity-based HRD program. Some display a kill-the-messenger approach that is simpler than making the effort to initiate change. Others have the capacity for denial, which adds to compliance. Still others are overconfident and mistakenly believe that senior management will never get rid of them. Any of these excuses leads to apathy and indifference, and is a serious barrier to the transformation process.

Your HRD colleagues will only alter their attitudes toward the transformation of HRD when they have the ability and appetite to do so (Conner, 1992). Ability involves possessing the necessary skills and knowing how to use them. Appetite involves possessing the motivation to engage in the transformation process and being willing to experience periods of discomfort as a more effective HRD program is installed. When your colleagues lack either ability or appetite, successful adaptation to change proves unlikely. Inadequate skills or knowledge causes deficiency in ability and should be addressed through developmental activities, mentoring, or selection. Lack of appetite for change stems from a lack of understanding or motivation and should be addressed through performance management and coaching.

You can raise the urgency level for transformation in a number of ways, including:

- Conduct a cost/benefit analysis that demonstrates how HRD adds value to the organization.
- Interview key decisionmakers and publish their comments regarding their perceptions of HRD.
- Hold focus groups to identify the strengths and weaknesses of HRD.
- Insist that HRD professionals be held accountable for business results.
- Make data available about stakeholder satisfaction.
- Insist that HRD professionals interact regularly with unsatisfied, unhappy, or disgruntled stakeholders.
- Hire an outside consultant to obtain the perceptions of stakeholders regarding HRD.
- Conduct an analysis of the linkage of HRD interventions and initiatives to the organization's strategic business goals and objectives.
- Question whether HRD is making a difference in the organization.

These should provide ample evidence of the lack of effectiveness of an activity-based HRD program.

Awareness and Understanding of Change

When your HRD colleagues learn about the possibility of the transformation of HRD, Conner (1992) cites two possible outcomes: confusion or understanding. Confusion reduces the probability of adequate preparation and favorable reception of change, whereas understanding advances the transformation process to the acceptance phase. Awareness does not necessarily mean that your colleagues have a complete understanding of the impact of change. For example, your colleagues may know that a change is coming but may be uncertain about the specific effects the change may have. They may be unclear about the nature, depth, breadth, or basic rationale for the change.

Acceptance.   The acceptance phase is a mental period of change in which your HRD colleagues struggle with the idea of altering their lives. It is characterized by two elements: understanding and positive perception.

Understanding.   Understanding the nature and intent of change is the first step in acceptance (Conner 1992). Your HRD colleagues who are aware of and comprehend a change can encourage and facilitate it. When this has occurred, they have crossed over the disposition threshold. There are two possible outcomes for the understanding stage:

- Negative perception—HRD colleagues who have a negative perception toward the transformation of HRD decrease their support for change and may demonstrate resistant behaviors and actions.
- Positive perception—HRD colleagues with a positive perception of change increase support for change, which enhances the likelihood of change acceptance.

Once employees perceive a change as positive, they must decide whether they are going to support it. It should be pointed out that a positive perception of change and the actions required to make change happen are quite different efforts (Gilley et al. 2001). For example, your HRD colleagues may not have the energy to implement change regardless of their perception of it. When your colleagues perceive a change as positive, however, they are better prepared to support the transformation of HRD.

Step 2: Providing Leadership for Change

The second step in the transformation of HRD is to provide leadership for change. This is critical since you are asking your colleagues to embrace and adopt a new way of executing HRD within your organization. Accordingly, you need to demonstrate ownership of the transformation process and publicly commit to its implementation. This may require you to gather the resources necessary to sustain change and invest your personal time and attention to the management of the transformation process.

You must also display an unswerving commitment to the goals of the transformation initiative and be dedicated to its success. You must demonstrate a willingness to be held accountable for achieving success through teamwork rather than through individual efforts. Moreover, you must assure your HRD colleagues that senior management is dedicated to the success of the transformation initiative and is facilitating and encouraging its adoption throughout the organization. You need to share with your employees your commitment to the transformation initiative and communicate the advantages and benefits for the HRD function, the organization, and your colleagues, which includes sharing what is in it for them. Next, provide highly visible leadership, which requires you to conduct "pulse check" conversations with your employees regarding their perspectives of the transformation and its progress.

During the early phases of the transformation initiative, you should try to do this with each employee at least once a week. Further, be clear with your HRD colleagues that you have as much to gain or to lose as they do; you are all in it together and your success depends on their success. Finally, ask your HRD colleagues for feedback on your performance during the transformation initiative. Try to do this informally at least once a month.

Creating the Guiding Coalition

Kotter (1996) suggests that a guiding coalition should be established for any significant change in an organization, for which the transformation of HRD qualifies. This group will help provide the leadership for change as well as the integrity, authority, and influence needed to successfully execute the transformation of HRD. The first step in putting together a guiding coalition is to find the right membership. Kotter (1996, 57) identifies four essential key characteristics needed of the guiding coalition team members: position power, expertise, credibility, and leadership. These four characteristics present in each member of the guiding coalition enables you to positively address the following questions:

1. Are enough key organizational leaders on board so that those left out cannot easily block progress?
2. Are the various points of view—in terms of discipline, work experience, and so forth—relevant to the transformation of HRD adequately represented so that informed, intelligent decisions can be made?
3. Does the group have enough people with good reputations so that executives and senior management will take its pronouncements seriously?
4. Does the group include enough proven leaders to be able to execute the transformation initiative?

The guiding coalition needs to have adequate management and leadership skills represented. Management skills enable leaders to organize and control the transformation process whereas leadership skills create commitment to and drive change. Both are essential in bringing about long-term systemic change.

Step 3: Creating Ownership and Support for Change

As a way of creating ownership and support for the transformation of HRD, you need to articulate a clear reason for the change and align the rationale for change to the organization's business goals and objectives. In this way, your HRD colleagues will better understand the reason for change, why it is important, and how it will help them and the organization in the short and long term.

Next, encourage as many of your colleagues, as early as possible, to become actively involved in planning and conducting the transformation effort. To achieve this end, involve several of your colleagues in the planning and implementing processes, and encourage others to share their ideas and concerns via informal or formally designed feedback systems. If possible, arrange a biweekly transformation initiative brown bag lunch series and encourage your HRD colleagues to attend and share their ideas, thoughts, feelings, and concerns. Use these meeting exchanges to share transformation initiative-related information, set goals for the transformation effort, monitor progress, and ensure the involvement of your HRD colleagues.

Hold regular meetings with the guiding coalition to debrief and ensure that everyone is up to date and on the same page. Keep minutes at all meetings (for example, brown bag luncheons and guiding coalition meetings), and disseminate minutes to all of your HRD colleagues. When an important message needs to be shared, use several media (such as memos, e-mail, and verbal announcements) to ensure that information filters do not cause misinterpretation. Above all, emphasize that you have an open door policy and encourage involvement.

Communicate the values and benefits of the transformation of HRD to all groups (leaders, managers, and employees) affected by the change. This may require you to hold regular update sessions as a part of the respective leadership team meetings. Approach these meetings as open forums for questions and transformation initiative–related discussion. Encourage leaders of the separate work groups or departments to answer all questions as candidly and honestly as possible, even if all the details surrounding the question or concern at hand are still being determined (Gilley et al. 2001). This helps relieve fear of the unknown.

Demonstrating Short-Term Successes

Kotter (1996, 123) believes that change is accepted more readily when short-term successes are evident. These are much like a small snowball that gathers momentum going down a hill and becomes a giant avalanche. They lay the foundation for sustainable long-term change and help the transformation of HRD in at least six ways:

- They provide evidence that sacrifices are worth the effort.
- They reward change participants by providing positive public recognition.
- They fine-tune the transformation vision and strategies by providing the guiding coalition with concrete data on the viability of their ideas.
- They undermine cynics and self-serving resisters by demonstrating the benefits of the transformation of HRD.
- They keep organizational leaders involved and supportive by providing evidence that the transformation is on track.
- They build momentum, thus turning neutrals into supporters, reluctant supporters into active helpers, and so forth.

Finally, Conner (1992, 155–160) provides six guidelines for obtaining employee and organizational commitment to the transformation of HRD. First, people respond to change at different intellectual and emotional rates, so adjust your expectation accordingly. Second, commitment is expensive, so demonstrate the cost-benefit relationship of the transformation. Third, do not assume that your HRD colleagues and other leaders will be committed to the transformation initiative without a plan of action. Fourth, keep in mind that building commitment is a developmental process, so encourage the natural reaction associated with personal and professional growth. Fifth, either build commitment and consensus or prepare for the negative consequences. Sixth, slow down to increase the speed of change.

Step 4: Creating a Shared Vision for Change

The fourth step in the transformation of HRD is developing a shared vision. Vision means a picture of the future with some implicit or explicit commentary on why other HRD professionals should strive to create that future. An effective vision statement is fairly short, memorable, and captures the essence of what you are trying to achieve.

In the transformation process, an exemplary vision serves three important purposes. First, it clarifies the general direction of the transformation of HRD. Second, an exemplary vision "acknowledges that sacrifices will be necessary but makes clear that these sacrifices will yield particular benefits and personal satisfactions that are far superior to those available today—or tomorrow—without attempting to change" (Kotter 1996, 70). Thus, an exemplary vision motivates HRD professionals to take action in the right direction and helps overcome their natural reluctance to change. Third, an exemplary vision coordinates the actions of your HRD colleagues by aligning them in a remarkably efficient way. Without a shared sense of direction, interdependent HRD professionals may constantly conflict, whereas a shared vision clarifies the direction of the transformation and helps your colleagues agree on its importance and value. Quite simply, Kotter (1996, 72) suggests that an exemplary vision is

> ... *imaginable* in that it conveys a picture of what the future will look like ... *desirable* because it appeals to the long-term interests of employees, customers, stockholders, and others who have a stake in the enterprise ... *feasible*, enabling organizations to develop realistic, attainable goals ... *focused*, providing guidance in decision making ... *flexible*, allowing individual initiative and alternative responses in light of changing conditions ... and is *communicable* in that it is easy to communicate.

As a way of developing a shared vision for the transformation of HRD, ask each of your HRD colleagues to draft a personal vision statement that captures what is important to them both personally and professionally about the HRD program's desired future state. Encourage them to sign their statements and display them in their work areas.

Another suggestion is to design and develop a banner or other promotional material that captures the transformation initiative vision statement. Display the banner or promotional material prominently in the most appropriate work area and encourage each of your colleagues to sign it as a public statement of their personal commitment to the successful transformation of HRD.

Three to six months after developing the transformation vision, all HRD professionals should attend a half-day or full-day retreat for the purpose of examining the progress that has been accomplished thus far. Dedicate a portion of this time to reexamining the transformation vision and determining whether it is still an accurate representation of the future. It is best to hold the retreat off-site, away from the constant distractions so common in most organizations.

Communicating the Change Vision

Next, create a communications plan that is designed to take advantage of every means possible to articulate the new transformation vision. An effective communication plan should be simple and jargon free; technical terms should be eliminated. Quite simply, it should paint a verbal picture worth a thousand words and incorporate all possible media forums (such as memos, e-mail, newsletters, and formal and informal interactions). Repeat information to establish messages in the subconscious of all HRD colleagues. An effective communication plan fosters two-way communication, which is always more powerful than one-way communication. Finally, an effective plan relies on leadership by example in that your behavior is consistent with the message being communicated (Kotter 1996, 90).

Empowering Broad-Based Action

Empowering broad-based action eliminates obstacles to the transformation of HRD, modifies systems or structures that undermine the transformation vision, and encourages risk taking and nontraditional ideas and actions. Kotter (1996, 115) identified five ways of encouraging HRD professionals to accept the transformation of HRD. They include:

- Communicating a sensible vision to all leaders, managers, employees, and HRD professionals.
- Making structures compatible with the vision.
- Providing training needed to obtain the appropriate knowledge and skills required to implement the transformed HRD program.
- Aligning information and human resource systems to the vision.
- Confronting leaders, managers, employees and HRD professionals who undercut needed transformation and request their cooperation.

In the future, the HRD program should hire, develop, and promote people who can embrace, support, and initiate results-driven HRD philosophy, strategies, tactics, and actions. Over time, every member of the HRD function will operate as change agents to modify systems, structures, and policies that do not fit together or align with the transformation vision. In this way HRD helps the organization achieve its business goals and objectives.

Step 5: Implementing and Managing Change

Before implementing the transformation process, identify the leaders, managers, employees, and HRD professionals who have decided to embrace the change. Once this occurs, Conner (1992) contends that the transformation initiative is now operational and has reached the commitment threshold. He suggests that the commitment phase consists of four subphases: installation, adoption, institutionalization, and internalization.

During the installation period, the transformation initiative is tested for the first time, which is sometimes referred to as the pilot-testing period. Problems and difficulties surface, providing opportunities to modify and adjust the transformation initiative. As problems and difficulties are resolved, a more realistic level of conviction toward the transformation develops, which allows commitment to advance to the adoption level.

During installation, some pessimism is common. Thus, you need to create a work environment that encourages dialogue, fosters open discussion, and allows for the expression of doubts and concerns. Such efforts facilitate and encourage problem-solving activities that build commitment.

The first opportunity for true, committed action arises during installation. In order to be successful, the transformation initiative requires consistency of purpose, an investment of resources, and the subordination of short-term objectives to long-range goals. Two outcomes are possible in the installation stage: change is aborted or adopted (Conner, 1992).

A considerable degree of commitment is required for your group to reach the adoption stage. During this subphase, a transformation initiative is still being evaluated and elimination is still possible. Therefore, you should assign all employees who are working on the transformation initiative to regularly update key constituents in the organization. These updates should be done both formally (meetings, presentations, or both) and informally (personal and small group discussions). Finally, establish a transformation initiative contact/liaison program to involve influential employees (not other HRD professionals) in making connections and providing transformation initiative-related information to all employees in their respective work areas.

Conner (1992, 152–153) identifies a number of reasons why many transformation initiatives are aborted at this stage, including:

- Logistic, economic, or political problems surface.
- The need that sparked the initial commitment may no longer exist.
- The overall strategic goals of the organization may have shifted and now do not include the transformation outcomes.
- People in key sponsorship positions may have left the organization or are not as active in the initiative as they once were.

At the conclusion of the adoption stage, terminate the transformation initiative or institutionalize it as standard operating procedure.

Institutionalization is the period in which all parties (for example, leaders, managers, supervisors, employees, and HRD professionals) no longer view the transformation of HRD as temporary. Once institutionalization occurs, the organizational system alters to accommodate the change. In short, after institutionalizing the transformation of HRD, the organization is never the same. Organizational members embrace the new results-driven HRD program as a matter of routine operation and perceive it as a way of daily life. Over time, the transformed HRD program becomes a part of the organizational culture and is adopted as an important value or guiding principle. The expanding use and integration of technology is a prime example.

Internalization of the transformation of HRD occurs when its philosophies are reflected in organizational members' interests, goals, or values (Conner 1992, 154). In other word, employees become deep-seated advocates who take personal responsibility for the success of the transformation of HRD. Internalization is also stronger than any organizational mandate because it generates enthusiasm, high-energy involvement, and persistence on the part of organizational members.

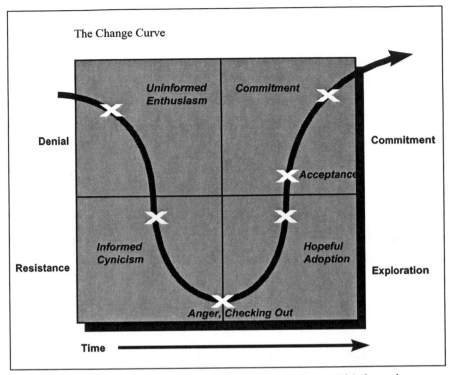

FIGURE 4.2   The Change Curve. Gilley, Quatro, Hoekstra, Whittle, and Maycunich. *The Manager as Change Agent.* Cambridge, Mass: Perseus Publishing (2001, 46).

Managing Through the Change Curve

As the leader of the transformation initiative, accept the fact that you are going to cause some level of disruption for those on the receiving end of the transformation (change). Individuals (leaders, managers, employees, and HRD professionals) who are most resistant to the transformation of HRD become the first persons that you must manage through the change curve. Their resistance can range from slight to downright offensive.

The Change Curve.   The best of helping others through the change curve requires understanding its elements. The first step involves identifying the behaviors and emotions that indicate where individuals are located on the curve at any given time. Next, employ strategies to help individuals move forward toward exploration, adoption, and commitment (Figure 4.2).

The change curve consists of four quadrants (Bibler 1989). The upper left corner represents denial, or the period of time in which most HRD professionals are feeling enthusiastic. Denial occurs when they believe that the change they are considering will have little if any impact on them. People feel comfortable when the change is perceived to be something that will happen to others, which is a typical symptom of a period of denial. Based on their lack of knowledge related to the transformation initiative, this quadrant is often called uninformed enthusiasm. On the other hand, this phase is sometimes referred to as the honeymoon—some of your HRD colleagues feel extremely positive about change stemming from naive enthusiasm based on insufficient data.

The second, lower left quadrant, is reached when the transformation becomes personal. It is a period when employees begin to doubt the appropriateness of the change opportunity. This often occurs as a result of receiving specific information or hearing the latest rumor about the transformation effort. Some HRD professionals finally realize that they will be affected by the transformation of HRD. Consequently, many begin to actively resist change as the transformation initiative formally enters a period of resistance.

The critical point in this change curve—checking out—occurs when your colleagues are located between resistance and exploration (Figure 4.2) In fact, they are halfway through the change curve without knowing it. This is typically where some HRD professionals choose to check out, emotionally and even physically, in a state of anger, frustration, and disappointment with the changes that they must endure. Some HRD professionals withdraw from the transformation initiative because they have serious reservations or a low tolerance for change.

Much of managing your colleagues through the change curve depends on providing them with information and reassurance as the transformation impacts them. Typically, HRD professionals, like most people, disregard formal information regarding the transformation at first because they have entered a period of informed cynicism. Do not let this throw you off course. Rather, continue to provide your colleagues with information to reinforce the seriousness of your intentions. Further, your colleagues need to go through this portion of the change curve before they can move toward accepting, adopting, and supporting the transformation initiative. Although informed cynicism is inevitable, checking out is not.

As the leader of the transformation initiative, you obviously want to minimize the number of your colleagues who check out, either temporarily or permanently, especially if they can help facilitate the transformation. On the other hand, in reality some of your colleagues will benefit personally or professionally by leaving the organization. What you must avoid are HRD colleagues who check out mentally and emotionally but physically remain in the organization. This can lead to open rebellion or undermining the entire transformation effort.

The third quadrant, in the lower right corner, is where progress can be realized in the journey toward acceptance and commitment of the transformation initiative. It is referred to as the exploration phase of change. During this phase, change is perceived more positively than negatively. It is a period of hopeful adoption, where your HRD colleagues accept the reality of the change that is occurring and start seeking positive outcomes.

Cynicism does not suddenly disappear, although it lessens as HRD professionals move into hopeful adoption. This is not a return to the "everything is wonderful days" of uninformed enthusiasm; it simply means that employees begin to understand the positive possibilities of the transformation.

As more and more concerns are resolved, your HRD colleagues become increasingly confident and move into the next stage, which is characterized by the acceptance of change as a positive growth and development opportunity. Stakeholders demonstrate their commitment to the transformation initiative by supporting and managing its implementation. Once this stage is reached, employees enter a period of equilibrium and tranquillity. Thus, the final stage is known as commitment, which is represented by the upper right quadrant. It is a period in which your colleagues accept the transformation of HRD from activity-based to results-driven. It is also the point where they are fully committed to the new way of doing things. In this place you and your colleagues collectively reenergize and realize the full positive impact of the transformation initiative. Unfortunately, some HRD changes never reach this stage because their HRD professionals are not helped through the previous three stages.

The leader of the transformation initiative creates an environment for confronting conflict in a constructive and positive way. By valuing diverse opinions and respecting the energy of dissent, everyone involved in the transformation process engages in honest conflict in a safe environment that nourishes all.

Step 6: Integrating Change into the Organizational Culture

Burke (1992) argues that a change initiative, like the transformation of HRD, is not permanent in an organization until it alters the culture. The culture of an organization is a powerful influence on human behavior, which can be difficult to change, and the near invisible nature of an organization's culture makes it hard to address directly (Kotter 1996, 150–151). Furthermore, shared values, which are less apparent but more deeply ingrained in culture, are more difficult to change than norms of behavior. An organization's culture proves powerful for three reasons: individuals are selected and indoctrinated so well, culture exerts itself through the actions of hundreds or thousands of people, and all of this happens without much conscious intent and, thus, is difficult to challenge or even discuss. When a change initiative (HRD transformation) is not compatible with the relevant culture it will be subject to regression or even attack. The initiative can unravel, even after years of effort, if it has not been anchored firmly in group norms and values via culture.

Making Change Last

Specific actions such as assigning accountabilities and time frames, and integrating multidirectional activities (top-down, side-to-side, and bottom-up) facilitate the transformation of HRD. Ulrich (1998, 138) believes that chances of success improve dramatically when you have developed short- and long-term plans to keep attention focused on the transformation initiative, its values and benefits, and have a plan for adapting the HRD transformation initiative over time. In short, you create an integrated culture-change action plan when you implement the seven steps of the successful transformation of HRD.

Several characteristics are crucial when examining the relationship between organizational culture and change. They include beliefs, behaviors, and assumptions.

- Beliefs are the set of integrated values and expectations that provide a framework for shaping what people hold to be true or false, relevant or irrelevant, good or bad about their environment.
- Behaviors are observable actions that constitute the way people actually operate on a daily basis. Whereas beliefs reflect intentions that are often difficult to discern, behaviors can be verified in a more objective manner.
- Assumptions are the unconscious rationales we use for continuing to apply certain beliefs or specific behaviors. When people develop belief and behavior patterns that are successful, they rely on those patterns when similar circumstances arise (Conner 1992, 164–165).

The prevailing beliefs, behaviors, and assumptions of an organization guide what are considered appropriate or inappropriate actions in which individuals and groups engage.

An organization's collective beliefs, behaviors, and assumptions affect daily interactions and decisions. They are present on two different levels: overt and covert. At the overt level, organizational beliefs, behaviors, and assumptions are observable, intentional, and directly influence operations (for example, goals, policies and procedures, and institutional vision and mission statements). At the overt level, an organization typically operates on beliefs and observable behaviors rather than on assumptions. At the covert level, an organization is influenced by employees' collective assumptions that are obscure, unintentional, and indirectly influence operations (such as informal ground rules, unofficial guidelines, or interactions) (Conner 1992, 166). At the covert level, the organization is influenced by employees' collective assumptions. Since the latter stem from personalities, institutional history, biases, and personal views, they are difficult to change. The overt and covert influencers combine to impact oral and written communications, institutional structure, power and status, policies and procedures, compensation and reward systems, and the design and use of physical facilities.

When an organization's current culture is congruent with a proposed change (transformation of HRD), it enhances the chances of successfully implementing that change. The odds of implementing the desired change diminishes when a disconnect exists between the present culture and the beliefs, behaviors, and assumptions required by the new initiative. Quite simply, organizations encounter minimum resistance when a change initiative is consistent with its culture. Moreover, Rummler and Brache (1995) believe that whenever a discrepancy exists between current organizational culture and the objectives of change, the current culture always wins. Therefore, effective management of organizational culture is an essential contributor to the success of a change initiative.

Because organizational culture is resistant to major change (see the Organizational Immune System, Chapter 6), a great deal of time, energy, effort, and resources must be used in its conversion. When implementing a change that requires significant alterations in organizational culture, Conner (1992, 178) believes you should do one of three things: modify the change to be more in line with existing beliefs, behaviors, and assumptions of the institution's culture; modify the beliefs, behaviors, and assumptions of the current culture to be more supportive of the change; or prepare for the change to fail.

Step 7: Measuring and Monitoring Change

Measuring and monitoring the transformation of HRD requires a means of evaluating its impact on your organization's culture. Benchmark progress of the transformation and evaluate whether your goals for the transformation initiative were accomplished. This includes determining whether milestone dates were achieved. Finally, use your stakeholders (leaders, managers,

---

Questions Useful in Implementing the Seven-Step Transformation Model

- To what extent have you communicated a sense of urgency for the transformation initiative?

- To what extent does the transformation initiative have a leader who will guide its success?

- To what extent do the key stakeholders (leaders, managers, supervisors, employees, and HRD professionals) essential to the success of the transformation initiative possess ownership and support for it?

- To what extent do key stakeholders understand the desired vision for the transformation initiative?

- To what extent are key stakeholders involved in implementing and managing the transformation initiative?

- To what extent do you have an action plan for integrating the transformation initiative into the organizational culture?

- To what extent are indicators in place to track progress of the transformation initiative?

TABLE 4.1   Questions Useful in Implementing the Seven-Step Transformation Model

employees, and HRD professionals) as sources of accountability and progress when tracking the transformation initiative.

A Guide for Monitoring Change

Resolving the paradox of change means transforming the seven steps to the successful transformation of HRD from a theoretical exercise into a managerial process. Using the questions in Table 4.1, the seven steps can be profiled. Addressing these questions ensures that the resources and actions needed to transform an HRD program will be available and initiated. The probabilities of implementing any change initiative improve dramatically when these seven questions are addressed.

Leaders of the transformation of HRD may erroneously believe that they must "own" all the actions to make change happen. In reality, your primary job is to shape the transformation process—guide organizational leaders, managers, employees, and your HRD colleagues in discussions using these questions as a guide. Afterward, a comprehensive action plan for making change happen can be developed.

Conclusion

We have provided you with an easy and proven seven-step approach to successfully transforming your organization's HRD program. Its implementation is critical to the success of HRD and its practitioners.

PART C

Six Transformational Roles in Results-Driven HRD

In the past, HRD professionals could simply buy training programs from vendors, schedule a training session, deliver the program, conduct simple reaction evaluations asking participants' opinions of the training event, and hope that somehow employee performance would improve. Although this is a negative description of an activity-based program, this behavior still exists far too often in today's organizations. Fortunately, many HRD professionals are dedicated, determined, and spend their time, energy, and effort helping their organizations develop learning cultures, create performance management systems, and implement change initiatives. These activities build developmental cultures, improve elements of the organizational system (structure, mission, strategy, leadership, managerial practices, processes, and work climates), and enhance HRD professionals' credibility within organizations.

HRD professionals may engage in one of two roles. The first role, transactional, focuses activity strategy where training is the cornerstone. The other role, transformational, promotes a results-driven strategy that is performance and organizationally centered (Robinson and Robinson 1989). In this role, you help the organization achieve its strategic business goals and objectives.

Transactional and transformational roles differ in their focus and contributions to an organization. Transactional professionals emphasize training whereas transformational professionals aim to maximize organizational performance and effectiveness. The first strategy embraces a business-as-usual approach, the latter is results-driven and requires you to adopt a new and exciting role.

Transactional Roles

Activity-based HRD practitioners engage in several different roles—the most common are trainer, instructional designer, needs analyst, and evaluator (McLagan 1989). When engaged in these roles, you provide services to an organization in the way of training programs, performance support material, needs assessment activities, training manuals, and the like. Typically, these roles are located in the centralized training and development or HRD department.

Trainers present the information associated with learning programs and training activities, identify learning needs, and develop appropriate activities and programs to address those needs. Finally, trainers evaluate the effectiveness of programs and activities by determining their effects on the organization and its learners.

Instructional designers design, develop, and evaluate learning programs and training activities, although most designers seldom implement them. Instructional designers are generally employed full-time by large organizations that can afford such specialization. Additionally, they are often the organization's media specialist, instructional writer, task analyst, and evaluator.

Needs analysts conduct needs assessments to identify training needs. Once identified, they often engage in instructional design activities useful in the development of training programs and materials. At the completion of a training event, they serve as learning evaluators. In this role, they determine the learning participants' reaction to training and, occasionally, conduct pre- and post-tests to ascertain whether learning occurred.

These roles are *transactional* because practitioners primarily engage in exchanges that result in services consumed by internal clients (for example, training programs). As a result, they participate in relatively short-term engagements that yield little strategic value. These activities are typically at the request of others and are based on nonempirical inquiry. In some respects, this process resembles a retail approach to providing HRD programs, where exchanges take place and value is exchanged between parties without the benefit of serious dialogue or evidence of integration or application. Over time, HRD programs may fall prey to the services-for-hire approach, which locks practitioners out of serious strategic discussions and engagements. When services are not needed or the organization encounters a difficult economic period, HRD activities are often outsourced or eliminated.

Many HRD programs are perceived to be outside the mainstream of the organization because they are viewed as merely internal training houses for employees (Brinkerhoff and Apking 2001; Brinkerhoff and Gill 1994). Because of this perception, training is not considered critical to the success of the organization, nor are HRD professionals taken seriously. Moreover, little attention is given to the outcomes of training or the impact it has on employee performance. As a result, the services provided by transactional practitioners are not often linked to the strategic business goals of the organization (Brinkerhoff and Gill 1994). Training is conducted in a vacuum, with little attention paid to the problems facing the organization and how training can be used to address them. Consequently, the organization fails to develop performance management systems that improve performance. Organizational performance fails to improve when training is not linked to the business needs of the firm. This type of training represents the hit-or-miss approach—some training is on target, but most is not.

Transactional Responsibilities

Transactional HRD professionals are primarily responsible for individual and career development interventions. Individual development commonly refers to training in which employees develop new knowledge, skills, or improved behaviors. Occasionally, this results in performance enhancement and improvement related to an employee's current job (training). Such interventions may involve formal and informal learning activities or informal, on-the-job training activities. Individual development is directed at a short-term orientation to performance improvement, which results in a micro level of organizational enhancement (Gilley, Eggland, and Maycunich 2002). Quite simply, improved knowledge, skills, or behaviors affect a single job or groups of jobs.

Career development involves identifying an employee's interests, values, competencies, activities, and assignments needed to develop skills for future jobs (development). Career development includes both individual and organizational activities. Individual activities include career planning, career awareness, and using career resource centers, whereas organizational activities include job posting systems, mentoring systems, career resource center development and maintenance, using managers as career counselors, providing career development workshops and seminars, human resource planning, performance appraisals, and career pathing programs (Simonsen 1997). Career development is more complex and focused on the long term than individual development. It has a greater impact on organizational efficiency because it is directed at providing employees with a continuous developmental approach to achieve ever-increasing levels of competency, which impacts the total operation of the organization (Walton 1999).

Transformational Roles

Although transactional roles provide an important service, today's HRD professionals need to adjust to ever-changing conditions and circumstances. The challenges facing organizations require you to adopt roles that can improve organizational performance, enhance competitive readiness, and facilitate renewal capacity and capability. These roles allow you the greatest opportunity for organizational influence and leadership (Figure C.1). These roles enable you to work directly with leaders and decisionmakers in an effort to dramatically alter the organization's operations and systems.

These roles are transformational in that you become a strategic instrument used to improve the organization's effectiveness, competitive readiness, and renewal capacity. As a transformational professional, you help managers develop diagnostic skills to approach specific performance problems and address how things are done rather than what tasks are performed. Transformational professionals examine organizational structure, job design, work flow, performance appraisal and review processes, employee attitudes, performance criteria and standards, and quality improvement processes for the purpose of identifying ways of improving performance.

When you serve as a transformational professional, you work directly with key decisionmakers and managers in the execution of performance improvement and change initiatives. This ultimately enables you to develop higher levels of credibility within your organization. As such, you serve in one of six roles:

1. Relationship builder (Chapter 5)
2. Organizational architect (Chapter 6)
3. Strategist (Chapter 7)
4. Performance engineer (Chapter 8)
5. Change champion (Chapter 9)
6. Political navigator (Chapter 10)

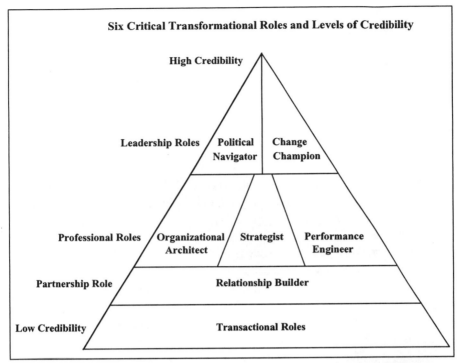

FIGURE C.1   Six Critical Transformational Roles and Levels of Credibility

The first, a partnership role, exists when you work toward building relationships with critical decisionmakers. The next three roles are professional roles, in which you demonstrate technical expertise, organizational understanding, and organizational analysis skills. The last two roles are leadership roles, in which you help guide the organization through difficult times employing your change management and political expertise.

Understanding the Levels of an Organization

In 1995, Garry Rummler and Alan Brache developed a model that reflects three levels of an organization and their interdependent relationships: organization, business process (departmental), and job/performer. Each level differs in terms of its goals, design, and management; however, they must be congruent and work in harmony to positively impact an organization's effectiveness and efficiency. Knowledge of these differing levels enables you to provide specialized recommendations and interventions for their improvement, and create integrated solutions that yield value through HRD practice (Ulrich 1997, 96).

Organization Level

At the organization level you examine the nature and direction of the business, including organizational goals, design, and management.

Organizational Goals.   Organizational goals are part of the business strategy at the organizational level. Organizations must establish clear systemwide goals that reflect decisions regarding the organization's competitive advantage(s), new services and new markets, emphasis it will place on its various products or services and markets, and resources it is prepared to invest in its operations and the return it expects to realize on these investments (Rummler and Brache 1998, 20).

Organizational Design.   This element focuses on the overall structure of the organization (see Chapter 6). Structure includes the reporting relationships between and among departments, how work gets done, and whether work relationships makes sense. In other words, the systems view of performance suggests that structure should include more than where departmental boundaries have been drawn and who reports to whom (see relationship mapping, Chapter 6).

Organizational Management.   Organizations must be managed appropriately to operate effectively and efficiently. Of course, the first step is to make certain that the organization's goals and design lead to effective management. At the organization level, management includes:

- Goal management: Creating functional subgoals that support achievement of overall organization goals.
- Performance management: Obtaining regular customer feedback, tracking actual performance along the measurement dimensions established in the goals, feeding back performance information to relevant subsystems, taking corrective action if performance is off target, and resetting goals so that the organization is continually adapting to external and internal reality.
- Resource management: Balancing the allocation of people, equipment, and budgets across the system.
- Interface management: Ensuring that the "white space" between functions is managed. In this capacity, managers resolve functional "turf" conflicts and establish infrastructures to support collaboration

that characterizes efficient, effective internal customer-supplier relationships (Rummler and Brache 1995, 21).

Business Process Level

Every large organization contains separate departments, sometimes referred to as functions or business processes. Each department performs specific duties and activities, which offer identity for employees and provide them a connection within the firm. The separateness of these functions occasionally hinders interaction between and among departments or the individuals within them. In fact, the "systems view does not enable us to understand the way work actually gets done, which is a necessary precursor to performance improvement" (Rummler and Brache 1995, 22). Most performance breakdowns or opportunities for efficiencies occur within cross-departmental processes such as order handling, billing, procurement, customer service, sales, and marketing, and product development. As a result, examining processes within an organization yields insight into the handoffs that occur between employees in different departments who are trying to produce a product or service for an internal or external customer. The aggregate of all performance activities, either within a department or across departments, is known as business processes (Rummler and Brache 1995).

Every department exists to serve the needs of one or more internal or external stakeholders. For external stakeholders, "the functions should measure the degree to which its products and services meet needs. If a function serves only internal stakeholders, it should be evaluated based on the way it meets stakeholders' needs and on the value it ultimately adds to the external stakeholder. In both cases, the key links to the customer are the processes to which the function contributes" (Rummler and Brache 1995, 22).

Process Goal.   Business processes are the means through which work is produced; therefore, you perform a valuable service by helping managers and their employees set goals for their business processes. Goals, whether directed at internal or external stakeholder needs, should be aligned with organizational goals and stakeholder requirements.

Process Design.   Effective organizational processes are structured (designed) to meet goals efficiently once process goals have been identified (Rummler 1998). Process design should be logical, efficient paths to the achievement of goals. Answering one simple question achieves this end: "Do the company's key processes consist of steps that enable it to meet process goals efficiently?" (Rummler and Brache 1995, 23).

Process Management.   Unless managed properly, any business process will be ineffective. Process management includes the same ingredients as organization management:

- Goal management: Establishing subgoals at each critical process step.
- Performance management: Regularly obtaining customer feedback on process outputs, tracking process performance along dimensions established in goals, feeding back performance information, identifying and correcting process deficiencies, and resetting process goals to reflect current customer requirements and internal constraints.
- Resource management: Supporting each process step with the equipment, staff, and budget needed to achieve goals and make expected contributions to overall process goals.
- Interface management: Managing the "white space" between process steps, especially those that pass between functions. As at the organization level, the greatest process improvement opportunities often lie between process steps (Rummler and Brache, 1995, 23).

Job/Performer Level

Organizations must effectively manage their human performance system to survive. Breakdowns will occur—regardless of how well organization and process levels are organized and managed in terms of goals, design, and management—unless employees perform at acceptable levels. Managers ultimately determine whether company strategy becomes reality. Although business processes are the means by which an organization produces outputs, employees (performers) are the means through which processes are executed.

Implications for the Levels of Organizations Approach

Although this model was specifically designed to improve the management of performance between levels of organizations and departments, it is helpful to understand the layers of organizational complexity that transformational professionals must manage to be effective.

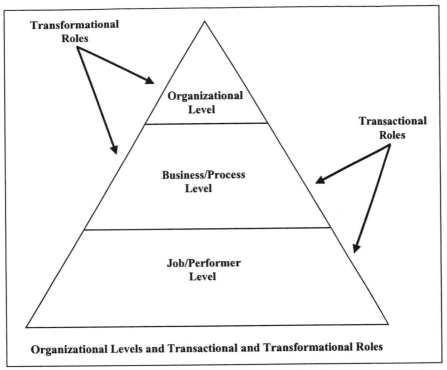

FIGURE C.2   Organizational Levels and Transactional and Transformational Roles

The Rummler and Brache model helps differentiate the responsibilities of transactional and transformational professionals. This model identifies the various levels at which transactional and transformational professionals focus their efforts. For example, transactional professionals spend a majority of their time working at the job/performer level (Figure C.2), which is evident by the type of activities in which they prefer to engage. On occasion, transactional professionals work directly with managers to execute a training event or conduct a needs assessment activity. Rarely, however, do transactional professionals work directly with senior managers or executives at the organizational level.

Transformational professionals spend a majority of their time interacting at the organizational level with senior managers and executives (Figure C.2). They are primarily responsible for developing performance management systems, facilitating organizational change initiatives, and engaging in quality improvement and system enhancement activities. They spend a significant amount of time working directly with managers at the business process level, helping them implement initiatives and interventions as well as evaluating their effectiveness. Transformational professionals spend little if any time at the job/performer level because this is the primary responsibility of managers. Since transformational professionals work with senior managers and executives, they need to develop organizational and political expertise to be effective and maneuver through the organizational maze (see Chapters 6 and 10). Finally, transformational professionals establish reporting relationships at the organizational level to create opportunities to have a seat at the executive table (Chapters 6–10).

Developing Front and Back Wheel Expertise

Improving credibility requires development of two types of competencies, which are professional expertise and interpersonal skills. To best illustrate this concept, visualize a bicycle (Figure C.3). A bicycle has two wheels: a front and back wheel. The back wheel provides the power to propel the bicycle forward, and represents your professional competency, expertise, and business/organizational understanding. In essence, the back wheel symbolizes the talents, skills, and competencies for which the organization hired you in the first place. These competencies are used to enhance the organization's strategic position and performance capacity. The front wheel provides steering, which allows you to maneuver the bicycle through difficult situations. It gives you the ability to avoid obstacles and guide the bicycle to your final destination. The front wheel represents your interpersonal skills, which are critical when working with executives, managers, and employees. These skills and competencies are useful in convincing individuals that change is needed or a performance improvement intervention is essential. They help you build long-term collaborative relationships with stakeholders throughout the firm. Quite simply, you need both front and back wheel competencies to become a successful transformational HRD professional.

Front wheel competencies are essential when engaging in the relationship building role, whereas back wheel competencies are demonstrated when you act as an organizational architect, strategist, or performance engineer. Serving as a change champion and political navigator require you to possess both front and back wheel competencies (Figure C. 3).

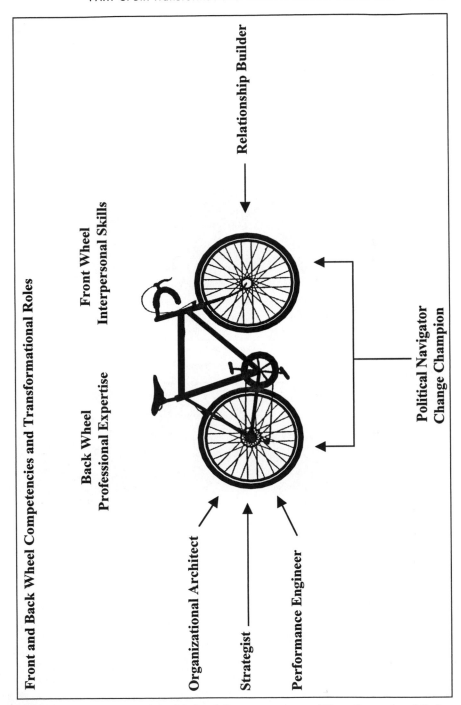

FIGURE C.3   Front and Back Wheel Competencies and Transformational Roles

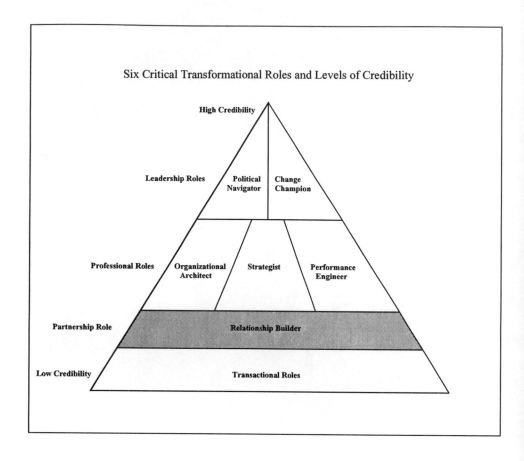

Six Critical Transformational Roles and Levels of Credibility

Relationship Builder

Some HRD programs falter because they are not based on the needs of the organization. Others falter because they are not perceived as helping the organization achieve its strategic business goals and objectives. The most common reason for the failure of HRD programs is due to HRD practitioners' lack of credibility in the organization. There are two reasons for this condition. First, some HRD practitioners fail to demonstrate an understanding of their organization and its business operations. This is evident by the fact that most HRD practitioners are never invited to participate in discussions regarding the strategic direction of the organization. As a result, they are perceived by many as a cost to the organization rather than as an investment. Thus, HRD is considered a staff function whose budget generates internal services instead of as revenue-generating. Second, some HRD practitioners fail to properly communicate the value and benefits of their interventions and initiatives to decisionmakers within the organization. Since vital decisionmakers are unaware of HRD's contributions, they believe that HRD is unable to help improve performance, quality, efficiency, or productivity. Over time, they view HRD as nonessential in accomplishing the organization's strategic goals and objectives. In short, many HRD practitioners lack credibility within the organization, hence their programs are destined to fail.

Communication and Interpersonal Strategies

Another front wheel skill is developing communication and interpersonal strategies appropriate to creating long-lasting client relationships. Since getting things done is often more about who you know than what you know, it is critical that you:

1. build rapport with clients
2. establish commonality and professional competence with clients
3. build client relationships through effective communicate techniques
4. identify your interpersonal style and develop strategies for improving interpersonal relationships
5. create a thirty-second commercial.

Armed with these strategies, you should be able to develop meaningful relationships with any potential client. Such relationships are fundamental to your success and the success of a result-driven HRD program.

Becoming a Conscious Competent

All of us want to be good at what we are doing. We want to perform well and we want to know why, which defines being a professional. A pro is a person who is competent, and fully aware of the *reasons* for that competence. When something goes wrong in practicing a skill, the pro knows why it went wrong and what should be done to prevent future occurrences. A pro is what we call a conscious competent (Figure 5.1).

The professional did not get there by chance. In fact, the pro may have started at the opposite end of the scale, as an unconscious incompetent. Years ago, the pro did not have the skill to perform and did not even know how to improve.

Occasionally, through trial, error, and intuition, one masters a skill and overcomes incompetence. Those who achieve success over time are unconsciously competent; they do not know why they are good. Since they do not know how they became competent, they do not know how to repeat the cycle or take corrective action if they get off course.

A conscious incompetent's performance is inconsistent. In some cases, people at this stage know how to perform effectively but elect not to do so. Over time, most of us learn what works and what does not. Eventually, you are conscious of what you do not know, which puts you on the road toward learning, toward becoming professionals.

Strategy 1: Building Rapport with Clients

Rapport is defined as an open, honest relationship between you and your client. This condition is not a superficial relationship but is based on a deep concern for the well-being of others. It is established through your sincere interest in and acceptance of the client.

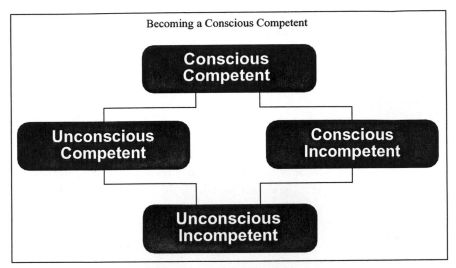

FIGURE 5.1   Becoming a Conscious Competent

The result of developing rapport is the creation of a definitive working relationship that enhances communication between you and your client. It can be observed when you demonstrate that you are equally concerned for the relationship you have with the client and for the well-being of HRD.

One of the most difficult processes for you to master is to become participatory, since it requires having the courage to relinquish control and dominance over clients. The participatory approach requires a gentle shift from authoritarian control to participation, which is less threatening to clients. Participation also allows clients to become active agents, which helps them support the decisions made.

The participatory approach requires you to recognize the importance of having a functional working relationship with clients. Moreover, you need to recognize that clients bring a great deal of experience to a situation, which is an invaluable asset to be acknowledged and tapped. Many practitioners, however, fail to recognize that this asset provides a wealth of information beneficial to a working relationship. Such recognition is indeed difficult but is essential in the development of positive rapport.

The first step in the development of a participatory approach is to create an environment in which a free exchange of ideas and feelings are encouraged. The benefit of this type of environment is that clients feel secure. Clients also recognize that the lines of two-way communication are open. A sharing environment goes beyond the superficial to demonstrate a deep concern for the well-being of clients, and is dedicated to improving organizational performance and effectiveness.

Elements in a Positive Relationship Environment.   A closer examination reveals that certain key elements are needed for development of a proper sharing environment. These ingredients are essential to your success, and include acceptance, attentiveness, empathy, genuineness, involvement, understanding, and credibility.

Acceptance

Acceptance is the basic attitude that you hold toward a client, and requires respect for the client as a person of worth. You demonstrate acceptance via your willingness to allow clients to differ from one another. This willingness is based on the belief that each client is a complex being comprised of different experiences, values, and attitudes. As Carl Rogers (1961) stated in his classic work *On Becoming a Person,* "by acceptance I mean a warm regard for him/her as a person of unconditional self-worth . . . an acceptance of and a regard for his/her attitudes . . . no matter how negative or positive."

Attentiveness

Attentiveness refers to the effort made by you to hear the message conveyed by clients. It requires skills in listening and observing. Too many HRD practitioners cannot wait until a client stops speaking so that they can present their own point of view. This diminishes the importance of the client's ideas and communicates a lack of respect. On the other hand, listening conveys to clients that you are interested in and sensitive to their feelings and thoughts.

Nonverbal communication is also important in establishing and maintaining an environment that is conducive to sharing. Many clients are quite aware of the nonverbal behavior of some HRD practitioners and often avoid certain topics and discussions as a result. In fact, this might even lead a client to avoid contact with a particular practitioner. A simple nonverbal technique such as proper eye contact can greatly improve the communication between you and your client.

Empathy

Typically, empathy has been described as putting oneself in the other person's shoes, attempting to see things from another person's vantage point. When you have the ability to feel and describe the thoughts and feelings of others, you are considered empathetic. Empathetic understanding is the ability to recognize, sense, and understand the feelings that another person communicates through his or her behavioral and verbal expressions, and to accurately communicate this understanding to that person. It is not enough to understand the behavior or feelings of clients, you must also communicate that understanding to them. True empathy is an active event rather than a passive one.

Genuineness

Genuineness refers to your ability to be yourself in all situations, rather than playing a part or role. Genuineness is demonstrated when you know your true feelings, act on them, and communicate them if necessary. Genuineness implies being honest and candid with yourself while functioning as an HRD practitioner, and not pretending to be something you are not. This also implies self-disclosure, but does not mean that one should totally unveil one's personal and private life. Clients want to believe in you. Honesty and candor provide the atmosphere for this to take place.

Involvement

A willingness to care and feel responsible for the other person is rightly called involvement. Although acceptance and understanding are passive, involvement implies action; it means active participation in the client's problems and needs. Only active participants become agents for change, engaging in activities that allow face-to-face contact with clients. Maintaining good records of interactions and training activities demonstrate the interest that you have in their clients.

Understanding

Understanding is recognizing and correctly interpreting the feelings, thinking, and behavior of another person. Although we acknowledge that no one fully understands their clients, it can be said that the path to understanding is essentially a process of sharing. Clients express themselves through verbal and nonverbal language that you attempt to interpret and put into words to clarify it for both of them. Understanding can be characterized as external or internal.

External understanding refers to an awareness of clients' behavior and actions on your part. This means being able to identify the actions of clients and account for the results. Internal understanding refers to your ability to step into the perceptual world of your clients. This is done in an effort to discover their internal world—their fears, successes, and failures. It is at this level that genuine communication begins.

Several other activities help you establish rapport with clients. These include turning assertions into questions, giving clients options, making meetings and reports meaningful, helping clients implement solutions and interventions, being accessible, and always, always adding value. We believe that one of the best ways of improving client relationships is helping them learn new skills and competencies. Learning enhances client self-esteem, which in turn improves client relationship. You can also enhance client relationships by encouraging development of critical thinking skills that improve clients' professional practices and result in better approaches to accomplishing work.

Strategy 2: Establishing Commonality and Professional Competence with Clients

When meeting with clients for the first time, it is extremely important to develop a positive working relationship. To achieve this end, you need to establish two things: commonality and competence. Commonality is achieved by discovering areas of similarity and mutual interest. Competence must be demonstrated before a potential client will be willing to trust your recommendations and suggestions.

- Attempt to identify with clients. This includes identifying with their interests and expectations, business customs and behavior, dress and manners, speech and language. You must be willing to communicate with clients at their level by using terminology with which clients relate. This is one of the fastest ways to build a relationship with a client. Further, communicate using terms that clients value, such as return on investment, profitability, operational results, cost effectiveness, improved efficiency, quality performance, or revenue enhancements. These simple terms help demonstrate your awareness of their organizational issues.
- Develop mutual interest with clients through self-disclosure or using open-ended questions that search out and highlight common history, ideas, and experiences. Third-party references also provide an excellent way to identify mutual interest. This technique identifies a common experience or mutual acquaintance. The process is not designed to trick clients or develop a superficial relationship with them; it should be a genuine attempt to explore commonality.

Summary of Communication Techniques

Active Listening	Hearing and clearly understanding what is being said, by concentrated involvement in the communication process with the employee
Clarifying	Getting others to elaborate on feelings or attitudes to benefit understanding
Encouraging	Supportive statements or gestures that let others know that you accept or empathize with their approach
Interpreting	Dealing with cause-and-effect relationships, derived from your own knowledge and the others' comments, to understand implications
Paraphrasing	Demonstrating understanding of an employee's ideas by restating them in your words
Questioning	Using inquiry to pull together the interaction
Silence	Intentional pauses that adjust the pace of interaction
Summarizing	Tentative overall conclusion of what has transpired in the interaction, to check levels of agreement and understanding by the participants
Reflecting	Mirroring another person's message content by stating what his or her feelings and attitudes are believed to be
Tentative Analysis	Partial conclusion based on initial public testing of one idea expressed by the other person

TABLE 5.1   Summary of Communication Techniques

- Demonstrate professional competence via your ability to solve clients' problems and meet their needs. You can do this without bragging. Share information about your professional experience, educational background, training, skills, and track record. Also communicate your understanding of the client's situation and the performance problems, changes, and developmental needs that other clients in similar situations face.

Strategy 3: Building Client Relationships Through Effective Communication Techniques

Effective relationship builders develop strong communication techniques. Table 5.1 outlines the techniques and links them to the goals that are typically sought through the communication process. Each technique can be learned by virtually anyone and is helpful in guiding the change management process. These particular skills help clients develop a sense of trust when implementing change for the first time, promote rapport, and enhance credibility so clients will be willing to accept your recommendations.

Relationship builders assume subroles to build client relationships: collaborator and communicator. As a collaborator, you establish credibility and gain confidence to implement change. Collaborators tailor communications to their audience, listen and ask appropriate questions, present ideas clearly and concisely via well-organized written and interpersonal communications, engage in informal communications that build support, and identify commonalities among their various client groups to determine shared interests.

One of the most important subroles is that of communicator. Important skills here include active listening, using silence, demonstrating understanding, establishing rapport, communicating empathy, clarifying statements, and appropriately employing summarization techniques.

Communication Techniques. We believe that using the following communication techniques help establish rapport with clients, which leads to more successful performance improvement interventions and change initiatives. These techniques can play a critical role in relating successfully with clients.

Active Listening

One of the agreed-upon keys to effective communications is to become a better listener. Good listening is an important bridge to understanding because it changes the entire relationship between you and the client. Some 70 to 80 percent of our waking hours are spent in communication and over half of that time involves listening. Feedback is also a necessary ingredient in effective communication and one that can be made accurate only through good listening.

The difference between active and inactive listening is the difference between listening and just hearing. The act of listening requires effort and concentration. Listening to clients intently helps you more readily capture content and intended meaning. Moreover, since you also convey respect through active listening, certain positive results can be predicted. That is, clients who are listened to attentively will tend to

- Consider their point of view to be more important.
- State their feelings and thinking more clearly.

- Listen to others more carefully when they speak.
- Become less quarrelsome.
- Become more receptive to different points of view.

To develop better listening skills, you should

- Concentrate all your physical and mental energies on listening.
- When possible, avoid interrupting the speaker.
- Demonstrate interest and alertness.
- Seek an area of agreement with the client.
- Search for meaning and avoid getting hung up on specific words.
- Demonstrate patience (you can "listen faster" than the client can speak).
- Provide clear and unambiguous feedback to the client.
- Repress the tendency to respond emotionally to what is said.
- Ask questions when you do not understand something.
- Withhold evaluation of the message until the client is finished and you are sure you understand the message.

Clarifying

Sometimes it is helpful to make clarifying statements in an attempt to place the client's feeling and attitudes in a clear, more recognizable form. Additionally, you may ask the client to elaborate on a particular point or statement, or provide an example or illustration to make the meaning more clearly understood. To this end, the client may be asked. It is important to remember that this technique should not be used in a direct effort to interpret the client's feelings or identify the cause of his or her problem; it should be used here only to "test" understanding. Using this technique involves asking questions such as "Are you angry at not being selected to participate in the restructuring project?"

Encouraging

This technique enables clients to continue to elaborate on their feelings and thoughts. Supportive remarks by you such as "I understand," "It's okay to feel that way," "That's interesting, tell me more," or "I hear you" are useful in countering feelings of inadequacy on the part of clients. They also prompt action by encouraging the client to continue the discussion. Another effective technique is a nod of the head or an "mm-hm," which serves to strengthen the client's response and his or her efforts to continue speaking, and lets the client know you are listening.

Interpreting

When using this technique, you go beyond the client's statement to explain cause-and-effect relationships and clarify implications. This approach enables clients to understand the full ramifications of what they are saying, and generally results in a greater awareness of what is involved. Use of interpreting requires you to draw a conclusion about the client's perception of a situation or event. Interpretation is subject to error; that is, the interpretation could be incorrect.

As a technique, interpreting provides a basis for publicly testing any assumptions made during a conversation. Thus, it allows the client the opportunity to acknowledge the correctness of your interpretation and verify his or her own point of view. Common statements such as "What I hear you saying, ... " and "Based upon what you have said, ... " can be used to introduce your interpretations.

Paraphrasing

With this technique you attempt to restate, in your own words, the client's basic message. The primary purpose of paraphrasing is to test your understanding of what has been said. Another purpose is to communicate to the client that you are trying to understand the basic message and, if the paraphrasing is successful, that you have been following what the client said. An example of paraphrasing would be: "You seem to be saying that his overbearing personality makes it difficult to accomplish the project."

Questioning

Questioning is a common and often overused communication technique. Questions should be used only to obtain specifically needed information or to direct the conversation into more constructive and informative channels. Basically, two types of questions are useful: open- and closed-ended. Questions may be directed at specific clients or at an entire group. Although questions are often overused, they remain powerful tools with which to facilitate group discussion, guide the flow and direction of conversation, and help you obtain specific information very quickly.

Open-ended questions generally require more than a few words to answer and encourage the client to expand the conversation in several different directions. They also help clients to widen their perceptual field and prepare them to consider divergent points of view. In short, open-ended questions open the doors to developing a positive relationship and good rapport. An open-ended question is less threatening to the client and allows that person to convey his or her point of view. An example might be "How do you feel about the effectiveness of the new marketing program?" Clients answering this type of question may take several different approaches.

Closed-ended questions, in contrast, can be answered in relatively few words and have specific responses. They are important for gathering essential information quickly and guiding the conversation. Examples of a closed-ended question might be "How long have you been in your current position?" or "Is this a problem you'd like to solve?" This type of question is not concerned with the effectiveness of the response or the feelings of the client but rather with gathering needed information.

Silence

Although a somewhat difficult technique to master, the use of silence enables a client to think through what has transpired and provide additional information or explanation if appropriate or needed. It is important to remember that even experienced HRD professionals are initially uncomfortable with silence as a technique. With practice, however, it becomes apparent that intentional silence provides clients with additional time to think about what they are going to say and allows them to explore their feelings more deeply. In addition, it may provide the less articulate clients with a feeling of worth. At the same time, silence can be overdone; more than a minute of silence, for example, often causes discomfort. Therefore, avoid extensive periods of silence as they may be misinterpreted and perceived as unresponsiveness. Silence is most useful when used in combination with other techniques such as encouraging and active listening.

Summarizing

Summarizing conveys to clients the essence of what has been said throughout the exchange. You may wish to ask clients to agree or disagree with your summary in order to make certain that both sides are understood. An example of a summarizing statement is "Let me take a moment to summarize our conversation. . . . " Summarizing differs from paraphrasing in that it is used as the discussion with clients is drawing to an end. A summarizing technique deals with several thoughts and concepts and helps you determine the most appropriate steps to follow for each client. Alternatively, consultants may wish to have clients summarize the discussion. Again, this is a check for accuracy and understanding.

Reflecting

Reflecting allows you to bring to the surface and verbalize the emotional or substantive content of the client's words. Its purpose is to reveal that you understand correctly what the client is feeling, thinking, or experiencing. It may actually verbalize the core of the client's attitudes when he or she has trouble putting thoughts into words.

Reflecting places the responsibility for feelings about and reactions to HRD services and activities with the person who has them. Reflection helps you guide the conversation and bring out into the open feelings and hidden agendas. This is important because deeply hidden feelings can affect virtually every thought or behavior of a client. These feelings often hinder the exchange process between you and your clients, and thus need to be brought to the surface to be dealt with effectively. This helps develop an open and honest exchange between you and your clients. An example of a summarizing statement would be "So you're looking for a training program to help you develop interpersonal skills to improve your effectiveness as a supervisor?"

Tentative Analysis

This is a "hunch" type of interpretation that is usually narrow in scope. A tentative analysis is usually stated in the form of a question because of its tentative nature. As such, it is a form of short summarization. It stops short of being comprehensive because it generally deals with one thought or concept instead of several. Its chief advantage is the way it communicates that you are attempting to test publicly a client's understanding of his or her messages. By doing this one step at a time, you demonstrate patience with and respect for the client's viewpoint. An example of tentative analysis would be "I have a feeling you're not very satisfied with the quality of the sales training program."

These ten techniques enable you to develop a comfortable working relationship with clients—one conducive to sharing ideas and feelings. Such a relationship is essential to the development of rapport with clients.

As you have seen, many things can impact the quality and effectiveness of any interpersonal interaction. You have control only over yourself as a

---

Questions Helpful in Improving Your Own Communication Effectiveness

- To what degree does my personal history affect this conversation?

- To what degree is my self-concept at risk?

- How threatened do I feel?

- Did I hear the other person correctly?

- Do I really understand what the other person is saying?

- Given my knowledge of the other person, to what degree might that person be distorting the interaction? In what probable direction?

- How threatened might the other person be at this moment?

- How might I reduce defensiveness?

- Have I made any unjustified assumptions about this interaction or its meaning?

- Does my attitude toward the other person distort my perceptions?

- What is the other person's interpersonal style? How does it match with my own?

- What adjustments might I have to make in order to accommodate this person's interpersonal style?

TABLE 5.2   Questions Helpful in Improving Your Own Communication
Effectiveness

speaker and listener. In order to improve your own communication effectiveness, use the questions in Table 5.2 when engaging in interpersonal interactions. When you have answered these questions, take appropriate actions. This should help improve the quality of your interpersonal communications.

Strategy 4: Identifying Your Interpersonal Style and Developing Strategies for Improving Interpersonal Relationships

Interpersonal relationships are difficult to develop and maintain. They can take a great toll on us personally and produce significant amounts of stress. However, they are absolutely critical to your success as a transformational HRD professional. Clearly, differences between people are not the only sources of interpersonal tension. They are, however, a major factor in much misunderstanding and conflict. Moreover, behavioral science researchers have discovered that 75 percent of the population is significantly different from any one person (Merrill and Reid 1981). Since other people are important to your success, it is important to discover why they think, make decisions, and use time differently than you.

Additionally, others may communicate, handle emotions, manage stress, and deal with conflicting opinions differently (Bolton and Bolton 1996, 3). This is not necessarily a bad thing, although these differences can lead to misunderstanding, resentment, and conflict.

Although there are a number of interpersonal methodologies, we believe the ones that are the most useful help you identify another's interpersonal style through observation. In most situations you have precious little time to analyze another person's behavior and make adjustment other than through observation. The genius of the interpersonal styles we recommend is that it requires you to focus on just two dimensions of behavior. Only two! Out of the multitude of signals given off by another person, you only have to observe two clusters of behavior to ascertain that person's behavioral style.

How is it possible to reduce hundreds of variables to just two and still be able to predict other people's behavior? A key to this breakthrough was the discovery that certain types of behaviors tend to be linked to each other in clusters of traits called syndromes (Bolton and Bolton, 1996).

In the 1960s, Dr. David Merrill identified two clusters of behavior: assertiveness and responsiveness. These two dominions are incredibly helpful in predicting how other people are likely to behave. These key dimensions of behavior combine to form the Interpersonal Grid (Figure 5.2).

Assertiveness.   In this model, assertiveness is the degree to which a person is perceived as attempting to influence the thoughts and actions of others. It is helpful to think of a continuum of assertiveness in which a person's behavior is typically more assertive or less assertive than that of half the population. The assertiveness continuum in Figure 5.2 is cut in half by a line or axis (the responsiveness continuum seen in Figure 5.2). People whose characteristic behavior is more assertive than half of the population are sometimes referred to as right of the line, which indicates location on the continuum. People on the left of the line are considered less assertive than half of the population and get their needs met by using a less forceful and less directive manner (Bolton and Bolton 1996).

Some mistakenly believe that individuals in the lower levels of assertiveness indicate submissive behavior. This is simply not true. Although some less assertive people are submissive, many simply use less forceful ways to get their needs met. What you need to focus on is whether a person's behavior appears less forceful and directive than it does for half the population. Fi-

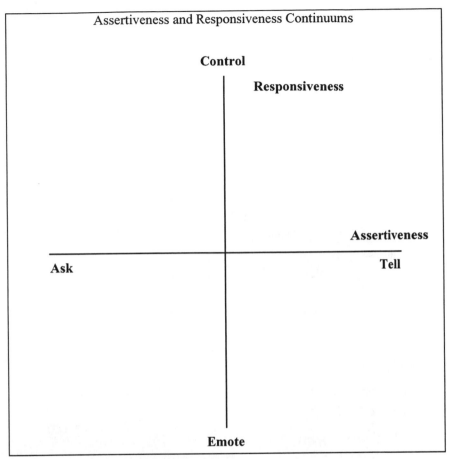

FIGURE 5.2   Assertiveness and Responsiveness Continuums (Merrill and
             Reid 1981)

nally, assertiveness is not an indication of a person's inner drive, ambition, or motivation. It is simply a reflection of how a person seeks to satisfy his or her needs (see Tables 5.3 and 5.4).

Responsiveness.   Responsiveness is the other crucial dimension of behavior in this model. Responsiveness is the degree to which a person is perceived as expressing feelings when relating with others. It is helpful to think of a continuum of responsiveness in which a person's behavior is typically more responsive or less responsive than that of half the population. The responsiveness continuum in Figure 5.2 is cut in half by a line or axis (the assertiveness continuum seen in Figure 5.2). People whose characteristic behavior is more responsive than half of the population are sometimes referred

Characteristic Behaviors of Less Assertive People

Less assertive people tend to:

- Demonstrate less energy
- Move slower
- Gesture less vigorously
- Have less intense eye contact
- Lean backward even when making a point
- Speak less rapidly
- Speak more softly
- Speak less often
- Be slower to address problems
- Decide less quickly
- Be less risk-oriented
- Be less confrontational
- Be less direct and less emphatic when expressing opinions, making requests, and giving directions
- Exert less pressure for making a decision or taking action
- Demonstrate anger less quickly

People who are less assertive than half the population exhibit most but not necessarily all of these characteristics.

TABLE 5.3   Characteristic Behaviors of Less Assertive People (Bolton and Bolton 1996)

to as bottom of the line because this is where they are located on the continuum. On the other hand, people on the top of the line are considered less responsive than half of the population and get their needs met by controlling their emotions, facial expression, and demeanor (see Tables 5.5 and 5.6).

Four Interpersonal Styles

Each individual's interpersonal style is his or her own unique blend of these two dimensions (Figure 5.3). Nevertheless, most people fall more or less into one or another of the four styles known as Driver, Expressive, Amiable, or Analytical (Bolton and Bolton 1996). These four styles can be described this way:

- Analytical style is perceived as ask-assertive/control-responsive. Analyticals are task oriented, precise, and thorough. Analyticals like

---

Characteristic Behaviors of More Assertive People

More assertive people tend to:

- Exude more energy
- Move faster
- Gesture more vigorously
- Have more intense eye contact
- Be erect or lean forward, especially when making a point
- Speak more rapidly, louder, and more often
- Address problems quicker
- Decide quicker
- Be more risk-oriented
- Be more confrontational
- Be more direct and emphatic when expressing opinions, making requests, and giving directions
- Exert more pressure for a decision or for taking action
- Demonstrate anger quicker

More assertive people exhibit most but not necessarily all of these characteristics.

TABLE 5.4   Characteristic Behaviors of More Assertive People (Bolton and Bolton 1996)

to deal in facts, work methodically, and use standard operating procedures.
- Driver style is perceived as tell-assertive/control-responsive. Drivers are goal oriented, disciplined, determined bottom-line thinkers who push for results and accomplishments. Drivers like control.
- Amiable style is perceived as ask-assertive/emote-responsive. Amiables are people oriented, friendly, accepting, cooperative, and like to be liked. Amiables are motivated to help others in a team effort.
- Expressive style is perceived as tell-assertive/emote-responsive. Expressives are idea oriented, vigorous, enthusiastic, and spontaneous. They like to initiate relationships and motivate others toward goals.

In communication, knowing what people want is half the battle. Developing versatility begins with understanding what drives or motivates each

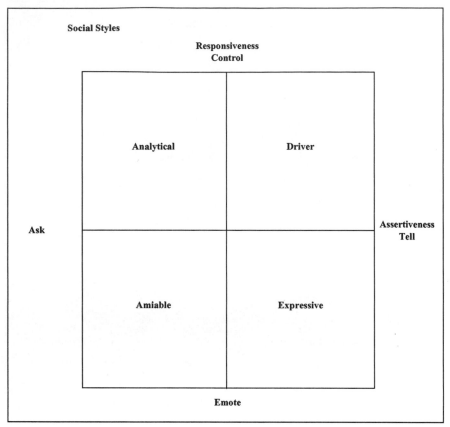

FIGURE 5.3   Social Styles (Merrill and Reid 1981)

individual interpersonal style. The following is a guide to relating most effectively to each interpersonal style.

Improving Interpersonal Relationships with Analyticals.   Analyticals are motivated by a need for respect. They value hard work and attention to detail. Things for them must be logical and carefully worked out. Their specialty is technical.

Working with Analyticals

Those working with analyticals should stick to business, use action words rather than feeling, and provide solid, realistic evidence and support for decisionmaking. Prepare your case in advance, approach them in a straightforward, direct way, and support their principles when possible. A thoughtful

Characteristic Behaviors of Less Responsive People

Compared to more responsive individuals, they tend to:

- Be less disclosing of feelings
- Appear more reserved
- Have less facial expressiveness
- Gesture less often
- Have less vocal inflection
- Be less interested in and less adept at "small talk"
- Use more facts and logic than anecdotes
- Be more task-oriented
- Prefer working alone
- Dress more formally
- Be more structured in their use of time

People who are less responsive than half the population exhibit most but not necessarily all of these characteristics.

TABLE 5.5   Characteristic Behaviors of Less Responsive People (Bolton and Bolton 1996)

Characteristic Behaviors of More Responsive People

Compared to less responsive individuals, the more responsive person tends to:

- Express feelings more openly
- Appear more friendly
- Be more facially expressive
- Gesture more freely
- Have more vocal inflection
- Be comfortable with small talk
- Use more anecdotes and stories
- Express more concern about the human aspect of issues
- Prefer working with people
- Dress more casually
- Be less structured in their use of time

More responsive people exhibit most but not necessarily all of these characteristics.

TABLE 5.6   Characteristic Behaviors of More Responsive People (Bolton and Bolton 1996)

approach is preferred, consisting of a list of pros and cons regarding your suggestions. Present materials in an organized manner, making certain that you clearly communicate important ideas and facts.

When preparing a schedule for implementing action, use a step-by-step timetable, assuring them there won't be surprises. When appropriate, give them time to make decisions and minimize risk by providing guarantees. When working with analyticals, avoid casual, loud, or informal conversations. You should not be vague or disorganized, and do not use opinion words (others' or your own) as evidence. Avoid making guesses and be accurate whenever possible. Do not be messy or rush the decisionmaking process, and avoid leaving things to chance or luck. Avoid pushing too hard, being unrealistic with deadlines, or being vague about what is expected of them, and always follow through.

Improving Interpersonal Relationships with Amiables. The payoff for amiables is approval. Amiables deal in building personal relationships. They want warmth, understanding, friendship, and trust in their communications. Their specialty is supportive.

Working with Amiables

Hold open meetings with a personal comment to break the ice and be casual and nonthreatening. Provide assurances and guarantees, especially for decisionmaking. Support their relationships and feelings, and show sincere interest in them. Be candid and open; listen carefully to what is being said and be responsive. Present your case softly, in a nonthreatening manner. Ask "how?" questions to draw their opinions. Watch carefully for possible areas of early disagreement or dissatisfaction. Move casually, informally. Define clearly (preferably in writing) individual contributions, and assure them that their decision will diminish risks and benefit them.

When working with amiables, do not rush into the business agenda or force them to respond quickly. Avoid being disagreeable and do not stick coldly or harshly to business. On the other hand, do not lose sight of goals by being too personal. Avoid making statements like "Here's how I see it." Avoid being domineering or demanding, and do not threaten them with positions of power. Recognize when you are manipulating or bullying them into agreeing because they probably won't fight back. Avoid debating facts and figures, do not be vague (rather, offer them options and probabilities), do not patronize or demean them by using subtlety, and do not be abrupt or rude.

Improving Interpersonal Relationships with Drivers. For drivers, the motivation is power. Drivers like to know they are in charge. They need information that allows them to make decisions quickly and get tangible results. Their specialty is control.

Working with Drivers

When working with drivers, be clear, specific, brief, and to the point. Always deal with the facts, packaging them for quick decisionmaking. When possible use results, support their conclusions and actions, and stick to business. Come prepared with all requirements, objectives, and support material in a well-organized presentation. Always present the facts logically and plan your presentation efficiently. Ask specific questions and provide alternatives and choices for making their own decisions. If you disagree, take issue with facts, not the person. If you agree, support results, not the person. Motivate and persuade by referring to objectives and results, at the same time supporting their conclusions. After concluding your business, depart graciously.

Avoid trying to build personal relations and do not waste their time. Do not be inefficient, ramble on, or be disorganized or messy. Avoid conversations that distract them from the business at hand, and don't ask rhetorical questions. Do not go to a meeting with a ready-made decision or offer guarantees and assurances where there is risk in meeting them. If you disagree, do not let it reflect on them personally. If you agree, do not reinforce with "I'm with YOU." Finally, never try to convince them to support an idea through "personal" appeals.

Improving Interpersonal Relationships with Expressives. Expressives thrive on recognition. They need to know you are with them in spirit. They appreciate information that allows them to move, create, or take action. Their specialty is social.

Working with Expressives

When working with expressives ask for their opinions and ideas, and support their dreams and intentions. Always talk about people and their goals and when possible give testimony and incentives for decisions. Leave time for relating and socializing and ask for their opinions and ideas regarding people. Allow plenty of time to be stimulating, fun loving, and fast moving. Provide testimonials from people they see as important and prominent. Offer special, immediate, and extra incentives for their willingness to take risks.

Three Types of Roles

Task Roles

- Initiator-contributor: Proposes new ideas or a changed way of regarding the group goal. This may include a new goal or a new definition of the problem. It may involve a suggested solution or a compromise.

- Information-seeker: Asks questions for clarification, information, and facts relevant to the problem under discussion.

- Opinion-seeker: Seeks information that is related not so much to factual data as to the values underlying the suggestions being considered.

- Opinion-giver: States beliefs or opinions relevant to a suggestion.

- Elaborator: Expands on suggestions with examples or restatements.

- Coordinator: Indicates the relationships among various ideas and suggestions and attempts to combine them.

- Orienter: Indicates the position of the group by summarizing current progress and deviations from agreed-upon directions.

- Evaluator: Compares the group's accomplishments to some criterion or standard.

- Procedural assistant: Helps the group by doing things such as distributing materials, rearranging the seating, and so on.

- Recorder: Writes down suggestions, records group discussion or decisions.

Socio-emotional Maintenance Roles:

- Encourager: Praises, shows interest in, or agrees with the contributions of others; displays warmth; listens attentively.

- Harmonizer: Mediates differences between group members; attempts to reconcile disagreements.

- Compromiser: Offers compromises when the group is in conflict.

- Gatekeeper/Expeditor: Attempts to keep communication channels open by encouraging the participation of some or by curbing the participation of others.

- Standard-setter: Expresses standards for the group or evaluates the quality of group processs (not group content—as the Evaluator).

- Observer: Keeps a record of various aspects of group processes (not content) and feeds this information back to the group.

- Follower: Goes along with the group; passively accepts the ideas of others.

(continued)

TABLE 5.7   Three Types of Roles

Avoid dealing with too many details or being dogmatic, cold, or tight-lipped. Never talk down to them, legislate, or present too many facts and figures. Avoid being boring and do not leave decisions hanging in the air. Do not waste time trying to be impersonal, judgmental, or too task-oriented.

Dysfunctional Roles

- Aggressor: Attacks other group members by deflating the status of others, disapproving of ideas or values, attacking the group's goal, and so forth.

- Blocker: Resists, disagrees, and opposes beyond reason; brings up dead issues after they've been rejected by the group.

- Recognition-seeker: Calls attention to self through boasting, reporting personal achievements, fighting to keep from being placed in an inferior position.

- Self-confessor: Uses the group as an opportunity to express personal, non–group related feelings, insights, or ideologies.

- Playboy: Actively displays lack of involvement in the task; nonchalant; cynical; engages in horseplay and "goofing off" behavior.

- Dominator: Tries to assert authority or superiority by manipulating others in the group; flatterer, asserting superior status; gives directions; frequently interrupts.

- Help-seeker: Attempts to get sympathy from other members of the group through expressions of insecurity, personal inadequacy, or self-criticism.

- Special-interest pleader: Speaks on behalf of some group such as "the oppressed," "labor," "business"; expresses personal biases or prejudices.

TABLE 5.7   Three Types of Roles (continued)

Task, Maintenance, and Dysfunctional Roles for Each Social Style. Regardless of social style, individuals primarily engage in three types of roles: task, maintenance, and dysfunctional (Table 5.7). Task roles are useful in achieving results whereas maintenance roles are helpful in creating positive feelings among group members. Dysfunctional roles are primarily negative and can prevent a group from achieving its objectives. They also create bad feelings and poor relations between group members.

As discussed previously, you demonstrate one of four social styles based on your expression of responsiveness and assertiveness. Each social style, therefore, has a natural tendency to embrace various task, maintenance, and dysfunctional roles (see Figure 5.4). Although this is not an exact science, you can enhance your interpersonal relationships by understanding these tendencies and developing strategies for dealing with each task, maintenance, and dysfunctional role described in Table 5.7.

Strategy 5: Creating a Thirty-Second Commercial

Relationship builders communicate quickly and effectively the mission, goals, objectives, purpose, and values of HRD activities, services, and expertise. One way of doing so is to create a short, concise, yet thorough message—a

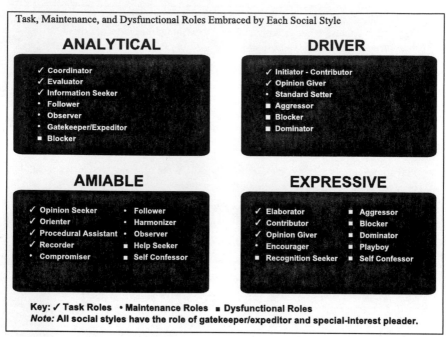

FIGURE 5.4   Task, Maintenance, and Dysfunctional Roles Embraced by Each
Social Style

"thirty-second commercial" about HRD—to share with interested and curious individuals throughout your firm. This message shares the advantages, benefits, and values of HRD to potential clients.

An effective thirty-second message includes the background of HRD, its mission, its overall goals or objectives, information about its HRD practitioners, the outcomes that HRD helps the organization realize, and the special way in which the transformational HRD professionals work with the organization to realize those outcomes. This is a great deal of information to work into a conversation of thirty seconds. However, it is important to communicate as much of this information in as concise and memorable a manner as possible. In fact, a better strategy might be to create a series of thirty-second commercials that can be used to promote each of the previously identified topic areas, so that you can communicate the most appropriate message to whomever the audience happens to be. Keeping the message short guards against information overload, which is a common flaw of promotional communications.

Thirty-second commercials may also be used in other promotional materials, such as brochures and HRD catalogs. These enable the promotional message to be communicated in a variety of forms and fashions. The most important message to be communicated reveals the value of HRD and how HRD practices, services, and programs help the organization realize its operational outcomes. Such a message should be the centerpiece of the thirty-second commercial strategy.

Conclusion

Working with people is the hardest thing you will ever do. Therefore, you must develop the interpersonal skills to work effectively with others. When this competency is developed adequately, you will have the power and maneuverability to take on any political terrain.

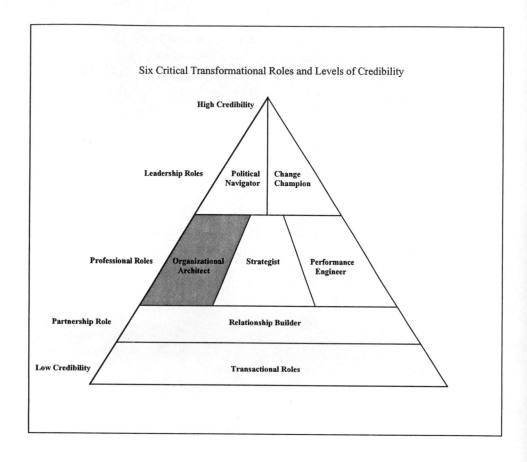

Six Critical Transformational Roles and Levels of Credibility

Organizational Architect

A critical transformational role in HRD is that of organizational architect. This role enables you to demonstrate knowledge of how multiple systems work in harmony to achieve targeted results. Organizational architects interact with senior managers and executives regarding the critical components of an organization and their congruency or incongruency, which ultimately determine the efficiency and effectiveness of operations. Finally, knowledge of organizations and their operations is a prerequisite to the leadership roles of strategic planner, performance engineer, and change champion, for which organizational knowledge proves essential.

Understanding the Formal and Informal Organization

Improving performance and implementing change requires HRD professionals to consider the scope and intensity of their efforts. French and Bell (1998) liken organizations to icebergs. Formal components of the organization represent the part of the iceberg seen above the water. Informal components lie beneath the water's surface—unseen, unknown, undetected, yet clearly an organizational element. They believe that the formal organization consists of publicly observable, structural components that include:

- span of control;
- hierarchical levels;
- the organization's mission, goals, and objectives;
- job descriptions and definitions;
- operating policies, procedures, and practices;
- human resource policies and practices;
- production and efficiency effectiveness measurements.

Informal organizational components are not observable and consist of personal perceptions of the organization; group sentiments and norms; the informal power structure; patterns of intergroup and intragroup relationships; and personal views of the organization and individual competencies. They also consist of perceptions of trust, openness, and risk-taking behaviors; individual role perceptions and value orientations; emotional feelings, needs, and desires; effective relationships between managers and employees; and satisfaction and development effectiveness measurements.

Both the formal and informal organization should be considered when implementing change and performance improvement initiatives. Why? The scope and intensity of organizational problems manifest themselves in the informal components of the organization (Tichy 1989). As a result, the depth of intended change refers to how far management is willing to go into the organizational iceberg to solve a problem. Furthermore, real change only occurs when the informal organization and all of its behaviors and practices are radically altered. Changes and improvements that occur in the formal organization rarely penetrate deep inside the firm to improve organizational system or performance capacity. The greater the depth of the intervention, the greater the risk of failure and the higher the cost of change. Consequently, you must be able to condition the organization and establish ownership for change prior to implementing interventions.

Managing the Organizational Immune System

One of the biggest mistakes that transformational professionals make involves developing a love affair with the formal organization. We are referring to the lure, temptation, or even lust to "transform" the visible organization via structural realignment or systemwide regeneration through a massive organizational change initiative. The transformational professional often needs to be perceived as the conquering hero—much like Caesar returning from a military campaign from the far reaches of the world. Simply said, many have an ego need for this type of dramatic conquest. Consequently, some transformational professionals lead the charge for altering the most visible components of an organization (formal) in pretense that radical change is in order.

Once engaged in this struggle, they quickly realize that changing the deck chairs on the *Titanic* is not the most appropriate action when the ship is sinking. They begin to understand that the internal problems plaguing the organization are not going to disappear by simply changing reporting relationships, assignments, or even the direction of the firm. The most powerful foe, however, now surfaces. Unseen by the unsuspecting transformational professional, it is invisible, yet omnipotent, able to kill any good idea and action about to be implemented. As though purposely sabotaging your good intentions, the organizational immune system prevents change from being implemented—regardless of its positive consequences. This stealth enemy resides in the informal organization, waiting to attack anything trying to alter the status quo.

Because many transformational professionals are preoccupied with altering the formal organization, they never suspect that something as innocuous as this could disrupt their perfectly designed intervention. This enemy is almost impossible to detect and nearly invisible to most who fail to realize such a powerful adversary exists. Many unsuspecting transformational professionals have fallen victim to its steady onslaught; quite simply, they never saw it coming.

Although altering the formal organization might be the most appropriate course of action, the organizational immune system must be taken into account prior to inciting action. Any change in the formal organization impacts the informal. As with the human body, the more change initiatives that fail, the more resistant the organization becomes to change.

Eventually, the organizational immune system builds up such a tolerance to change that it kills even those changes needed to maintain organizational competitiveness and viability. Over time, it weakens the firm's competitive advantage and could lead to the death of the organization. In fact, the corporate graveyard is full of many examples of organizations unable to embrace change.

Successful defense against the organizational immune system requires several actions. The most important is acknowledgment of the existence of the enemy, followed by planning accordingly. Look for symptoms of its presence, and make adjustments or implement contingency plans. Rely on the formal and informal communication system to deliver clear and understandable messages regarding the intent of the change initiative, and provide reassurance that everything is going to be okay, which serve as antibodies useful in battling this foe. Address elements of the informal organization when a change initiative is implemented and prepare for the inevitable resistance that occurs whenever change is introduced. Finally, take advantage of the power of the organizational immune system. Learn how to use this system to eliminate cynicism, negativity, and criticism, which poison positive change efforts. In this way, you enter an alliance to help the organization implement needed change without the negative effects so common with such initiatives.

Understanding the Organization as a System

The complexity of organizations varies greatly. Organizational architects are expected to deal with this complexity with relative ease. To do so, we recommend adopting an approach that is reliable regardless of the size or complexity of the organization, and one that is applicable to even the smallest work group (work team or project team). We recommend two such blueprints: relationship mapping and the organizational system blueprint (Figures 6.1 and 6.2).

Relationship Mapping

The principal danger of arranging jobs into separate, individual departments is that they become windowless structures that are tall, thick, and prevent interaction between peers at low and midlevels (Rummler and Brache 1995, 7). The silo structure forces managers to resolve low-level issues, taking their time away from higher priority customers and competitive concerns. It forces employees to adopt culture, language, and customs common to their department rather than that of the organization as a whole. Such behavior prevents crossdepartmental interaction, thereby inhibiting communications, decision-making, performance, and quality. Operating within silo structures produces an organization's Tower of Babel. Similar to the biblical metaphor, the Tower of Babel indicates a time when confusion reigns within an organization or society as a result of specialized culturalization. When this occurs, people from different departments (cultures) fail to communicate or maintain a common language, which leads to isolation and employees operating from a narrow departmental perspective. Employees are prevented from working across departmental lines to achieve desired business goals when the organizational Tower of Babel exists. As organizational decisions are pushed up to the highest level, teamwork or crossdepartmental cooperation are hindered (Rummler and Brache 1995, 65). Guarding against inappropriate or illogical departmentalization prevents a firm from achieving its ultimate business goals and objectives.

Eliminating the silo culture remains one of the best ways of improving organizational systems. Understanding their crossdepartmental interactions and dependencies can be facilitated through a methodology known as relationship mapping (Rummler and Brache 1995). Figure 6.1 shows a relationship map for a medium-size dental office, reflecting the dependencies of various departments on one another.

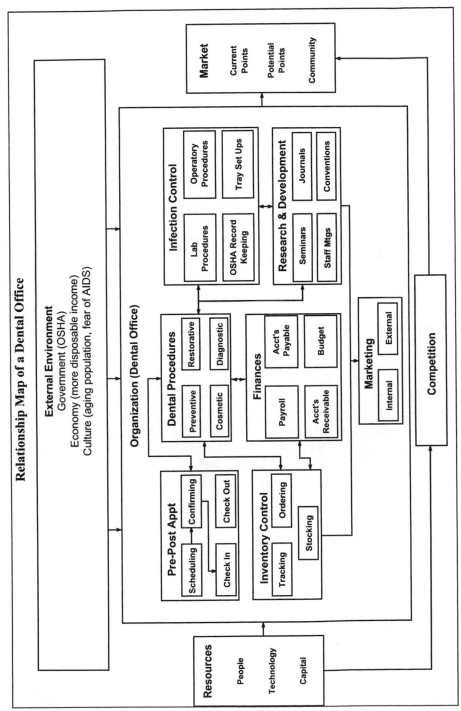

FIGURE 6.1   Relationship Map of a Dental Office

A relationship map demonstrates that organizations are indeed systems. Figure 6.1 reveals the grouping of elements that individually establish relationships with each other, as well as those that interact with their environment, both individually and collectively (Gibson, Ivancevich, and Donnelly 1999). As a system, the organization relies on inputs (resources) and processes (interdependent tasks and activities) to produce desired results and outputs (products, services, or deliverables). The most important function of relationship mapping is identifying connections between various departments.

The greatest opportunity for performance improvement often lies in functional interfaces—those points at which activities are passed from one department to another (Rummler and Brache 1995, 9). Consequently, organizational architects help the organization understand the need to create more efficient and effective interdepartmental relationships—ones that improve organizational performance capacity and effectiveness.

Another way of thinking about crossdepartmental processes is to consider the actions that occur during a relay race. Each runner is responsible for successfully completing his or her segment of the race and handing the baton to the next runner. This process continues until the final runner (anchor) finishes the race. In this example, external stakeholders are members of the overall team, the sponsor of the team, and its fans. Their primary concern is how the "relay team" finishes the race as a measure of success. Internal stakeholders represent the relay team members who actually run the race. Each runner is concerned with executing his or her individual responsibilities, the quality performance, and whether it contributes to a successful outcome. Internal stakeholders measure success very differently than external stakeholders. They are often more interested in the execution of the race itself as opposed to the ultimate outcome. For the actual runners, success (winning) is a by-product of excellent execution. They are concerned with their individual performance and the quality of the baton handoff rather than winning the race. In fact, most serious athletes contend that the proper execution of their specific responsibilities at a high level ultimately result in winning a majority of the races run.

Applying this example to organizational performance focuses on the quality of the handoff between employees as similar to execution of a job. In this way, you direct your attention to the area where the majority of mistakes are made or precious time is lost, which ultimately affects the outcomes of product or service delivery. As with a relay race, handoffs between employees determine the outcome of performance in terms of effectiveness and efficiency.

Relationship mapping allows you to demonstrate the interconnection between departments responsible for generating products and services. It is a tool that rearranges the organizational chart in such a way to demonstrate dependency relationships rather than reporting relationships. Relationship mapping reveals the importance of teamwork, cooperation, performance partnerships, and accountabilities. Quite simply, this tool identifies performance breakdowns and the value of teamwork. In turn, relationship mapping enables employees to better understand how they affect production or service delivery, which helps them develop a sense of accountability and ownership.

Organizational System Blueprint

Organizations have been compared with human organisms. Just as humans have digestive, circulatory, skeletal, and nervous systems, organizations have similar subsystems that enable them to remain alive. Typically, organizations are diagrammed in such a way to describe connections between various departments, both vertically and horizontally. On the horizontal plane, various departments represent functions such as finance, marketing, manufacturing, customer service, and so forth. On the vertical plane, organizations are divided into subparts of various departments, usually indicating individual titles and specific reporting relationships.

Let us further consider the similarity of human organisms and the organizational system. Human anatomy consists of a number of complex internal systems working in harmony. If you strip away the outer skin and muscles that house the human body, you are left with a skeletal structure and vital organs that comprise the elements essential for life. As with an organization, the formal organization constitutes the outer skin and muscular frame. This is typically all we recognize about an organization. Granted, this outward manifestation gives the organization its texture, depth, and breadth, although seldom does the outward appearance of an organization reveal its daily operations. Quite simply, what an organization appears to be seldom mirrors reality. Organizations, like the human body, consist of vital organs and structures that give them strength, rigidity, form, and function—components critical to an organization's life.

The organizational blueprint helps architects

1. develop a profile of an organization and its areas of strength and weakness.
2. examine the components of the organization for areas of congruency or incongruency.

3. act as troubleshooters by using this diagnostic tool to isolate current or possible breakdowns, difficulties, or inefficiencies within an organization.
4. build or reinforce infrastructures, reconfigure the organization, and make other needed corrections.

The organizational system consists of interdependent functions on which the organization is dependent in order to remain viable. These eight interdependent functions include:

1. leadership
2. organizational culture
3. mission and strategy
4. organizational structure
5. work climate
6. managerial practices
7. policies and procedures
8. organizational processes (communication and decisionmaking).

In Figure 6.2, each of the eight functions is dependent on the others, as represented by the arrows. Each function represents an independent component of the organization, not unlike the vital organs of the human body. The arrows in both directions convey an open system principle—changes in one factor eventually impacts others (Burke 1992). The organizational system must be intact, healthy, and vibrant to positively impact other systems within the firm. In a healthy organization producing positive results, these eight interdependent functions work in harmony. When an organization fails to achieve desired results or is ill equipped to meet the competitive demands of the global marketplace, it is helpful to look within each of these functions or their relationships to one another to determine whether their symptoms reveal decline, inadequacy, or failure. Thus, you can analyze the relationship between various functions within the organizational system to reveal potential breakdowns or areas of weakness. Change interventions can be targeted to improve various functions for the entire organizational system. Thus, you have a systematic approach to examining weaknesses as well as looking for opportunities for continued growth and development essential to organizational renewal.

Using an organizational system blueprint is important for many reasons. First, this blueprint enables you to approach organizational change from both micro and macro perspectives. Approaching change from a micro perspective requires reliance on the blueprint to help isolate components that

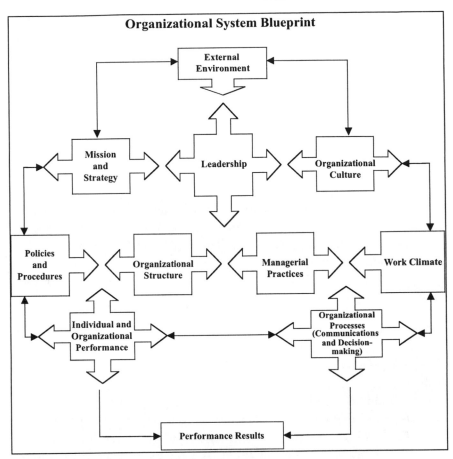

FIGURE 6.2   Organizational System Blueprint

affect organizational performance (see Chapter 8). At the macro level, the blueprint isolates breakdowns within the organizational system as a whole. Second, you can analyze the relationships between various functions within the organizational system to determine potential breakdowns or areas of weakness. Third, when looking for symptoms of poor performance or organizational breakdown, a combination of these eight functions can be examined to determine whether one, a few, or all are contributing to the performance problem or breakdown. Fourth, you can better develop change interventions by focusing on the most appropriate functions and their interdependencies. Fifth, this blueprint identifies appropriate layers or groupings within each respective system or across system lines. Sixth, the organizational system as a whole may be treated as a separate entity requiring a more comprehensive change management initiative.

As previously discussed, an organizational system consists of eight independent yet interdependent functions, each of which serves as a universal language across departments and divisions. Although departments maintain separate identities, languages, and customs, the eight components are common to all. Members of the marketing and finance departments may have different languages, practices, and customs, but they are unified when taking into account each of these eight components.

Organizational Leadership. A variety of definitions attempt to illustrate leadership. Simply defined, leadership is the process of making decisions regarding how to interact with employees in order to motivate them, then translating those decisions into actions. Although this definition does not take into account the various types of leadership within an organization, it does describe its primary purpose. Leadership can be described as "the behavior of managers and executives that provides direction and encourages others to take needed action" (Burke 1992, 130).

When examined carefully, a host of leadership theories surface that contribute to a better understanding of organizational systems. Gibson, Ivancevich, and Donnelly (1999, 307–314) identify four major leadership theories applicable in today's organizations; Gilley and Maycunich (2000b) added a fifth, which is developmental leadership.

Attribution leadership theory examines the relationship between individuals' perceptions and interpersonal behavior. Thus, leaders' perceptions determine the way they interact with employees and vice versa. This theory of leadership suggests that knowing those events' causal explanations (Gibson, Ivancevich, and Donnelly 1999, 307) enhances understanding of and ability to predict how employees react to events.

Charismatic leadership is the ability to influence employees via one's extraordinary gifts and persuasive powers. Based on this theory, leaders are most effective when they communicate their vision, build trust, and demonstrate the means of achieving their vision via role blueprinting, empowerment, and unconventional tactics. Two types of charismatic leaders exist based on the leader's emphasis on the future: visionary charismatic leaders focus on the long term; crisis-based charismatic leaders focus on the short term (310).

Transactional leadership adapts to the situation and emerges as the result of interactions with constituents. This style defines what employees want or prefer, and helps them achieve the level of performance that results in rewards. They focus on goal setting and providing appropriate resources to achieve performance goals. They rely on contingent reward and on management by exception (313).

Transformational leadership consists of the ability to inspire and motivate fellow employees to achieve results greater than originally planned, and helps employees obtain intrinsic satisfaction from their accomplishments (Gibson, Ivancevich, and Donnelly 1999, 307). Additionally, "transformational leadership occurs when managers broaden and elevate the interests of their workers, when they generate awareness and acceptance of the purposes and mission of the group, and when they motivate their people to look beyond their own self-interests for the good of the whole group" (Rolls 1995, 108). Since transformational leaders have the ability to create meaning for their employees, they have an extraordinary effect on their behavior. These leaders provide essential conditions under which employees can develop, transform, grow, and flourish.

Organizations need leaders who have been through their own personal transformation to facilitate the transformation of others. Quite simply, senior managers and executives need to adopt transformational leadership practices and principles to be effective in the twenty-first century.

Organizations need leaders who "value people, growth, and learning, and who can help employees tap into inner reserves, re-invent themselves, become more attuned to interrelationship, connect to and value their own wisdom, and work with colleagues in co-creation. Without these leaders, it be difficult to build a high performance organization" (Rolls 1995, 105–106).

Transformational leaders manifest the characteristics of the five disciplines as identified by Senge (1990) (personal mastery, mental blueprints, shared vision, team learning, and systems thinking). Transformational leaders have deeply examined their core values and beliefs and have identified several leadership qualities that are most in demand (Schwandt 1995). These include integrity, vulnerability, awareness of the human spirit, courage in relationships, curiosity, predictability, breadth, and comfort with ambiguity and presence. Moreover, transformational leaders establish a stronger platform from which to conduct their lives and their interactions with others through self-reflection.

Transformational leaders invite employees to interpret the ideal future in terms of their roles and to determine how to close the gaps between current and future states. They create conditions in which employees can experience "self esteem, connection, dignity and security, where they can create and feel alive, be listened to and cared for, become, live their values, self discover, risk in an environment of safety—where they can live with meaning and meaningfully contribute to the art and practice of the learning organization" (Rolls 1995, 103–108).

Developmental leadership is based on the belief that leaders encourage, support, and promote their employees, helping them grow and develop to the fullest. These leaders accept responsibility for others' career development by working tirelessly to help employees grow and develop, and assist workers as they struggle to become the best they can be (Gilley and Maycunich 2000b). Developmental leaders understand that, as individuals grow and develop, so does the organization. They share organizational success with subordinates and make certain that other decisionmakers in the organization are aware of employee contributions to achieving desired business results. These leaders accept responsibility for their employees' failures and celebrate their successes. Above all, developmental leaders operate without regard for their own well-being or career advancement because they believe their employees are the organization's most important asset.

Developmental leadership is based on the principles of servantship. This approach implies a willingness to work for the betterment of others and a personal philosophy of humility but does not mean that leaders are weak or unable to make difficult decisions (Greenleaf 1996). Such leaders help their organization by advocating, assisting, growing, and developing its most important asset: its people. Simply stated, servantship means being a caretaker without regard for one's own personal needs or the rewards that are typically afforded leaders responsible for the professional lives of others. This is called the law of legacy, whereby a leader's lasting value is measured by succession: "a legacy is created only when a leader puts his/her organization into position to do great things without him/her" (Maxwell 1998, 215–221).

Developmental leaders truly understand that they will receive credit for a job well done since part of their job was being delegated. Consequently, they delegate tasks and responsibilities to others because they realize that such assignments facilitate growth and development in their employees. Additionally, developmental leaders believe that creating personal relationships with their employees encourages them to honestly discuss important issues without fear of negative repercussions or reprisals. As a result, employees are willing to become vulnerable and exposed rather than guarded and controlled.

Organizational Architect's Responsibility in Examining Organizational Leadership

Organizational leadership is the greatest determinant of organizational success (Collins 2001). The type and quality of leadership has a tremendous affect on organizational culture, the type of organizational structure, the mission and strategy, and managerial practices. As an organizational architect, you are responsible for determining the type of leadership that exists within your organization. Armed with this information, you will be better prepared to facilitate change and performance improvement initiatives and recommend integrated solutions designed to improve and enhance other components of the organizational system. Finally, this information provides you with a wealth of knowledge regarding the type of opportunities that exist within your organization and how to proceed accordingly.

Organizational Culture.   As we discussed previously, organizational culture can be simply defined as "the way we do things around here" (Burke 1992, 130). Organizational culture is often a collection of artifacts, creations, rules, values, principles, and assumptions that guide organizational behavior. Culture is strongly influenced by history, customs, and practices. It could be said that organizational culture is what employees perceive to be the pattern of beliefs, values, and expectations that guide behavior and practice within an organization.

Organizational culture is perhaps one of the most important components of an organizational system (French, Bell, and Zawacki 1999). The type of organizational culture that exists often depends on the type of organization in which one works. Some say that collaborative organizations present the optimal organizational culture. Collaborative organizational cultures exhibit the following characteristics:

1. Growth and development of organizational members is just as important as making a profit or staying within budget.
2. Equal opportunity and fairness for people within the organization is commonplace—the rule rather than the exception.
3. Managers exercise their authority more participatively than unilaterally or arbitrarily, and authority is associated more with knowledge and competence than role or status.
4. Cooperative behavior is rewarded more than competitive behavior.
5. Organizational members are kept informed or at least have access to information, especially concerning matters that directly impact their jobs or them personally.
6. Members feel a sense of ownership of the organization's mission and objectives.
7. Conflict is dealt with openly and systematically rather than ignored, avoided, or handled in a typical win-lose fashion.
8. Rewards are based on a system of quality, fairness, and equitable merit.
9. Organizational members are given as much autonomy and freedom to do their respective jobs as possible, ensuring both a high degree of individual motivation and the accomplishment of the organization's strategic goals and objectives (Burke 1992, 196–197).

Adopting the characteristics of a collaborative organization is extremely important to attracting and retaining human resources. This is even more true when employees possess exceptional talent or potential. As a result of this effort, organizations gain competitive advantage over their competitors. Organizations further enhance their competitive advantage by:

- developing each employee's knowledge and skills
- creating structures and systems that focus and support each individual's ability to contribute
- gaining individual commitment to the vision and objectives of the organization (Dean 1999).

Organizational long-term ability to compete in the marketplace depends on the competence, creativity, and commitment of its employees, which are enormously important in building a developmental culture (Morris 1995).

Socialization

Considering organizational culture from an HRD perspective, it makes a great deal of sense to look at the issue of socialization. Socialization can be defined as a process by which organizations bring new people into the culture (Gibson, Ivancevich, and Donnelly 1999). Unfortunately, too many organizations fail to meet their socialization responsibilities because many employees are left on their own to sink or swim within the muck and mire of organizational culture. Examining socialization more closely reveals that effective organizations practice more efficient techniques of socialization than traditional firms (see Table 6.1).

Phases of Socialization

Three phases of socialization predominate within organizations: anticipatory, accommodation, and role management (Feldman 1967). To increase an employee's chances of enjoying a successful career within an organization, you need to execute different activities and undertakings for each phase.

Anticipatory Socialization

When employees think about working for an organization, they typically consider two questions: What will it be like to work for the organization? Are they qualified for the job available within the organization? Effective organizations anticipate these questions and attempt to address them prior to hir-

---

Characteristics of Effective Socialization

Effective organizations focus their attention on enhancing employee socialization by providing five meaningful activities, including:

- Tailor-made and individualized orientation programs

- Social and technical skill training

- Performance evaluations designed to provide supportive and accurate performance feedback

- Challenging work assignments that stretch an employee's abilities and talents

- Demanding but fair managers who practice effective performance coaching techniques.

Each of these activities reduces tension and conflict within the organization while improving employee retention.

TABLE 6.1   Characteristics of Effective Socialization

ing the individual. They realize that first impressions are typically lasting ones and if addressed correctly, employees feel a heightened sense of satisfaction and loyalty as they begin employment.

Accommodation Socialization

After an employee becomes a member of the organization, he or she enters the second phase of socialization. During this phase, employees discover the "real" organization, its people and its jobs. This phase begins with a honeymoon period in which employees are treated as guests. This period of tranquillity quickly fades as employees become regular members of the organization. Four common events constitute the accommodation phase:

1. establishing new interpersonal relations with coworkers and managers
2. learning the tasks required to perform the job
3. clarifying one's role within the organization via formal and informal groups
4. evaluating one's progress toward satisfying demands of the job and the role (Gibson, Ivancevich, and Donnelly 1999).

Regrettably, this period can be very stressful for many individuals because they feel a need to demonstrate their competence as a performer on the job. If all goes well during this phase, employees feel a sense of accomplishment and acceptance by coworkers and superiors while gaining confidence in performing their jobs.

Role Management

Role management socialization refers to the organization's ability to address and resolve conflicts between employees and the management of the organization. Conflict may involve job performance, interpersonal relationships with coworkers or managers, inadequate development opportunities, insufficient job assignments, misinterpretation of rules or regulations, and so on. As an organizational architect, you have a responsibility to successfully resolve conflict regardless of the root cause. Doing so successfully results in positive perceptions of the organization, whereas unresolved or negative resolution may cause resentment, poor attitudes, or lukewarm cooperation on the part of employees. Effective organizations focus on resolving conflict in a positive way to enhance relationships and build organizational esprit de corps.

Organizational Architect's Responsibility in Examining Organizational Culture

Effective organizational architects understand fully the damage caused by conflict within the firm. As a result, you need to be ready to provide professional counseling opportunities when conflicts arise. Encourage managers to accept roles as career counselors and performance confronters so employees have a forum and persons with which to discuss career opportunities as well as difficulties on the job.

Organizational architects are fully aware of the organization's culture and design orientation programs that facilitate an employee's transition from outsider to fully engaged member. This includes interpreting the culture for new employees so their transition is positive. Knowledge of the culture helps mediate differences among departments and divisions by providing insight into the way things get done in the organization, which improves the efficiency and effectiveness of performance.

Mission and Strategy. The mission of an organization is what executives, managers, and employees believe to be its central purpose. Establishing an organizational mission is a time-consuming, soul-searching process. Each member of the organization may hold a different perspective of what the organization is attempting to accomplish; however, it is essential that each individual ultimately agrees with and supports the organization's mission. A well-defined mission statement gives everyone a sense of purpose, direction, significance, and achievement. In short, a mission statement acts as an invisible hand that guides scattered organizational members to work independently but collectively toward the realization of the organization's strategic business goals and objectives.

Strategy refers to how an organization intends to achieve its purposes over an extended period of time. Historically, a long-term strategy attempts to define roles and responsibilities within the organization, thus dictating how work is to be accomplished. Strategy can be considered the organization's game plan, to be embraced and executed by all members while remaining flexible, adaptive, and taking into consideration unique circumstances and events.

Organizational Architect's Responsibility in Examining Mission and Strategy

Organizational architects address the following questions when examining the organization's mission:

1. What is our purpose?
2. What direction do we want to strive toward?
3. Who are our customers (both internal and external)?
4. What are we trying to achieve?
5. What significance are we attempting to accomplish?
6. What will be our future purpose?

Organizational architects examine how the organization intends to achieve its mission, and determine the most appropriate course of action. Although this is typically an activity reserved for senior managers and executives, you need to examine their efforts to determine the correctness of fit and ascertain whether changes are in order. Organizational architects demonstrate the capacity and competence equal to any senior administrator, otherwise they fail to possess the credibility to recommend integrated solutions useful in improving the organizational system.

Organizational Structure. Organizational structure consists of departments, divisions, and units responsible for achieving the organization's ultimate objectives. As such, the structure of an organization is like that of the human skeletal system because it provides the rigidity necessary to support the organization's weight and strength during periods of uncertainty or crisis. The organizational structure, like a human skeleton, provides definition and organization. In other words, there is a place for everything and everything in its place.

Most organizations are divided into centralized or decentralized operations. The degree to which organizations divide into centralized or decentralized bases depends largely on communication, structure in place, and the extent to which organizations rely on formal policies and procedures when making decisions. Some organizations are arranging work units according to projects, customer service, or both. This approach is used to be more responsive to client needs on a short-term project orientation or long-term customer satisfaction basis.

The strongest structure has no walls—no barriers between people, departments, or customers (Boyett and Boyett 1995). In fact, the most effective organization structure

> has no boundaries . . . it has been compared to a solar system, a symphony orchestra, a spider's web. . . . It is open, adaptive, and infinitely flat. It is both centralized and decentralized, and perhaps most importantly, it is virtual. . . . It is fluid and free-form. It is hard to depict with lines on a chart. It requires motion and movement, because it is constantly changing and reforming itself . . . it takes a million different forms, so there is no single "it" to describe (Burke 1992, 63).

Organizational structure also refers to the arrangement of work functions and employees in specific areas and levels of responsibility, decisionmaking authority, and relationships for the business to achieve its strategic business goals. Creating an organizational structure involves three important variables:

1. Departmentalization—the process by which a firm is divided by combining jobs in accordance with shared characteristics.
2. Division of labor—the process of dividing work into specialized areas.
3. Span of control—the number of employees who report to specific managers or executives.

Departmentalization

Combining jobs within a department according to some shared characteristic is known as departmentalization. It is the most common element of organization structure and its primary purposes involve maximizing economies of scale and assembling individuals who possess similar backgrounds or shared characteristics to magnify productivity or enhance performance.

Five types of departmentalization occur within organizations, which include being:

- organized around functions common to their industry (for example, production, marketing, finance, accounting, and human resource).
- divided into regional departments whereby geographical areas determine how the business is organized—very common in large national and international manufacturers, consulting firms, and insurance companies.
- divided into product divisions.
- divided into customer- or client-based groupings.
- divided into both functional and product-based approaches—these are referred to as matrix organizations, which enable firms to be product- or project-based and organized around various functions vis-à-vis specific products or projects improving communications, employee involvement, and decisionmaking (Gibson, Ivancevich, and Donnelly 1999).

Organizations must guard against selecting a departmentalization strategy based solely on the enhancement of productivity or profitability. It makes more sense to organize in ways that give employees new, challenging job assignments in order to enhance growth and development. Regardless of their departmentalization, each has its advantages and disadvantages. For example, a product, customer, or matrix approach allows for the most crossdepartmental cooperation while advocating a synergistic approach to achieving business goals and objectives. Using a functional or territorial departmentalization approach can be effective; however, organizations must make certain that employee growth and development are paramount in a long-term strategy.

Division of Labor

To achieve a differential advantage over the competition and to increase quality and efficiency, many organizations divide work into relatively specialized jobs. Typically, division of labor occurs in one of three ways:

1. Work can be divided into professional specializations, often referred to as a sense of occupational professional identity (for example, accountants, engineers, human resource professionals, and so forth).
2. Jobs can be divided into separate activities based on the sequence of work an organization completes (such as the claim division of an insurance company).
3. Jobs can be divided based on a hierarchy of authority from the lowest to highest levels within the organization.

Traditionally, division of labor helps an organization achieve its strategic business goals and objectives. Organizations that promote a developmental culture incorporate an additional element (Simonsen 1997)—they arrange jobs in ways that enhance and encourage employee growth and development. This is because most employees are desirous of identifying an occupation in which they can enhance their skills and abilities. They want to avoid being placed in work groups that limit their learning and growth opportunities.

Span of Control

Span of control is based on the number of people a given manager can effectively oversee; the difficulty is in determining an appropriate number. Mercer Human Resource Consulting Inc., a large compensation, benefits, and human resources consulting firm, addressed this issue by establishing a policy whereby consulting offices should not exceed 100 members. When an office reached this threshold, it was divided into separate operational units. Accordingly, "the philosophy behind this approach was that the effectiveness of a senior consultant to manage and interact with other consultants reached a point of diminishing returns at or about one hundred staff members. To maintain effective communications, decision-making, and interaction, the organization made certain that offices did not exceed this limit" (Gilley and Maycunich 2000b, 106).

Organizational Architect's Responsibility in Examining Organizational Structure

Organizational architects improve their organizations by creating structures that embrace performance and quality. This helps organizations focus on continuous improvement, further developing and using the diverse capabilities and potential of all employees. As such, you should create work environments that meet the critical and changing needs of every employee.

As an organizational architect, you are also responsible for helping organizational leaders determine the most appropriate departmentalization, division of labor, and span of control. Departmentalization aims to help leaders construct the most efficient and effective architects that promote positive interaction, teamwork, and cooperation. Such architects provide employee growth and development, with continuous organizational renewal as a critical outcome.

Effective division of labor helps organizations examine issues to guarantee that decisionmaking focuses on processes that advocate employee growth and development in addition to achieving desired business results. Regardless of how an organization divides its labor force, employee growth and development are essential.

When span of control has expanded to a point where face-to-face interaction is no longer possible, a manager's ability to provide reinforcement and feedback are greatly diminished.

Therefore, it is critical that you help your organization strike the correct balance between efficiency and cost effectiveness, whereby the number of managers are controlled and they maximize the ability to facilitate and manage individual employee growth and development interventions. Identifying the optimal span of control enables employees to have an opportunity to discuss their developmental needs and career aspirations, and communicate face-to-face with managers and leaders. Consequently, organizations wrestle with the issues of span of control and identifying an acceptable threshold while meeting their employees' developmental requirements.

Organization design represents the configuration used to transform resources into products or services to create competitive advantage. Competitive advantage occurs when one organization is more successful than another in influencing the decisions of three key constituencies: customers, suppliers of capital and funds, and current and potential employees (Jewell and Jewell 1992). It improves by understanding where an organization does or can have leverage over its competitors, and then devising strategies and operational procedures to maximize this leverage. An organization achieves competitive advantage by providing greater perceived value for its products and services than its competitors do. This allows an organization to gain market share, broaden its customer base, and force competitors to adjust their strategy. Another way is by providing higher return on investment for risk taking. When successful, organizations influence their financial partners (suppliers of internal and external funds) to underwrite key initiative and strategies. As a result, organizations have greater access to the funds they need to grow.

Work Climate. Work climate can be best determined by examining employees' impressions, expectations, and feelings concerning the work environment. Work climate can be affected by organizational leadership, coworkers, the type of organization, economic factors, and departmental stability within the organization. Accordingly, organizations can be divided into four types: passive, hierarchical, competitive, and collaborative according to how employees are viewed, the relationship employees have with the firm, or both.

- Passive organizations do not perceive their employees as important and are not committed to their well-being. These organizations fail to rely on the talent, skills, and abilities of their employees to solve problems or make essential decisions and contributions. Examples often include retail operations and small businesses.
- Hierarchical organizations believe that most employees are committed to the welfare of the organization, but that only a few have the critical talent, skills, and abilities to make informed, critical decisions. Hierarchical organizations are historically large and consist of many layers. Examples are most Fortune 500 companies, governmental agencies, and universities.
- Competitive organizations consist of many talented, skilled employees, although only a few are loyal to the organization. Employees often possess high levels of education and many years of experience in this type of organization. Most are able to find employment in a number of competitive firms, placing extreme pressure on management and organizational leaders to meet or exceed their needs. Examples include professional service and consulting firms.
- Collaborative organizations view employees as important and committed, allowing them to participate in all critical decisions. The firm's culture fosters loyalty and involvement, and management encourages and supports organizational development activities. Examples are some employee-owned organizations and those with unique, progressive leadership (French and Bell 1998).

Organizational Architect's Responsibility in Examining Work Climate

As an organizational architect, your primary responsibility, when examining the work climate, is to determine your organization's type. To do so, you need to address two important questions: Are most employees perceived to have important resources to offer? Are most employees committed to the organization's welfare? An analysis of these two questions results in the following breakdown:

- Question 1: Positive; Question 2: Positive—collaborative organization
- Question 1: Positive; Question 2: Negative—hierarchical organization
- Question 1: Negative; Question 2: Positive—competitive organization
- Question 1: Negative; Question 2: Negative—passive organization
  (Neilsen 1984).

Once an organization's type has been determined, architects begin the process of reversing its negatives. They implement a strategy that allows the organization to exhibit the characteristics of a collaborative firm. In passive organizations, senior managers and executives need to view human resources as important and provide incentives that enhance employee commitment to the organization. Competitive organizations must improve employee commitment. Hierarchical organizations need to understand the importance of employee involvement and loyalty and improve management's perception of its people.

Managerial Practices. Managerial practices encompass the normal activities used by managers to implement organizational strategy, including the use of human and material resources and daily contact with employees. Managerial practices can be seen in all interactions with employees, including delegating work tasks, managing projects, implementing organizational change interventions, managing employee conflicts, and confronting poor performance. These practices define the way managers accomplish organizational objectives through people.

Unfortunately, most managers are still not good at getting results through people. Many managers do not know how to communicate with employees, provide feedback, confront employees' poor performance, enhance employee self-esteem, or reward their performance. When these behaviors are present managers create a serious problem for the organization—one referred to as managerial malpractice (Gilley and Boughton 1996).

Managerial malpractice involves encouraging and supporting practices that produce unprofessional, unproductive, or incompetent managers. Symptoms of managerial malpractice include: keeping managers who are not good at getting results through people, promoting unqualified people to management, selecting new managers because they are the best performers or producers without regard to their people skills, spending valuable time fixing managerial incompetence instead of hiring qualified managers, keeping managers who preach the importance of teamwork but then reward individuals who stand out from the crowd, and allowing managers to say one thing and do another (Gilley and Boughton 1996). Managerial malpractice is also present when there is a significant difference between what is said is important and what is actually done. Common misbehaviors of managers include:

- failing to conduct performance appraisals;
- failing to provide performance standards;
- failing to delegate work assignments;
- failing to develop their employees;
- lacking patience with employees;
- criticizing employees rather than their performance;
- changing priorities and work requirements;
- creating paranoid working environments.

Why Improve Managerial Practices?

One of the most critical questions architects address is "Why improve managerial practice?" At least four reasons for improving managerial practices surface. First, organizations are unable to improve their performance capacity or effectiveness until they improve the quality of managers and their respective practices. This is true because managers are essential to achieving favorable business results. They are the only organizational members who communicate daily with employees and have the opportunity to observe performance. Consequently, performance improvement can really only occur through a daily ritual of observation, feedback, and application. Perfect practice makes perfect performance, which is the primary responsibility of managers.

Second, managers are the lifeblood of the organization, the interpreters of the organization's vision and the executors of its strategy. Managers mediate and translate organizational policies and procedures for employees while developing work climates conducive for improving productivity and quality. They help employees maneuver through the organizational maze and develop an appreciation and understanding of the organization's culture. In short, managers are the only leadership most employees interact with during their tenure in an organization.

Third, managers are the gatekeepers of quality and performance improvement because they are the overlords of the learning and compensation and rewards systems. Consequently, managers are responsible for developing employees' performance capacity, helping them apply new knowledge and skills, delivering performance feedback, appraising performance, and rewarding employees for improving. Consequently, managers hold the keys to maximizing organizational performance.

Fourth, managers are the primary conduit used to improve employee motivation and satisfaction. Managers are the individuals responsible for enhancing employees' self-esteem by involving them in activities and projects that allow a sense of achievement, accomplishment, power, influence, or mastery. Managers are truly the only persons in the organization capable of demonstrating appreciation and concern for the well-being of employees.

Authority

One of the hidden elements of managerial practice is that of authority. Authority refers to an individual's rights to make important job decisions without approval from senior management or direct obedience to another.

Most organizations maintain either a centralized or decentralized authority. Centralized authority is most useful in avoiding duplication of effort and improving the efficiency and effectiveness of decisionmaking. Many senior managers are accustomed to making decisions, and resist delegating authority to their subordinates. Finally, the cost of reviewing or auditing decisions made by individual employees can be quite extensive. As a result, it is financially expedient to use a centralized authority approach.

In a decentralized environment, employees are given permission to make appropriate decisions. This may require some to gain additional decision-making skills and problem-solving abilities required of such a responsibility. When job specialization is high, decentralized authority is often the most efficient approach because employees are perceived as authorities within a professional practice and are, therefore, granted a certain level of respect and freedom to make decisions.

International organizations' employees are often scattered throughout the world. Hence, it makes sense to grant individuals the authority to make decisions when and if appropriate. Under these circumstances, the ability to deal with autonomy and freedom is of paramount importance; individuals must feel as though they have the right or justification to make certain decisions in isolation.

Decentralized authority provides the greatest opportunity for employee growth and development. For example, participating in the decisionmaking process helps employees develop analytical and rationale skills, which enhance their self-esteem and sense of accomplishment. In turn, this improves their personal job satisfaction and enhances loyalty to the organization. Moreover, it allows employees to examine new ways of enhancing their knowledge and skills.

Organizational Architects' Responsibility in Examining Managerial Practices

Managerial malpractice, when allowed to flourish, causes the organization's performance, quality, productivity, and effectiveness to suffer greatly. One way of overcoming managerial malpractice entails creating management development partnerships throughout the firm. These are joint ventures between you and the organization designed to improve the competencies and skills of managers. Such partnerships enhance the quality and professionalism of managers in order to improve problem-solving, increase employee performance and quality, and achieve better business results.

Improve Problem-Solving

Management development partnerships help organizations by providing managers with a problem-solving process. This process consists of the following six steps:

1. Identifying the conditions and factors that contribute to the problem.
2. Identifying the root cause of the problem.
3. Identifying the solutions to the problem and analyzing each.
4. Selecting the solution that best resolves the problem.
5. Implementing the solution.
6. Evaluating the solution to determine whether it solved the problem.

Increase Employee Performance and Quality

Improving performance is a three-stage process that begins by identifying performance standards and communicating them to employees. These standards serve as criteria to determine whether a job is being conducted correctly. They also serve as a guide in executing the job or task (Gilley and Boughton 1996).

The second stage involves measuring current performance against established performance standards to determine whether a difference exists between actual and desired performance. Once deficiencies have been identified, managers are ready for the third stage, which is making changes in the way a job is being performed. Changes might include new tasks, procedures, or processes. Actual performance sometimes exceeds established performance standards; however, changes still might be necessary to ensure that long-term productivity continues. When no significant difference between actual performance and desired performance exists, managers should consider possible adjustments to ensure continuous improvement.

Achieve Better Business Results

Organizations are often not concerned with how results are obtained, they simply want them achieved. Managers are responsible for results, from increased revenues and more units of production to improved client service or increased market share. Results remain crucial. Managers cannot, however, obtain these results by themselves; they rely on their employees. Managers must get results through people.

Developing management development partnerships enables the organization to replace traditional roles of planning, directing, organizing, and controlling with performance coaching skills. Such a transformation can be achieved by selecting better qualified managers, training managers to become performance coaches, and holding managers accountable for getting results through their people. When these three activities have been completed, managers should be able to demonstrate seven performance coaching behaviors, which include:

1. creating positive relationships with their employees
2. training and developing their employees
3. providing career coaching for employees
4. confronting employees' performance when it falls below established performance standards
5. mentoring employees
6. enhancing employees' self-esteem
7. rewarding and recognizing employees' performance.

By embracing the transformation to performance coaching, organizations make a serious commitment to improving the way managers are selected, trained, and evaluated. Such a transformation has an immediate impact on the organization by helping improve its performance capacity and effectiveness, which ultimately improve the bottom line.

Policies and Procedures. Policies and procedures encompass an organization's rules and regulations. Policies are perceived to be the established set of rules that employees must follow, whereas procedures prescribe how employees implement daily work activities. Policies and procedures provide structure for the organization, allowing the firm to align employees around its central focus and mission. Policies and procedures govern organizational behavior, providing a means of norming practice.

When effectively written, policies and procedures create a sense of group cohesion. They also provide a code of conduct and behavior, developed and shared among employees, which increases their willingness to participate in projects and assignments. Policies and procedures should be flexible enough to allow for employee input, at the same time sufficiently structured to provide guidance and direction for employees when uncertainty rules.

Organizational Architects' Responsibility in Examining Policies and Procedures

Policies and procedures provide a clear roadmap for how decisions are made in an organization. Therefore, your primary responsibility is to make certain that the organization's policies and procedures make sense and enhance organizational efficiency and effectiveness. Although this appears to be a relatively easy task it is not. A thorough understanding of the organization and its other components is needed before undertaking this responsibility. Second, determine the exact consequences of each policy and procedure and project the outcomes once changed. This challenging and time-consuming task enhances your credibility as an organizational architect.

Organizational Processes—Communications and Decisionmaking. Two organizational processes must be accounted for when analyzing the organizational system—communications and decisionmaking.

Organizational Communications

Collectively these processes involve and affect every employee, and contribute to the success of the organization. Failure to address these processes affects employee morale and motivation since they contribute to an employee's sense of belonging and shared ownership.

Every aspect of a manager's job involves communication. Although every manager communicates, not every manager is an effective communicator.

Overcoming this deficiency requires managers to understand the four distinct directions of communication:

- Downward communication—flows from higher to lower levels in an organization, including managerial policies, instructions, and official communiqués.
- Upward communication—flows from the lower to the higher levels in an organization, including suggestion boxes, group meetings, and grievances procedures.
- Horizontal communication—flows across functions in an organization; necessary for coordinating and integrating diverse organizational functions.
- Diagonal communication—cuts across functions and levels in an organization; important when members cannot communicate through upward, downward, or horizontal channels (Gibson, Ivancevich, and Donnelly 1999).

All four types of communication are necessary to improve effectiveness within organizations.

Decisionmaking

Making effective decisions can be a complex process. The decisionmaking process consists of two types: programmed—routine, frequent, and repetitive decisions based on current policies, rules, and definite procedures; nonprogrammed—novel and unstructured cause-and-effect relationships necessary for creativity, intuition, and creative problem solving. Regardless of the type of decisions being made, the process consist of eight steps:

1. Establishing specific goals and objectives
2. Identifying problems
3. Developing alternatives
4. Evaluating alternatives
5. Choosing an alternative
6. Implementing the decision
7. Controlling and evaluating
8. Measuring results.

Decisionmaking can be affected by the values of the decisionmaker. These are the basic guidelines and beliefs that a decisionmaker uses when confronted with a situation requiring choice (Gibson, Ivancevich, and Donnelly 1999). Additionally, their personality, attitude toward risk taking, and predisposition to cognitive dissonance affect a decisionmaker's ability to render a decision.

Organizational Architects' Responsibility in Examining Organizational Processes

When examining organizational processes, your primary responsibilities are to identify the barriers to effective communications and decisionmaking, and identify strategies to overcome them. Several barriers to organizational communications can be identified, which include:

- Frame of reference of the listener
- Selective listening
- Value judgments made by the listener
- Source credibility of the sender
- Semantic problems
- Filtering of information
- Specialized or technical language
- Status difference between sender and receiver
- Time pressures
- Communication overload (Gibson, Ivancevich, and Donnelly 1999).

Communications can be improved by implementing better follow-up procedures to make certain one's message is not misunderstood and whenever possible attempting to determine the intent of a message. Next, implement processes that help regulate information flow and use feedback to enhance understanding. Repetition of information ensures that messages are clearly received and understood. You can improve communications by simplifying the language of a message and presenting it at the most opportune time for listeners to receive and understand it. Whenever possible, encourage face-to-face interaction, which builds mutual trust and involvement.

When addressing the decisionmaking process within an organization, examine how decisions are made and by whom. Next, introduce new data-gathering techniques:

- Creative brainstorming—promotes creativity by encouraging idea generation through noncritical discussion.

- Delphi process—encourages creativity by using anonymous judgment of ideas to reach a consensus.
- Nominal group—enhances creativity by bringing people together in a structured meeting that allows little verbal communication, where group decision is the mathematically pooled outcome of individual votes (Gibson, Ivancevich, and Donnelly 1999).

These techniques enhance the generation of ideas and improve the interaction between employees.

Conclusion

Relationship mapping and the organizational system blueprint are two useful tools to guide and direct your actions as an organizational architect. They provide insight into operations at both the macro and micro levels of an organization. These blueprints provide a universal language that crosses departmental, division, and unit lines, thereby improving organizational performance capacity and effectiveness. Finally, these blueprints are useful in enhancing organizational communications, fostering organizational change, and improving organizational operations.

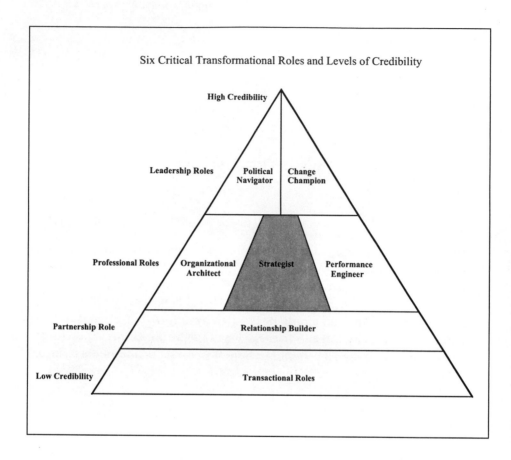

Six Critical Transformational Roles and Levels of Credibility

High Credibility

Leadership Roles / Political Navigator | Change Champion

Professional Roles | Organizational Architect | Strategist | Performance Engineer

Partnership Role | Relationship Builder

Low Credibility | Transactional Roles

7
Strategist

One of the most important transformational roles is that of strategist. This critical leadership role enables you to facilitate change. As a strategist you provide services that are valued by senior managers and executives, which enables you to improve your credibility within the organization, become a strategic business partner, enhance client relationships, better understand the organization, create an attitude of continuous improvement and change within the firm, develop learning, performance, and change partnerships, create a mechanism for executing the organizational effectiveness strategy, formulate a long-term decisionmaking strategy, and foster change.

Genesis of Strategic Planning

Marketing professionals maintain that all products, services, and ideas have a distinct beginning. The same is true of strategic planning within organizations. Every organization faces four different types of environmental conditions: overconfidence, growth, equilibrium, and crisis (Gilley and Boughton 1996).

Overconfidence is a condition in which perceived reality greatly exceeds results, which leads managers and executives to believe they are invincible. In this type of environment, organizational leaders are not receptive to new ideas or ways of improving organizational performance and effectiveness. Equilibrium is a period in organizational life similar to that of a calm lake in early morning. Actual and needed results are mirror reflections of each other. During this time, new ideas and innovations are often resisted as unnecessary—after all, why rock the boat? There is a strongly held belief that managers and executives are satisfied with the organization's position and future. Growth is marked by a period in which today's results are not considered adequate to sustain future operations. A discrepancy exists between desired results and to-day's reality. During this time, all organizational activities are focused on clos-ing the gap, and most managers and executives are receptive to new and innovative ideas for improving organizational performance and effectiveness. Crisis conditions are marked by organizational results that are significantly below those needed to sustain acceptable levels of operation. This period entails extreme stress and anxiety for all members of the firm. In a crisis, man-agers and executives desperately seek ways to dramatically improve organiza-tional performance and effectiveness.

During periods of overconfidence and equilibrium, strategists and the ac-tivities they perform are not generally accepted with open arms by executives and senior managers, since no need is perceived. Growth and crisis situations force vastly different attitudes on senior managers, urging them to pursue so-lutions to performance problems and inefficiencies with a vengeance. Strate-gists, then, are ideally suited for organizations facing these two conditions. Though some argue that strategic planning is an effective process regardless of the economic conditions challenging an organization, most organizations resist until they are feeling the heat of their indecisiveness (Kaufman, Rojas, and Mayer 1992).

Effective strategists develop organizational awareness skills sufficient to identify the economic conditions facing them. In this way, they are better able to identify opportunities for implementing strategic planning activities.

Strategic planning efforts need not be an organizationwide activity. Therefore, strategists need to resist the temptation to limit strategic plan-ning to an organizational restructuring tactic. These activities can also im-prove internal organizational performance at the micro level. By embracing this philosophy, more opportunities to participate in strategic planning will present themselves.

Improving Organizational Effectiveness Through Strategic Planning

Webster's *New American Dictionary* defines strategy as the "skillful employ-ment and coordination of tactics" and "artful planning and management." Strategists, then, provide focus and unity within an organization.

Strategists encourage everyone in the organization to participate in deci-sionmaking, and thus to make a personal impact on the organization's future (Simerly 1987). Consequently, strategists help improve and enhance the self-esteem of employees. Make no mistake, strategists engage in activities that are designed to re-create and reinvent organizations by helping them establish a new vision and purpose, which greatly improves organizational effectiveness.

As strategists, you produce an end product—usually a written document that enables all decisionmakers, stakeholders, and influencers to comprehend, analyze, and critique the organization's mission, goals, objectives, and strategies. These documents help the organization achieve its desired business results. Consequently, strategic planning is both a process and a product. The two are interrelated in such complex ways that it is almost impossible to analyze one without considering the other (Michael 1973).

The best example illustrating the importance of strategic planning was offered in the book *Alice in Wonderland*.

> "Cheshire puss," she began, rather timidly, and she did not at all know whether it would like the name; however, it only grinned a little wider. It's pleased so far, thought Alice and she went on, "Would you please tell me, please, which way I ought to go from here?" "That depends a good deal on where you want to get to," said the cat. "I don't much care where," says Alice. "Then it doesn't matter which way you go," says the cat. "So long as I get somewhere," Alice added as an explanation. "Oh, you're sure to do that," says the cat, "if you only walk long enough."

This simple passage demonstrates a lack of strategic planning, without which an organization is certain to end up somewhere, though it may not be the destination desired.

The strategic planning process is simply a systematic way of organizing the future. As such, strategists are the instruments used to help an organization identify the direction it wants to go, define the outcomes it wants to achieve, and outline how to get there.

Why Is Strategic Planning Important?

Some believe strategic planning is as much a process as it is a plan (Gilley and Coffern, 1994; Simerly, 1987). Many organizations view strategic planning as a once-a-year activity done to formulate well-written and well-meaning mission statements that, sadly, are quickly forgotten in the heat of organizational competition. When strategic planning is treated in this manner it is not part of the organization's management philosophy. Strategic planning should be a minute-by-minute, day-by-day process of planning and managing financial, material, and human resources. Furthermore, it should be used as a tool to help organizations maintain viability. In short, the strategic planning process provides a vehicle to improve current and future organizational effectiveness.

When organizations employ strategists to develop a common purpose for their employees, the results are improved and enhanced communications, organizational culture, and performance. Strategists provide a snapshot of currently available opportunities, as well as a way of identifying barriers that impede performance. This information helps organizational leaders make better, more informed decisions.

HRD professionals benefit from the strategist role in several ways. First, participating improves your credibility within the organization and provides opportunities to develop performance partnerships. Second, you benefit by demonstrating a willingness to listen to clients and help them solve challenging problems. Third, understanding of the organization is improved by working with departments, divisions, and units with whom you previously had no access. Fourth, implementing ongoing strategic planning activities fosters an attitude of continuous improvement and change within the firm. Fifth, strategic planning serves as a mechanism for further analysis of the organizational system discussed in Chapter 6. Sixth, you can help the organization formulate a long-term decisionmaking plan—one that has the approval and blessing of senior management—designed to foster change within the organization.

In some ways, strategists are team builders who force loose confederations of individuals to collectively analyze the organization's culture, identify its mission, develop organizational goals and objectives, and select action plans for change. Perhaps the best definition, then, of the strategic planning process is that it helps organizations identify and keep in focus its primary objective, which is continuous organizational improvement.

How Strategic Planning Differs from Needs Assessment

Strategic planning and needs assessment are quite different processes; however, they use many of the same strategies and techniques to identify gaps between current and desired results. The primary difference between the two may be best understood by examining their end products. In the case of needs assessment, the final product is the identification of skills, knowledge, or attitudes in which employees are currently deficient. Consequently, interventions are designed to provide these individuals with the necessary skills, knowledge, or attitudes to improve performance. Although strategic planning uses an analysis process similar to that of needs assessment, its primary product is the identification of gaps in business results that prevent the organization from operating in an effective manner. Also, strategic planning can be conducted at two different levels—micro or macro. Strategic planning aimed at the micro level is concerned with the quality of an organization's deliverables that are used by internal clients (Kaufman, Rojas, and Mayer 1992). Therefore, micro-strategic planning is designed to improve the internal operations of an organization (organizational performance). Macro-strategic planning is focused on the quality of an organization's deliverables to external clients. It is essentially designed to improve organizational effectiveness.

Although HRD professionals have long been used to identify performance needs within an organization, they have seldom been allowed to participate in micro- and macro-strategic planning activities. This is the result of the old philosophy of HRD—that is, training for training's sake. In order to create results-driven programs, attention must be focused on strategic planning activities that are designed to improve the internal and external operations of an organization. We do not wish to minimize the importance of needs assessments since it serves a useful function within an organization. However, as a strategist, you need to understand the differences between needs assessment and strategic planning, and then make decisions accordingly.

The Five Strategic Planning Phases Used by Strategists

Strategists use a forward-thinking process that helps organizational leaders shape the future through intelligent, informed, and innovative actions. The process gives purpose and direction to an organization by allowing it to ascertain, in advance, what it wishes to accomplish and the means by which it can achieve its ends.

The strategic planning process consists of five separate but interrelated phases, which include scoping, analyzing, visualizing, planning, and implementing and evaluating (Figure 7.1). As a way of positioning strategic planning as both a process and a product, we will identify a number of its major characteristics (see Table 7.1). These components serve as the ingredients of a properly designed, implemented, and evaluated strategic plan.

Scoping

Strategic planning begins by identifying the important issues facing an organization. During this phase, strategists determine the nature of conditions challenging the firm. An effective approach involves asking the question,

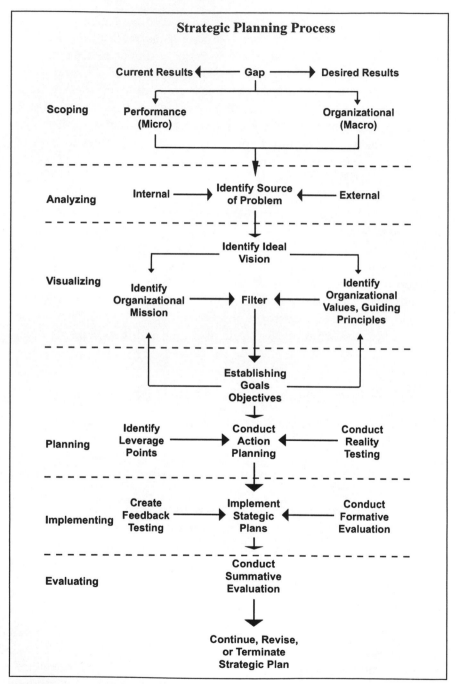

FIGURE 7.1   Strategic Planning Process

Characteristics of the Strategic Planning Process

1. Identifying the nature and scope of the business problem(s) facing an organization;

2. Examining the strengths, weaknesses, opportunities, and threats (SWOT) of an organization;

3. Formulating the organization's ideal vision;

4. Identifying organizational problems and needs;

5. Comparing current performance results with desired results in order to ascertain performance gaps;

6. Identifying an organizational mission;

7. Identifying organizational values and guiding principles;

8. Filtering an organization's ideal vision through its mission, values, and guiding principles;

9. Establishing organizational goals and objectives;

10. Developing action plans that bring about lasting, meaningful change;

11. Locating places within the organization where readiness for change is acute;

12. Conducting reality testing activities to make certain that strategic plans are attainable and practical;

13. Implementing strategic plans in a timely, efficient manner;

14. Establishing a formal feedback system that gathers immediate reactions from decision makers and employees;

15. Conducting formative and summative evaluations to determine the overall success of a strategic plan.

TABLE 7.1   Characteristics of the Strategic Planning Process

"Where is the pain?" The scoping process is designed to ascertain whether a real problem exists—not unlike that of a physician determining the exact cause of an ailment by examining a patient's symptoms.

One source of confusion during the scoping phase entails the lack of a generally accepted, useful, and substantive definition of the problem. Simply put, a problem is a gap between a current set of circumstances and the desired set of circumstances. That is, a problem exists when there is a difference between what is and what should be. This simple but clear definition can be used when examining individual or organizational performance. The scoping phase is complete when a gap has been identified—which serves as justification for the ensuing strategic planning process.

Analyzing

The second phase of the strategic planning process involves conducting an analysis of the organization's internal and external environments. During this phase, you must evaluate the strengths and weaknesses (internal environment) and the opportunities and threats (external environment) facing the organization. Another purpose of the analysis phase is to determine which contingencies will help an organization carry out its mission and which will hinder it. Based on this analysis, you can help the organization make adjustments that compensate for weaknesses and threats, at the same time finding means to help the organization build on strengths and capitalize on opportunities.

Internal Environment. Examination of the internal environment allows for identification of the organization's strengths and weaknesses, which obviously affects execution of its mission. When examining the internal environment, a number of areas must be considered. These include:

- financial condition of the organization;
- managerial aptitudes and abilities;
- current organizational facilities;
- quality of technology; quantity and quality of material resources;
- quantity and quality of human resources;
- departmental and division images;
- organizational structure;
- organizational culture;
- work climate;
- policies and procedures;
- managerial practices;
- organizational mission and strategy;
- leadership;
- job and work design;
- organizational learning system;
- compensation and reward system;
- performance appraisal process;
- performance coaching process.

Questions to Determine the Strengths and Weaknesses of an Organization

1. What is the financial condition of the organization?

2. What are the aptitudes and abilities of managers and employees?

3. What is the current condition of facilities?

4. What is the current state and quality of technology?

5. What is the quantity and quality of material resources?

6. What is the quantity and quality of human resources?

7. What are the current images of various departments and their visions?

8. How is the organization structured?

9. Describe the company's culture.

10. Describe the work climate within the organization.

11. Identify policies and procedures that improve or impede organizational performance and effectiveness.

12. Describe managerial practices within the organization.

13. Describe organizational leadership.

14. Identify the organization's mission and strategy.

15. Describe the job and work design.

16. Describe the learning system.

17. Describe the compensation and reward system.

18. Describe the performance appraisal process.

19. Describe the current usefulness of performance coaching within the organization.

TABLE 7.2   Questions to Determine the Strengths and Weaknesses of an Organization

Several questions should be asked to determine the strengths and weaknesses of an organization (see Table 7.2).

Once these areas have been examined, describe each relationship in terms of its strengths and weaknesses. It is recommended that several data collection methods be used when conducting such an analysis (for example, questionnaires, interviews, observations, and focus groups). Combining methodologies ensures a more accurate picture of the internal state of the organization. Gathered data can be used to better allocate material, financial, and human resources in the execution of an organization's goals, objectives, and mission.

External Environment. External environmental analyses identify the long-term conditions facing the organization and encompass several important variables, including current economic condition; the legal and political environment; social and cultural values; resource availability; the organization's competitive rank; image in the marketplace; and performance and organizational gaps. In Table 7.3, we identify a number of questions that are useful in determining the external environment facing an organization.

This information reveals the economic health of an organization, its values, political climate, use of technology and resources, competitive rank within its industry, overall image, and areas requiring improvement. Each category provides a wealth of information useful in making decisions regarding the allocation of material, financial, and human resources. Once you have identified opportunities or constraints challenging the organization, they are armed with information critical to long-term viability. External analysis also provides information regarding the critical financial and human resources available for expansion and growth.

To remain viable in the marketplace, many organizations need to maintain aggressive research and development programs. An external environmental analysis helps identify the opportunities and threats facing an organization in a given industry, vis-à-vis the amount, type, and quality of technology needed to remain competitive. With the continued escalation of technology, such an analysis will be extremely important to the long-term competitiveness of most organizations and, ultimately, their long-term success.

Visualizing

Developing a strategic vision for the organization requires strategists to direct attention to the organization's future. Thus, you will be able to help leaders anticipate business trends and processes and break them down into manageable units for others to understand and implement. By dismantling business trends and processes into manageable components, you generate a variety of solutions that narrow the gap between what is needed and what is delivered, making the necessary adjustments to ensure organizational success.

As a strategist, you help organizational leaders develop a clear vision for their organizations in both human and financial terms, which allows employees to focus on a common set of goals and outcomes that give their daily

---

Questions Useful in Examining the External Environment

1. What are the economic conditions of the nation, region, and local community?

2. What social and cultural values predominate within the industry and its geographic locations?

3. What quantity and quality of technology does the organization employ to achieve its business results?

4. What external financial, material, and human resources are available?

5. What is the organization's image in the marketplace?

6. What is the company's competitive rank within the industry?

7. What performance gaps exist within the organization?

8. What organizational effectiveness gaps exist?

TABLE 7.3   Questions Useful in Examining the External Environment

activities serious meaning and determine an organization's success or failure. Moreover, you help them identify what they want to achieve and how employees can better serve their internal and external stakeholders.

Strategists are successful in helping organizational leaders communicate their organization's purpose and create an environment built on employee support and involvement. Employees participate in the creation of this vision, share their opinions and ideas, and accept responsibility for activities that help the organization realize its dreams because you use an inclusive approach when designing and developing organizational vision. Accordingly, you generate the support necessary for the collaborative vision to resonate throughout the organization, thereby creating an environment of employee and organizational success.

Creating a vision helps the organization do three things: identify an ideal organizational vision; create a mission; and develop values and guiding principles.

Identifying Ideal Vision.   Senior managers and executives must identify the type of organization to be developed. One way is to create an ideal vision of what the organization should look like in the future. An ideal vision depicts the "perfect" future for the firm. This exercise looks at the best-case scenario rather than practical realities. The ideal vision becomes the target on which the organization focuses its collective energy. It is a form of commitment to its employees and customers. Without an ideal, an organization might limit itself to the easily achievable, although not necessarily desirable, future (Kaufman, Rojas, and Mayer 1992). With an ideal, organizations stretch toward a continuously improving future. An ideal vision is not academic but practical (Senge 1990).

Many organizational leaders are reluctant to identify an ideal vision, believing they will be forced to achieve it. But the process of striving will produce benefits far greater than the failure to establish an aggressive target. An ideal vision will help an organization determine what it will deliver and commit to, which in turn promotes organizational mission, goals, and objectives. By identifying an ideal vision and comparing it with current results, performance and organizational needs can be identified. Comparing these needs with those identified during the scoping phase highlights similarities and differences. The more similar needs are, the more focused the strategic planning process becomes. Differences may indicate a failure to conduct an appropriate initial analysis.

Identifying Organizational Mission. Although vision describes what an organization would like to accomplish ideally, a mission statement clearly specifies what can be accomplished measurably as an organization moves systematically toward the ideal (Kaufman, Rojas, and Mayer 1992). Developing an organizational mission can be a soul-searching, time-consuming process. Each member of the organization has an opportunity to contribute to the creation of the mission since each must ultimately agree with and support it. A well-defined mission gives everyone within the organization a sense of purpose, direction, significance, and achievement.

By defining an organization's mission, you give the company a sense of purpose and direction. Accordingly, an organizational mission statement can help

1. organize employees within the firm around a common outcome;
2. serve as a guide to help organizational leaders in decisionmaking;
3. focus roles and responsibilities;
4. communicate types of changes necessary to improve profitability, competitiveness, and effectiveness;
5. guide the development of goals and objectives;
6. specify targets achievable within a specific time frame (Gilley and Coffern 1994).

Questions Helpful in Creating a Mission Statement for Your Organization

1. Is the mission statement long-term oriented?

2. What role will departments and divisions play in achieving the organization's mission?

3. Has the mission been communicated to all employees?

4. Is the mission clear, concise, and easily understood?

5. Is the mission written for employees as well as customers?

6. Does the mission support the values and guiding principles of the organization?

7. Have organizational members been given the opportunity to participate in the development of the mission?

TABLE 7.4   Questions Helpful in Creating a Mission Statement for Your Organization

The following guidelines will help in writing a mission statement, which should never be stated only in financial terms; set a future direction for the organization; be clear and concise in order to appeal to as wide a constituency as possible; and have an inspirational quality to it (Simerly 1987, 17). Additionally, we provide a few questions that will help you develop a mission statement in Table 7.4.

Identifying Organizational Values and Guiding Principles.   For strategic plans to be effectively implemented, organizational values and guiding principles must be identified. Strategic plans inconsistent with the organization's values and guiding principles stand little chance of success. It is best to consider these as tools that help direct organizational decisionmaking.

Identifying organizational values and guiding principles is critical because they directly influence people's behavior. During this phase of the strategic planning process, you should help the organization identify the most important feelings, beliefs, and attitudes of employees, managers, and executives. Quite simply, a composite of these values make up organizational culture.

Organizational culture is, perhaps, the most powerful internal force affecting the behavior of an organization. Culture defines expectations about behavior, how work is done, how decisions are made, how social interactions are structured, and how people communicate (Schein 1992).

Another component of organizational values and guiding principles is the role leaders play in developing and keeping organizational culture. One of the chief characteristics of high-performance organizations is that they have strong organizational cultures driven by a central core of values and guiding principles shared by employees (Simerly 1987). Successful leaders in high-performance organizations spend considerable time discussing and reinforcing organizational culture. These leaders are successful in monitoring and scanning the organizational environment to demonstrate accountability and responsiveness to their major constituents.

One way of helping you identify the organization's values and guiding principles is by interviewing a cross-section of employees, managers, and executives within the organization. Interviews should include a large number of organizational leaders in order to gain insights about the culture's evolution and its operation in the present environment. While interviewing, it is important to identify the role of organizational leadership as well as outside influences that impact the company's values and guiding principles.

Interviews should begin with a list of common questions asked of each employee, manager, or executive (see Table 7.5). However, it is just as important to provide these individuals with an opportunity to express their ideas and perspectives regarding the things they believe to be critical to the development of organizational culture; therefore, you should provide for open dialogue. This two-phased interviewing approach enables the gathering of as much information as possible regarding values and guiding principles, at the same time maintaining consistency from one person to another. This approach allows individuals to express themselves in greater detail. The questions asked should help you identify employees' perceptions concerning the work process, performance improvement criteria, quality issues, and interpersonal interactions—thus, the organization's values and guiding principles.

Planning

Planning provides a framework by which an organization identifies where it wants to go. During the planning phase, strategists help the organization establish its strategic goals and objectives, conduct action planning, identify leverage points where change can be implemented, and conduct reality testing to determine the practicality of the strategic plan.

Establishing Goals and Objectives. Once you have analyzed the strengths, weaknesses, opportunities, and threats facing the organization, identified an ideal vision and organizational mission, and have ascertained organizational

---

Questions Useful in Identifying Organizational Values and Guiding Principles

1. What are the guiding principles of the organization?

2. What behavioral expectations do managers have of their employees?

3. What performance expectations do managers have of their employees?

4. What behavioral expectations do employees have of their managers?

5. Do managers and supervisors provide specific, meaningful, and timely feedback?

6. Do managers and supervisors encourage employee participation in problem-solving and decision making?

7. Do managers and supervisors have a "desire" to communicate with employees?

8. Is upward communication encouraged within the organization?

9. What role do leaders play in determining or maintaining organizational culture?

10. Do employees and managers feel that their work "makes a difference?"

11. Do employees and managers feel that the organization positively rewards their efforts?

12. Does the organization reward process or task orientations?

13. Does the organization reward long-term solutions?

14. Does the organization reward entrepreneurship?

15. Does the organization reward performance improvement and quality efforts?

16. Does the organization reward teamwork and cooperation?

17. Are employees valued and appreciated by the organization?

18. What is the relationship between employees and managers?

19. How are decisions made within the organization?

20. Does the organization encourage employees' and managers' recommendations regarding performance improvement?

TABLE 7.5   Questions Useful in Identifying Organizational Values and Guiding Principles

values and guiding principles, it is time to develop strategic goals and objectives. Goals and objectives differ from mission statements in that mission statements suggest from where the organization is coming, whereas goals and objectives indicate where the organization is going and how it is going to get there (Gilley, Eggland, and Maycunich Gilley 2002). In other words, strategic goals help organizations decide where they are headed, and objectives identify how the goal is to be implemented. Without specific objectives, goals remain only idealized visions that fail to be realized.

A strategic goal is a large, generalized statement that indicates an organization's future direction. Generally, a goal statement should be broad enough that it cannot be easily measured in terms of time and space, though also short and easily understandable. Goal statements should be one or two sentences that describe where the organization is headed. An objective, on the other hand, is a subset of a goal. The characteristics of an objective are that it can be: measured in time and space; delegated to someone for implementation; and assigned a deadline for completion (Simerly 1987). In other words, strategic planning involves establishing goals and then developing specific objectives to achieve each goal.

The strategic goals and objectives of an organization can vary from year to year, depending on the problems and issues facing the company. The purpose of each goal and objective, however, is to carry out the broader mission of the organization while keeping its values and guiding principles. We believe that organizations that do not filter their strategic goals and objectives through their mission, values, and guiding principles will find themselves off course, and will realize they are engaged in activities they were not intended or qualified to do. In fact, the most frequent errors in writing mission statements are not providing specific and measurable objectives to achieve goals, and not developing feedback mechanisms that regularly monitor peoples' progress (Simerly 1987).

Strategic goals and objectives should be written in a way that helps employees, managers, and executives focus on achieving the overall company mission while creating commitment and agreement on how targets will be met. Effective goals and objectives satisfy six characteristics: they should be specific, measurable, agreed upon, realistic, timely, and written (S.M.A.R.T.w.) (Table 7.6).

The following questions build the foundation when writing strategic goals and objectives:

- What are the organization's primary, short-term business needs?
- What does the organization wish to accomplish in the next few years?
- Where does the organization want to be long-term—in five years, ten years, and beyond?
- What is the HRD program's role and responsibility in helping the organization achieve its strategic business goals and objectives?

S.M.A.R.T. w. Criteria

- *Specific:* Strategic goals and objectives should be well - defined and clear, so that anyone with basic knowledge of the organization can read and understand them and know what they are trying to do.

- *Measurable:* Every strategic goal and objective must be measured. Some recommended standards that can be used in measuring any goal or objective are quantity, quality, time, and cost.

- *Agreed upon:* Members of the organization must agree on the strategic goals and objectives. The more agreement and clarification reached up front, the easier it will be to develop an action plan to improve organizational effectiveness. Agreement also makes it easier to respond to changes that may need to occur during implementation of the strategic plan.

- *Realistic:* All too often organizations set goals and objectives that are impossible to achieve given there sources and time available. Unrealistic goals and objectives set the organization up for frustration and failure. Making goals and objectives realistic may mean adjusting the goal, deadline, or resources.

- *Timely:* All strategic goals and objectives must be tied to a timetable. Although this may be difficult when writing goals, it is an important criteria because at some point the strategic goals must be achieved. Setting a general date for completion may be appropriate.

- *Written:* All strategic goals and objectives should be written to articulate and record desired outcomes that, in turn, focus energies during economically difficult, stressful periods. Written goals and objectives communicate commitment to their completion, which encourages organizational members to reciprocate.

TABLE 7.6 S.M.A.R.T. w. Criteria

Conducting Action Planning. An essential part of strategic planning is the creation of an action plan to be used when implementing all strategic goals and objectives. Action plans address two basic issues: What are the possible problem areas in implementing the strategic plan? How will new strategies be developed if the primary plan falters? Several important points must be considered when developing this phase of the strategic plan. How will the comprehensive plan be implemented?

Who will be in charge of its implementation? What is the basic timetable for implementation? How will the plan's success be measured?

An action plan drives the strategic planning process and thus is critical to its success. In turn, the steps involved in creating an action plan are driven by the strategic goals and objectives.

Identifying Leverage Points. There are certain points in the organization where change is more likely to succeed. Change should be introduced at these penetration points and be allowed to spread to the rest of the organization over time. We refer to these as areas of organizational readiness, or leverage points. Either these points are most receptive to change or they possess the ability to influence others to accept change. It is extremely important for you to identify these entry points since this is where the organization should focus its attention when implementing change.

Conducting Reality Testing. When creating a strategic plan, strategists may become so future oriented and visionary that they lose touch with everyday reality. To prevent the strategic planning process from becoming an academic, theoretical, and unrealistic nightmare, it is important to answer the following question: Are the strategic goals and objectives realistic and attainable given the practical constraints and organizational barriers present today? As you answer this question, you are engaging in a process known as reality testing. In Table 7.7, we identify additional questions that can be helpful when conducting reality testing activities.

In fact, "the reality testing phase is the last opportunity for the organization to modify their strategic goals, objectives, and mission before implementing the strategic plan" (Gilley and Coffern 1994, 106). Therefore, it is absolutely crucial that you conduct reality tests of the strategic plan prior to implementation. Testing helps ensure success.

Implementing

Strategic planning, although undeniably beneficial, remains a difficult process to implement given the many players and constraints involved. The following ten recommendations assist in successful implementation:

1. Obtain high-level management support for the implementation of the strategic plan.
2. Create organizational readiness for implementing the plan.
3. Create an implementation committee responsible for guiding the process.
4. Allocate an appropriate amount of time for implementing the plan.
5. Monitor implementation.
6. Remain flexible during implementation.
7. Manage high-level conflict when it occurs.
8. Support the total concept of strategic planning.
9. Reward participants.

Questions Used to Conduct Reality Testing Activities

- What financial, material, and human resources does the organization need to accomplish its strategic goals, objectives, and mission?

- If needed resources do not exist, how can they be acquired?

- Who can help acquire necessary resources?

- What barriers will prevent the organization from achieving its strategic goals, objectives, and mission?

- How do organizations overcome these barriers?

- How do organizations deal with conflict during implementation of the strategic plan?

- Does the organization need to rethink or rework the strategic plan?

- Does the organization need to rethink or rework the action plan?

TABLE 7.7   Questions Used to Conduct Reality Testing Activities

10. Establish the philosophy that strategic planning is a continuous process.

These recommendations assist strategists in two ways. First, they help successfully implement the strategic plan. Second, they serve as a constant reminder that strategic planning is not complete until it has been successfully implemented and change has occurred within the organization. Do not take anything for granted—strategic planning can be ordered or abandoned at any point in the process. Implementation is "where the rubber meets the road," and you should always guard against the possibility that strategic plans could be compromised.

Creating a Feedback System.   A feedback system enhances implementation of the strategic plan. Feedback systems provide information about the success or failure of the plan, which helps in designing future strategic plans that are better suited to realizing desired results. One means of developing a feedback system is to seek answers to the questions provided in Table 7.8.

Conducting Formative Evaluations.   Formative evaluation is developmental, providing feedback during implementation of the plan that facilitates choosing from among possible modifications. Formative evaluations should be used as a basis for constructively modifying the strategic planning effort and making

Questions Helpful in Developing a Feedback System

- How will people be rewarded for reaching the organization's strategic goals?

- How will employees celebrate when the organization has achieved its strategic goals?

- How will feedback be reported or measured?

- Can a feedback system be designed to assist in developing strategic plans?

- How will the organization measure progress of strategic plans?

- What alternative plans are available if the original strategic plan fails?

TABLE 7.8   Questions Helpful in Developing a Feedback System

recommendations for future implementations. These evaluations are not simply the basis for keeping the strategic plan alive and alternatively completing the process, but aid you in the implementation of the strategic plan.

Evaluating

Conducting Summative Evaluations.   At the completion of the strategic planning process, summative evaluation proves a valuable tool. This type of evaluation assesses the overall outcomes of the strategic planning effort and guides decisions to either continue, revise, or terminate the activity. Summative evaluations should not be conducted for at least three to six months after the strategic plan has been implemented, for the full impact of the strategic plan will not be known.

Formative and summative evaluations differ in their purpose and intent, although both provide feedback that is crucial for the successful implementation of the plan. They capture vital information that can be used to make adjustments during the process and reveal the ultimate outcomes produced by the strategic plan.

Continuing, Revising, or Terminating.   After completion of the strategic planning process, strategists help the organization proceed in one of three ways. First, the organization can elect to continue the strategic planning process on an ongoing basis. Second, the organization can opt to revise the strategic plan and make modifications deemed appropriate or necessary. Modifications may be made in any of the component areas of the strategic plan, including the company's ideal vision. Third, the organization may decide to terminate the strategic planning process due to failure to accomplish its ultimate aims. Regardless of how the organization elects to proceed, the strategic planning process, to be successful, must help the organization achieve its primary goal: to reduce the discrepancy between current and desired results.

Core Competencies

Strategic planning proves incomplete absent analysis of an organization's core competencies, which represent areas of superior performance by a firm. Strategists serve their organizations by leading inquiry and analysis of their strengths—what it does well, what it is known for, its source(s) of competitive advantage, and so forth.

Treacy and Wiersema's (1993) study identified three basic dimensions that drive organizational excellence and therefore, represent core competencies: product leadership, customer intimacy, and operational excellence. In short, firms offer products, services, or operational efficiency (cost) to their customers. Reengineering and processes are about how to run the race; strategy is about which race to run. Core competencies provide the vehicle to get you across the finish line.

Product Leadership

Organizations whose core competencies encompass product leadership offer their customers the best, latest, most advanced, or sophisticated items available. Product leaders are known for their quality, technology, innovation, and ability to satisfy rapidly changing customer needs. Organizations known for their product leadership include Sony, Disney, and Nike.

Customer Intimacy

Customer-intimate organizations thoroughly know and understand their customers and tailor products and services to meet the needs of individuals or small groups of clients. These organizations specialize in satisfying their customers' needs by providing value for the short and long term. Examples of customer-intimate organizations are Home Depot, MBNA, and USAA.

Operational Excellence

Operational excellence manifests itself in a firm's ability to lead in price, value, and convenience. Customers feel confident they are purchasing reliable products at a reasonable price—the result of optimized business processes (for example, efficient systems, supplier management, volume buying, inventory control). Wal-Mart and Dell represent operationally excellent organizations.

Interestingly, organizational members' perspectives of their performance in any or all of the above areas of core competence are often quite different from that of customers. Effective analysis, then, explores the perceptions of internal (employees, managers, executives) and external (customers, vendors) stakeholders via surveys, customer satisfaction questionnaires, focus groups, formal and informal discussions, complaint trends, and so forth. Customers and organizational members often possess quite different perceptions regarding a firm's products, operational efficiency (convenience, cost), or service. For customers, perception is reality; hence, their responses carry more weight than those of internal organization members.

The difference between customers' and organizational members' perceptions of performance reveals whether and where true core competencies exist. Organizations that are legends in their own minds fail to maintain viability in the face of fierce competition. These differences, or gaps in perception, pose opportunities for firms to enhance their offerings. Thus, strategists play a key role in shaping future direction.

Some organizations attempt to be all things to all people—a fantasy at best. Sears is a prime example of an organization that has struggled for years to create a cohesive strategy built on strengths, mistakenly believing that its core competencies lie in all three areas (product, service/customer intimacy, and cost/efficiency). In reality, Sears is mediocre at best in only one area—product excellence in its Craftsman tools. As a result, Sears' performance has declined steadily in past decades.

Can a company excel in two of the dimensions, or three? Rarely. Three companies are recognized as being world class in two dimensions at once: USAA (customer intimate and operationally excellent), Staples (operationally excellent and customer intimate for client companies with fewer than fifty employees), and Toyota (operationally excellent and customer intimate) (Treacy and Wiersema 1993).

No company is recognized as being world class in all three dimensions. In reality, the mere attempt to do so all but ensures failure as it proves nearly impossible to optimize so many variables. Fortunately, dominance of or core competency status in one dimension solidly entrenches an organization in the marketplace. Strategists remind their organizations of this fact, and help them focus on areas of strength to satisfy stakeholder needs and position the firm for long-term success. Core competencies represent an organization's strengths; strategists guide efforts to maximize strengths through analysis, recommendations, and implementation of collaborative, forward-thinking plans and initiatives.

Conclusion

As a strategist, you can help an organization achieve desired goals and objectives during a specific period of time. As much a philosophy as a plan, strategic planning is an ongoing activity within the organization, not a one-time event. In some organizations, the principal benefit derived from strategic planning is participating in the process itself. Employees, managers, and organizational leaders engage in unique dialogue designed to improve the viability of the firm. Organizational readiness for change is enhanced far greater than by any other type of activity or intervention conducted by a transformational professional. Consequently, strategic planning is the quintessential organizational effectiveness strategy of choice. It is wise to embrace this role within organizations whenever possible.

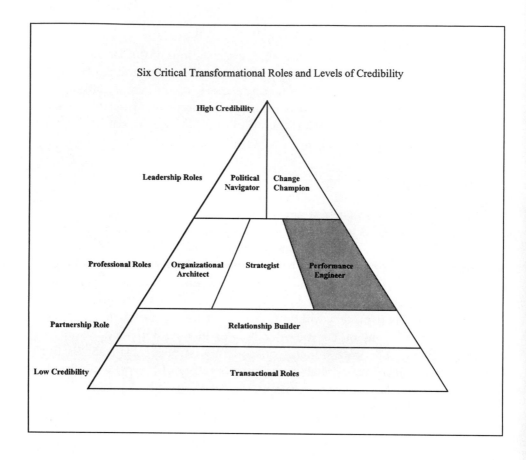

Six Critical Transformational Roles and Levels of Credibility

Performance Engineer

8

Several roles define and separate activity-based HRD from results-driven—one of the most pronounced is that of performance engineer. This role relies heavily on analysis and systems thinking as primary areas of expertise in achieving organizational results.

Performance Engineers in Organizations

The idea of performance engineering was first embraced in the late seventies (Gilbert 1978, 1996). It was based on the belief that human performance could be engineered given suitable conditions, environment, materials, organizational inputs (values, goals, climate), feedback and incentive systems, management action, analysis and evaluation techniques, and human capacity. Other disciplines can be engineered (chemical, electrical, civil), so too can human competence. Several names have been attached to this concept, most notably performance consultant (Robinson and Robinson 1996), human performance technologist (Stolovitch and Keeps 1999, 1992), and human performance enhancer (Rothwell, 1996). We prefer the term performance engineer (Dean 1999) because it communicates exactly your intentions, which are to engineer performance. Further, we believe that results-driven programs must clearly and specifically communicate their intentions so that organizational leaders fully comprehend their intent.

Performance engineers possess a very different perspective from transactional HRD practitioners. Their focus is on helping organizations achieve goals and objectives by improving overall organizational performance. Thus, performance engineers rely on performance management and systems thinking skills to bring about organizational change. The emphasis on the overall human performance system rather than on individuals within the system enable performance engineers to represent a macro perspective of organizational improvement. Performance engineers view the organization as a system containing inputs such as financial, physical, and human resources that produce outputs such as products and services through a series of business processes.

Regardless of title, performance engineers are in the business of improving performance in organizations. Like all transformational roles, you have no direct authority over organizational performance improvement or change; you rely on indirect leadership skills to convince others of the need for services. As a performance engineer you conduct analyses, identify the consequences of employee performance responses (rewards and punishments) to uncover root causes of performance inadequacy, provide recommendations, eliminate barriers to exemplary performance, and evaluate the impact of solutions on organizational performance. Serving in this capacity, you are a strategic troubleshooter responsible for identifying causes of performance gaps between workers and their performance environments and troubleshooting causes of gaps in work or work flow (Rossett 1999b).

Performance engineers have the ability to identify the "importance of gaps between what is and what should be in the organization's interactions with the external environment, within the organization, in work processing, between what workers can do and what they should be able to do" (Rothwell 1996, 149). You demonstrate understanding of organizational structure, culture, work climate, and policies and procedures to discover real or perceived problems (see Chapter 6). Further, you lead, coordinate, or participate in matching work requirements to worker competencies, which is demonstrated by your ability to answer the questions in Table 8.1.

Performance engineers build partnerships with senior managers and organizational leaders to identify performance improvement initiatives that address business needs (Robinson and Robinson 1996, 287). Performance engineers encourage organizational leaders to take action to improve organizational performance, partner with stakeholders (organizational leaders, managers, and employees) to provide services, determine what must be accomplished, and ensure that business problems are resolved to their satisfaction (Fuller and Farrington 1999).

Outputs of Performance Engineers

Performance engineers are responsible for generating five important job outputs, which include:

- Forming and growing partnerships with sustained clients;
- Identifying and qualifying opportunities for performance improvement;

**Questions Helpful in Matching Work Requirements
to Worker Competencies**

- What competencies *are* available among workers to function effectively in the organization's internal and external environment and deal with work processing requirements?

- What competencies *should be* available among workers to function effectively in the organization's internal and external environment and deal with work processing requirements?

- What gaps exist between worker competencies *required* now and those *available* now?

- What gaps exist between worker competencies required in the *future* and those available *now?*

- How important are the gaps in worker competencies?

- What consequences stem from — or are expected to stem from — these competency gaps?

TABLE 8.1   Questions Helpful in Matching Work Requirements to Worker
Competencies
Source: Rothwell 1996, 152-154

- Conducting performance assessments, including performance models, competence models, process models, gap analysis, cause analysis, and data-reporting meetings;
- Managing multiple performance-change interventions;
- Measuring the results of performance improvement interventions (Robinson and Robinson 1999).

Skills of Performance Engineers

Accomplishing these outputs requires development of competencies that demonstrate several characteristics (see Table 8.2). These include:

- Technical skills are used to conduct performance and causal analyses, design and develop performance improvement interventions, perform change management activities, manage projects, and conduct evaluations.

- Observation skills examine a performance situation, dissect it into various elements, and determine and explain the relationships among them.
- Analysis skills explore the organizational system, define business issues with their clients, obtain permission to proceed with a performance analysis and other performance improvement activities, and decide what measures determine whether the performance improvement or management initiative has been successful.
- Root cause identification skills determine whether the root cause is a gap caused by the organization, its people, their behavior, consequences for performance, feedback, or other environmental factors (Fuller and Farrington 1999).
- Consulting skills are used to enter into discussions with potential clients, determine what services and results clients require, and formulate contracts with clients (Fuller and Farrington 1999; Neilson 1999; Gilley and Maycunich 1998; Hale 1998).
- Performance relationship mapping skills are used to illustrate the relationship between business goals, performance requirements, training, and work environment needs, determine the performance needed if business goals are to be realized as well as the current capability of individuals to demonstrate this required performance, and determine the training and work environment actions needed to change performance (Robinson and Robinson 1996, 53–54).
- Management skills are used to conduct stakeholder relationship building activities, interviews, project management planning, intervention identification and selection, evaluation activities, and follow-up and project termination activities.
- Project management skills lead performance improvement interventions and initiatives (projects) from beginning to end.
- Change management skills are used to implement and manage change, deal with resistance to change, create work environments that are conducive to change, and enlist the support and cooperation of organizational leaders, advocates, team members, and others involved with performance improvement.
- Communication and interpersonal skills are used to interact with stakeholders, colleagues, and all other persons potentially affected by the scope of performance engineering.

Characteristics of Performance Engineers

According to Sink (1992, 566–567) and Stolovitch, Keeps, and Rodrigue (1999, 158), performance engineers demonstrate six characteristics that distinguish them from transactional HRD practitioners.

- Results-driven. "Outstanding [performance engineers] are results-oriented. They solve human performance problems…[they] do not become so intrigued with the processes and procedures of [performance engineering] that they lose sight of the true problem and the desired results" (Sink 1992, 566).

- *Investigative.* They possess the art of being able to ask "the critical few questions" and know where to look for information (Stolovitch, Keeps, and Rodrigue 1999, 158).

- *Know how to set and maintain standards.* From "the start of an intervention, the experienced [performance engineer] sets expectations for standards of quality… [and] institutes quality checks at all key points in aproject" (Sink 1992, 567).

- *Cooperative/collaborative.* "Successful [performance engineers] display and encourage collaboration with clients, subordinates, peers, and other practitioners" (Stolovitch, Keeps, and Rodrigue 1999, 158).

- *Flexible while maintaining key principles.* "Talented [performance engineers] easily adapt to new contexts and shifting priorities, deal with sudden constraints or increased scope, apply their systematic processes, and stay with what is best for the client and for the ultimate success of the project" (Stolovitch, Keeps, and Rodrigue 1999, 158).

- *Willing and able to add value.* "Successful [performance engineers] go beyond doing a good job by educating clients about performance improvement principles, providing them with new resources, or introducing them to technologies that have impact beyond the current project" (Stolovitch, Keeps, and Rodrigue 1999, 158).

TABLE 8.2   Characteristics of Performance Engineers

Performance Improvement Model

Performance engineers "should be able to conduct appropriate performance analyses, design/develop interventions, and establish operational plans for implementing, monitoring, and evaluating interventions with a high degree of skill and confidence" (Stolovitch, Keeps, and Rodrigue 1999, 148). They ensure that the intervention plan is implemented as designed and that corrective actions are applied at appropriate moments, which requires organizational and project management competencies and skills.

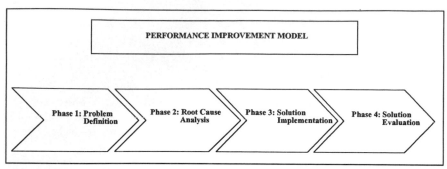

FIGURE 8.1   Performance Improvement Model

Although there have been a large number of performance improvement models introduced over the years, most contain the essential elements of problem definition, root cause analysis, solution implementation, and solution evaluation. A simple, straightforward, performance improvement model based on these elements is outlined in Figure 8.1.

Phase 1: Problem Definition

The performance improvement process begins with a phase known as problem definition. The purpose of problem definition is to identify the seriousness of the problem that you are trying to resolve. During this phase, you identify the organization's business needs. Focusing on this aspect enables you to define desired outcomes of the initiative and identify evidence that the project has met its goals. Next, analyze the current organizational system to determine the effects that leadership, managerial practice, structure, culture, mission and strategy, and policy and procedures might have on the issue at hand (see Chapter 6, Organizational System). Finally, determine the levels of performance necessary from employees. Comparing current performance with the desired performance to identify gaps accomplishes this outcome. This helps you avoid creating performance improvement solutions when none are needed.

During the problem definition phase, performance engineers partner with stakeholders to build a strong relationship, assess performance to gather data, develop performance models, identify performance strengths, gaps, and causes, and analyze data for patterns and connections. Additionally, they collaborate with clients to identify impacts on business goals, and secure agreement on actions to be taken and measures of success. Two types of analysis activities identify performance gaps—job analysis and performance analysis.

Job Analysis. One way to identify performance gaps is to conduct a job analysis, which reveals the requirements for each job within the organization or department under review. Such data create a solid basis on which to make performance-related decisions (Schneider and Konz 1989). This helps you establish future interviewing and selection criteria, and standards to conduct performance appraisals that can become the basis for promotional decisions. Job analysis clarifies job requirements and the relationships among jobs, forecasts human resource needs, and identifies training, transfer, and promotion requirements. Further, job analysis evaluates employee performance and conducts compensation reviews, recruits future employees, improves labor relations, and enhances career planning. It improves job design, develops job classifications, improves career-counseling activities, and resolves grievances and jurisdictional disputes. Finally, it improves working methods and identifies job classifications useful in developing selection, training, and compensation systems (Cascio 1997).

Performance Analysis. Performance analysis is "a process of identifying the organization's performance requirements and comparing them to its objectives and capabilities" (Rosenberg 1996, 6). The purpose of performance analysis is to measure the gap between desired and actual performance. A performance engineer measures actual performance and conducts a comprehensive assessment of employees' current capabilities. Next, you compare these results with desired performance levels and capabilities levels. Once accomplished, you have identified the performance and capabilities gaps respectively.

Performance analysis is critically important because organizations cannot afford to waste scarce resources on interventions that fail to solve performance problems. Since performance engineers devote a significant portion of their time, energy, and effort to designing performance improvement interventions that address stakeholders' needs, it is critical that these interventions be on target.

Performance analysis uncovers the causes of a performance problem by examining why differences exist among performers, whether performance is acceptable, unacceptable, or below standard. It also helps determine whether jobs are designed correctly and the effects of motivational strategies on performance.

Performance analysis reveals the seriousness of the performance gap. Answering four key questions can do this:

1. What results (performance outcomes) are being achieved?

Questions Helpful in Determining the Seriousness of Performance Problems

- What is the desired situation versus the actual situation?

- What is the performance gap or difference?

- Who is affected by the performance gap? Is it one person, a group, an organization, or a work process?

- When and where did the performance gap first occur—or when and where is it expected to begin?

- When and where were its effects, side effects (symptoms), and aftereffects (consequences) first noticed?

- Have they been noticed consistently or inconsistently?

- How has the gap been affecting the organization?

- Have the effects been widespread or limited?

- Is the performance gap traceable to individuals, work groups, locations, departments, divisions, suppliers, distributors, customers, or others?

- What are the immediate and direct results of the gap?

- How much has the gap cost the organization?

- How can the tangible economic impact of the gap best be calculated?

- How can the intangible impact of the gap be calculated in lost customer goodwill or worker morale?

(Rothwell 1996, 13)

TABLE 8.3   Questions Helpful in Determining the Seriousness of Performance Problems

2. What results are desired?
3. How large is the performance gap?
4. What is the impact of the performance gap? (Rossett 1999b, 13)

In Table 8.3 we have identified several additional questions to reveal the seriousness of performance problems.

Performance analysis is a partnering activity that requires stakeholders' involvement to be conducted correctly. Performance analysis involves reaching out for several perspectives on a problem or opportunity, and determining any and all barriers to successful performance.

Nine strategies for speeding up the performance analysis planning process have been identified and are sometimes referred to as "quick and dirty analyses." They summarize the importance of soliciting and presenting opinions based on discussions with your stakeholders. The strategies are as follows:

1. Know what you are doing.
2. Use existing data rather than gathering new.
3. Give your source something to respond to. Time is lost when people can't readily explain what they do or know.
4. Offer your stakeholders a chance to agree, disagree, or elaborate rather than expecting them to come forth with descriptions.
5. Make educated guesses; test with experts.
6. Be proactive; don't wait for stakeholders to ask for help.
7. Use one source to frame possibilities; validate with others.
8. Bring key players together to answer critical questions at the beginning rather than building a systematic process.
9. Use web sites and other electronic information databases to expedite the analysis process (Rossett, 1999b).

Phase 2: Root Cause Analysis

A common mistake made during the performance improvement process is moving too quickly to adopt a solution or intervention (such as training). It is critical that the underlying cause(s) of a performance problem be identified. Quite simply, root cause analysis uncovers the real reason(s) a performance problem or gap exists.

Root cause analysis identifies factors impeding and contributing to performance. Performance engineers identify each barrier (knowledge, motivation, and environment) to ascertain its contribution to a performance breakdown and impacts on performance. In Table 8.4 we provide several questions to determine the cause(s) of performance gaps.

Phase 3: Solution Implementation

Once isolated, valid root causes are targets of performance improvement solutions. Thus, eliminating root causes of poor performance allows employees to achieve desired performance, which allows the organization's business goals to be accomplished. Thus, your mission is to identify solutions that eliminate identified root causes as efficiently and effectively as possible. Additionally, the cost of eliminating performance barriers should be weighed against the benefit of achieving business goals.

Since performance problems are often multicausal, they may require a combination of interventions. We (2000a, 275) believe that "training combined with changes in the work environment (structure) or motivation strategy

---

Questions Helpful in Determining the Cause(s) of Performance Gaps

- Do employees have the knowledge, ability, skills, time, and other resources necessary to perform?
- What are employees' expectations of performance?
- Are employees motivated to perform adequately?
- Do performers possess the ability to perform their jobs correctly?
- What is the adequacy of environmental support and feedback?
- Are employees providing sufficient data and information regarding their performance?
- What are the rewards and incentives for performing correctly, and are they adequate to motivate acceptable performance?
- What are the results and consequences for performing inadequately?
- Are performers penalized or otherwise given disincentives for achieving desired work results?
- How well are people given the data, information, or feedback they need to perform at the time they need it?
- Are performers given important information they need to perform on a timely basis?
- How well are performers supported in what they do by appropriate environmental support, resources, equipment, or tools?
- Do performers have the necessary job aids and working conditions to perform satisfactorily?
- How well are individuals or groups able to perform?
- Do performers want to achieve desired results?
- What payoffs do they expect?
- How realistic are their expectations?

(Rothwell 1996, 13–14)

TABLE 8.4   Questions Helpful in Determining the Cause(s) of Performance Gaps

(compensation system) is more likely to be successful." When addressing complex performance problems, performance improvement efforts involving a simple fix such as training alone are not appropriate. A solution to a complex performance problem may require numerous interventions and changes across several layers and levels of the organization (Rummler 1998). The changes needed to bring performance up to an acceptable level may include training, performance coaching, motivational strategies, environmental change, and so forth.

Prior to implementing solutions, performance engineers engage in four activities:

1. Develop written agreements that outline performance improvement interventions and how they address the need of stakeholders.
2. Develop internal and external partnerships used to help facilitate performance improvement.
3. Develop the performance improvement actions that stakeholders will implement and support.
4. Identify the expected outcomes of an intervention to ascertain how success will be measured (Robb 1998, 253).

Implementing solutions should be undertaken with attention to implementation management and change management issues. Furthermore, the effectiveness of the performance improvement initiative should be evaluated based on achieving the original business goals identified in the performance analysis phase.

Recommending and Implementing Solutions.   Recommended solutions should be instrumental in eliminating the barriers to performance by addressing root causes, which requires a fluent knowledge of the human performance system and an ability to match interventions with types of root causes (Rossett 1999b).

The first step of this phase is to select a solution to close the performance gap. Solutions can either be instructional or noninstructional. Instructional interventions primarily require training and learning activities, transfer of learning efforts, and evaluation. Noninstructional interventions are those designed by you or in cooperation with others, which do not require participating in a formal learning activity. They include writing job descriptions, creating feedback systems, redesigning incentive or pay systems, using process engineering, making cultural changes, and using change management and information or knowledge engineering.

During this phase, you are responsible for designing, developing, and implementing intervention solutions. Once implemented, employees need to demonstrate on-the-job behaviors that bring about required outputs, skills and knowledge needed to perform successfully throughout the performance consulting process, and use systems, tools, and processes needed to perform successfully.

The best ways to think about interventions and to work with them is to organize them into four major categories:

- Human resource development emphasizes improving individual employee performance via training, career development, individual feedback, incentives, and rewards.
- Organizational development centers on improving the performance of groups or teams. It involves organizational design, team building, culture change, group feedback, incentives, and rewards.
- Human resource management is concerned with coaching and managing individual and group performance, as well as recruiting and staffing. Intervention topics include supervision, leadership, succession planning, and personnel selection.
- Environmental engineering focuses on providing tools and facilities for improving performance. Examples include ergonomics, job aids, electronic resources, systems design, job and organizational design, and facilities design (Rosenberg 1996).

Phase 4: Solution Evaluation

Evaluating interventions allows you to determine whether the performance gap between actual and desired has been closed. In other words, evaluation reveals whether an intervention has made a difference, what activities were useful, whether on-the-job behavior has changed, and whether changes in specific knowledge, skills, and attitudes have been sufficient to alter behavior.

Effective evaluations properly target the subject for change (employees and their performance) and the intervention (the means to an end) and answers these key questions:

- Did results match intentions?
- Was a human performance gap eliminated or a human performance improvement opportunity realized?
- Were organizational needs met? (Rothwell 1996a, 15).

Purpose of Evaluation

Evaluations are designed to determine how much change and how much improvement occurred and answers the following questions: What were the impacts of the intervention strategy? What value was added in economic and noneconomic terms? (Rothwell 1996). Further, they ask several additional questions to help determine the purpose of an evaluation. They include:

- What decisions need to be made?
- Who has to make them?
- When will decisions be made?
- Based on what criteria? (Guba and Lincoln 1988).

Evaluation is the process of "delineating, obtaining, and applying descriptive and judgmental information . . . concerning some object's merit; as revealed by its goals, structure, process, and product; and for some useful purpose such as decision making or accountability" (Stufflebeam 1975, 19). From this definition two major purposes of evaluation can be identified. First, evaluation involves producing information for improvement and guides choosing among possible modifications. This is often referred to as proactive evaluation (Rothwell and Cookson 1997), which is characterized as developmental. Thus, information gathered during an evaluation is used as the basis for constructively modifying the intervention or initiative, not simply to keep it alive or, alternatively, complete the process. The second purpose of evaluation is to justify the intervention's value to employers, managers, organizational leaders, and the organization, which is sometimes referred to as retroactive evaluation (Rothwell and Cookson 1997). This type of evaluation involves gathering information after program completion to describe and defend its achievements. Quite simply, summative evaluations are used to establish accountability for the outcomes of an intervention or initiative. Thus, they assess overall outcomes of an intervention and support a decision to continue or terminate the process.

Several important but less common purposes of evaluation can also be identified. These include:

- Fulfilling one's HRD responsibility regarding organizational performance improvement.
- Improving the quality of the organizational performance improvement process.
- Improving project management execution.
- Educating organizational leaders to the values and benefits of organizational performance improvement.
- Demonstrating one's capacity and capability.
- Improving intervention design and development, guiding HRD practice and improving its effectiveness (Brinkerhoff 1999).

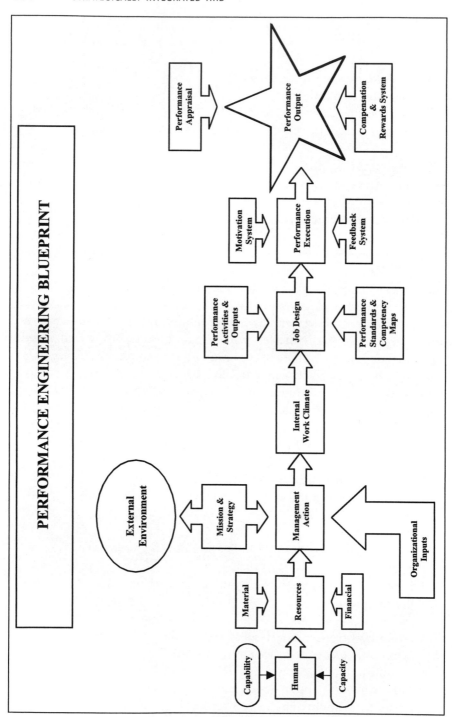

FIGURE 8.2   Performance Engineering Blueprint

Performance Engineering Blueprint

Engineering performance requires insight into how materials, people, tasks, environments, management actions, incentives, feedback, and information work in combination to generate desired outcomes (Figure 8.2). Accordingly, take a total system (systemic) approach to organizational performance, as opposed to making piecemeal interventions such as training activities. It could be said that performance engineers take a "holistic viewpoint with respect to performance problems, which means that [you] examine any given problem (defined as the gap between desired and actual states) within the broader context of the subsystem in which it is situated, within other interacting subsystems, and, ultimately, within the overall system where it occurs" (Stolovitch and Keeps 1999, 5).

Although not every performance problem requires endless examination of all systems, they do necessitate exploration of each performance problem in relation to the mission of the organization, which links actions to a context for improvement. Thus, the performance engineering blueprint approach blends the entire performance management process into one cohesive system (Figure 8.2). It links resources, management action, environmental factors, job design, behavior, and performance to outputs and thus serves as a blueprint for engineering performance.

Performance models such as the performance engineering blueprint define performance that is causally linked to accomplishment of business goals (Robinson and Robinson 1996). The business goals of the organization are the targets to which performance models are directed. Furthermore, it is critical for you to fully comprehend their organization's business goals. Without this understanding, you risk developing inaccurate or incomplete approach to performance improvement.

One of the primary purposes of the performance engineering blueprint is to provide a roadmap to continuously develop and improve the organization's performance management process. In this way, organizational effectiveness can be enhanced on an ongoing basis.

Resources

The performance engineering process begins by identifying the resources required to perform a specific job or set of jobs; these include human, material, and financial resources.

Human Resources.   How do organizations produce successful results? Simple. They have a plan for having the right people in the right place at the right time. Therefore, the first step of the performance engineering process involves identifying the human resources needed to accomplish the work. Consequently, human resources are the beginning of the performance engineering process.

An element of human resource planning is human resource forecasting. Its purpose is to estimate human resource requirements at some future date (Cascio 1997). Forecasting includes:

- identifying the conditions inside an organization;
- examining the external labor market as a whole to accurately project the quantity and quality of future human resources.

Additionally, we believe that human resource planning is a process of systematically organizing the future, of putting into place a plan designed to address upcoming performance problems or productivity and quality requirement. Human resource planning should be integrated with the organization's strategic plan and other organizationwide initiatives. Such planning activities are an integrative approach with other activities like recruitment, selection, orientation, placement, performance management, the learning and change process, career development, and compensation and rewards. Absent this approach, you will be unable to acquire the type and quality of employees needed to ensure organizational success.

Three things influence human resource planning: business needs of the organization, competitive pressure, and future HR requirements.

- Business needs comprise increased business revenue, profitability, quality, effectiveness, efficiency, safety, customer satisfaction, and so forth.
- Competitive pressures—every organization must respond to competitive pressure or be crushed by it. Therefore, organizations are continuously examining themselves to determine whether they can adequately respond to their competitors.
- Future HR requirements—the necessity to forecast the number, kind, and type of employees required in the future (Gilley and Maycunich 2000b).

These factors cause performance engineers to analyze the situation carefully and make projections accordingly.

As a performance engineer, you have two critical responsibilities with respect to human resources. First, you enhance their individual capabilities, which include expanding their personal and professional potential, awareness, and insight. One of the best ways to facilitate individual capability is to create learning systems that focus on strengths and manage employee weaknesses within the organization (Buckingham and Coffman 1999). Effective learning systems encourage employees to continue to develop their strengths via advanced training, new assignments, or challenging projects that increase their skills. At the same time, strategies should be identified and incorporated that help employees manage their weaknesses through partnering, preventing, and delegating (Clifton and Nelson 1992).

A performance engineer's second key responsibility involves increasing human resource capacity, which includes employees' collective skills, knowledge, and abilities. This task requires identification of employees' specialized training, current employment information, significant work experiences, educational background (including degrees, licenses, and certifications), language skills, growth and development plans (past and present), professional association leadership, and awards received. Identifying the capacity of an organization enables you to distinguish employee proficiencies and establish a reliable baseline of human capital. Once established, performance assignment decisions are made regarding the specific capacity of individual employees or the aggregate of employees' competencies. Accordingly, you can make decisions regarding future external recruiting efforts necessary to improve skill and knowledge gaps.

One approach that is commonly used to plan for future human resource need is career planning. Career planning is a long-term effort designed to maximize the skills and abilities of employees. Career planning enables organizations to hold on to their most important assets, their people, by charting an employee's career. This function differs from career coaching, which is a process used by managers to help employees review and explore their interests, abilities, and beliefs regarding their present and future career paths (Gilley and Boughton 1996). Quite simply, career coaching helps employees better understand their personal career interests and abilities.

Career planning enhances an organization by identifying employee performance deficiencies. This can be accomplished via skill and interest inventories as well as observation and performance. Moreover, career planning promotes overall organizational performance through better allocation of human resources. That is, organizations help themselves by placing the right person in the right job at the right time. It enables employees to better understand career choices and their associated feelings, which helps employees make a greater commitment to their career and the organization. We contend that improved loyalty enhances the attitudes of all employees and significantly impacts the quality of work produced. Thus, career planning efforts protect the organization from investing too much time and money in employees who are not suited for specific jobs or responsibilities.

Career planning activities help employees gain greater insight into the organization. Over time, this knowledge helps employees feel more a part of the organization, rather than just one of its disposable workers, which can improve teamwork, cooperation, and help foster an ownership attitude. Finally, career planning encourages employees' self-sufficiency and independence. These skills are essential for building self-directed and empowered work teams. Well-designed career planning activities pay off nicely in improved quality, efficiency, and organizational performance.

Material Resources.   Material resources include the tools, equipment, technology, and information necessary for employees to perform their jobs. Material resources include anything critical to the generation of products or services and can also include computers, component parts, and other vital elements of the production and service process. We also include time and interaction exchanges between working parties in the equation because they are essential factors in the production and service process. Most critically, material resources must be available in the quantity and quality sufficient to produce outputs (products and services) at acceptable levels. Finally, they must be available in a timely manner so as to expedite the production/service process.

Financial Resources.   One of the most important resources in the performance engineering process is financial. This resource determines the support available for each job classification within an organization, as well as the freedom and flexibility allowed when improving or reengineering performance processes and procedures. Financial resources primary include cash and other remunerations used to underwrite the cost of production. Typically, financial resources are linked to revenue growth and increased profitability. Finally, they are directly related to the mission and strategy of an organization and the execution of its business plan.

Management Action

Management action is simply the process of removing performance barriers, providing resources, redesigning jobs, and establishing appropriate compensation and reward systems that promote performance improvement. Unfortunately, many organizational leaders strive to guarantee organizational subservience to employees' efforts to improve productivity, efficiencies, and approaches essential to competitive readiness and organizational renewal. They do this by placing the contributions, involvement, and loyalty of employees above those of the organization. Most important, organizational leaders need to get out of the way and allow employees to work effectively and efficiently. This enables employees to demonstrate creative, insightful, and innovative approaches to business problems and performance difficulties. Organization leaders need to understand that the way they treat their employees determines performance, productivity, loyalty, growth, and development.

It was once said, "putting a good employee against a bad system; the system wins every time" (Rummler and Brache 1995). When organizational leaders get in the way of employees' positive contributions, ideas, and efforts, they diminish employees' importance and value. In essence, organizational leaders are conveying that the firm is more important and valuable than their employees. As a result, employee turnover, disloyalty, and mistrust increase and performance, productivity, and morale fall. Ultimately, the organization misses opportunities to improve its growth, efficiency, and profitability.

When an organization is out of control, performance engineers are able to provide guidance via four critical strategies:

1. Eliminating managerial malpractice, which is the custom of maintaining and using managers who are unqualified, poorly trained, misguided, or inadequately prepared (Gilley and Boughton 1996, 4). These poor managers lack the interpersonal skills necessary to enhance employee commitment and improve organizational performance. Quite simply, they do not have the ability to get results through people.
2. Implementing improved operational actions involves designing organizational structures to enhance performance, and using managers as learning and development champions.
3. Initiating innovative human resource practices entails four actions: communicating to all employees that performance improvement and change are critical to business success; defining the deliverables for all performance engineers and holding them accountable for results; investing new technologies that enhance performance management; and insisting on increased professionalism among all HRD personnel.
4. Implementing developmental strategies includes championing performance improvement and change, developing effective learning systems, establishing long-term career management and planning programs, and creating mentoring programs that facilitate employee growth and development.

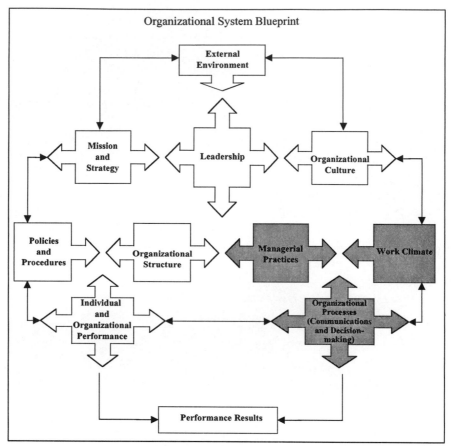

FIGURE 8.3   Organizational System Blueprint (A)

In Chapter 6 we discussed the use of the organizational system framework to effectively manage the components of your organization. Again, this framework is helpful in revealing the relationships among several of its components (Figure 8.3). For example, to affect management actions you need to adjust an organization's managerial practices, policies and procedures, and work climate. Additionally, this tool can be used to communicate exactly what areas need attention so that key stakeholders are able to visualize the potential end result.

Factors Affecting Management Action.   Management action is affected by three factors: organizational inputs, mission and strategy, and external environment (Figure 8.2). Each profoundly influences the ability of an organization to mediate and influence management action.

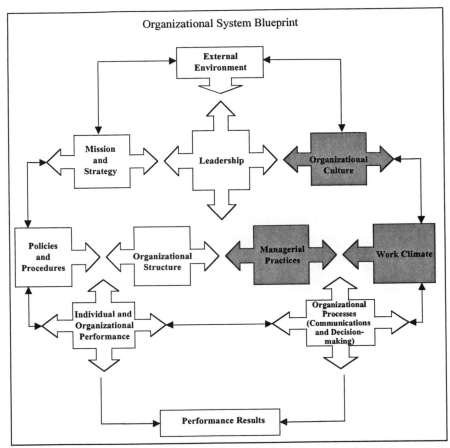

FIGURE 8.4   Organizational System Blueprint (B)

Organizational Inputs.   Management action is greatly affected by organizational culture. These include: the organizational culture, information system, and standards and expectations. All of these affect the way employees perform.

Organizational Culture

Organizational culture refers to norms of behavior and shared values among a group of people. It dictates how work is to be done and how employees treat one another. It is commonplace for individuals who fail to abide by culture to be punished (socially) by other members of the organization, elect to leave because they do not fit in, or be dismissed for failing to demonstrate a willingness to adopt accordingly.

Again, the organization system framework demonstrates the relationship between the firm's culture, managerial practices, and work climate (Figure 8.4). Quite simply, effective management action results when these three components are combined, which creates a healthy atmosphere within an organization. The more positive the atmosphere, the better employee performance. The opposite is true when the atmosphere is perceived as negative.

Information System

Of fundamental importance is how an organization obtains information from its internal and external stakeholders regarding their needs and expectations. The way an organization captures this information is known as its information system, which helps an organization improve and manage its performance.

A poorly executed information system may lead to poor communications and loss of external customers, turnover among employees, or poor partnerships. Evaluating an organization's informational input proves more effective when the following questions are posed:

- How is the organization obtaining information about customers', employees', and partners' needs?
- How are decisionmakers and prospective change participants using that information?
- How should they be using that information to make adaptive or even proactive change to meet or exceed customer, employee, and partner requirements?
- How is or should performance improvement intervention supporting efforts obtain and use information to meet or exceed customer, employee, or partner requirements? (Rothwell and Cookson 1997, 107).

Standards and Expectations

Standards and expectations measure the quality of the organizational culture and information system. Standards represent the excellence criteria used in measuring quality of the organizational culture and information system; expectations measure the anticipated consistency of the organizational culture and information system. Unless standards and expectations are established for these factors, employees cannot possibly generate performance outputs or execute performance activities acceptable to internal or external stakeholders.

Mission and Strategy.   Suspended between management action and the external environment is the organization's mission and strategy. Mission is simply what the organization wants to achieve; strategy entails the tactics employed to achieve a desired end. Mission and strategy affect and are affected by both of these other elements. As a result, the interplay between these two shapes the organization's mission and strategy.

As the organization's mission and strategy change, so should management action. This creates a direct link between these elements and the performance management process remains stable. If management action does not reflect changes in the mission and strategy, the organization's business goals and objectives are in jeopardy. Therefore, monitor the tension between the two elements to make certain they are in concert with each other.

External Environment

The external environment reveals the health of the overall economy. It greatly affects an organization, its values, political climate, use of technology and resources, competitive rank within its industry, overall image, and areas requiring improvement. This type of information is extremely valuable to you when making decisions regarding the engineering of performance within your organization.

To assess the external environment, refer to the list of questions provided in Table 7.3 (Chapter 7, Strategist) under external environment. The answers to these questions reveal the opportunities and threats facing your organization, which allows you to avoid costly mistakes during the performance engineering process.

Internal Work Climate

Although the external environment consists of everything outside the organization, the internal work climate is everything inside the work-unit of a firm. These factors have the potential to seriously impede performance even if resources and management actions are of the highest quality. A critical step in improving human performance involves taking into account the environment in which performance occurs.

Creating an appropriate work climate is critical to generating appropriate performance results. Analysis of organizational culture and managerial prac-

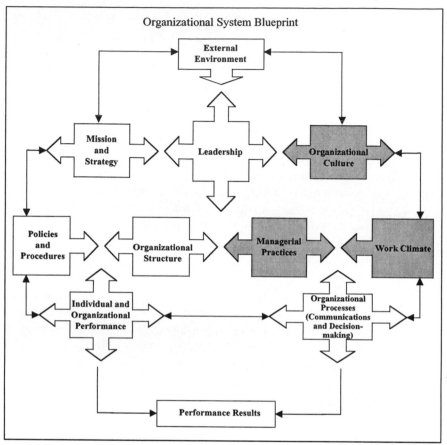

FIGURE 8.5   Organizational System Blueprint (C)

tices determines whether they are conducive to creating the best possible work climate (Figure 8.5). If not, appropriate adjustments are warranted.

Performance engineers focus serious attention on the socialization of employees into the workplace and to the organization as a whole (see Chapter 6 for more information). Socialization is commonly referred to as a process by which organizations bring new people into the culture. Thus, you are responsible for positively influencing the socialization process and improving organizational morale and thus performance.

The questions in Table 7.2 (Chapter 7, Strategist) promote evaluation of the work climate. Again, the answers to these questions reveal the strengths and weaknesses of the organization, which allows you to avoid costly mistakes during the performance engineering process.

Finally, the questions provided for the external environment and the internal work climate helps you identify the forces, within and outside the control

---

Five Interrelated Components of Job Design

- *Performance outputs* represent the deliverables that employee generate.

- Performance activities are the steps that employees engage in to create performance outputs and consist of micro tasks, which collectively form an employee's job.

- *Job descriptions* demonstrate the relationship between performance outputs and activities by clearly identifying performance outputs for each job, performance activities required by employees to produce deliverables, and the relationship between activities and outputs.

- *Performance standards* represent targets used to measure the quality of employee outputs and the efficiency of their performance activities and serve as excellence criteria used to measure product and service quality and worker efficiency.

- *Competency maps* consist of the skills, knowledge, and attitudes needed to perform performance activities used to generate performance outputs and are useful in recruiting and selecting employees for given job classifications.

(Gilley 1998; Rummler and Brache 1995)

TABLE 8.5   Five Interrelated Components of Job Design

of the organization, to encourage or inhibit the accomplishment of each performance result. Forces outside the organization force you to develop coping techniques and skills that optimize positive factors and overcome negative influences. Internal factors need to be managed or eliminated.

Job Design

Reshaping, reorganizing, redefining, replacing, or improving job design may be in order when organizations fail to accomplish their sales revenue, market share, or profitability goals. Quite simply, job design is defined as the series of steps used in producing a product or service (Rummler and Brache 1995).

The first step in the job design process is job analysis, which is used to identify requirements for a specific job classification within the organization (Schneider and Konz 1989). Job analysis reveals the relationships among jobs, enhances career planning, forecasts human resource needs, evaluates employee performance, conducts compensation reviews, and identifies training, transfer, and promotion requirements (Casico 1997). Job analysis allows organizations to establish important elements of a performance management system, which includes creating job classifications useful in developing selection requirements, providing training, developing feedback and motivation systems, creating performance appraisal systems, and developing compensation systems.

Job analysis involves identifying the interfaces between various departments within an organization to eliminate breakdowns or isolate areas of improvement that ultimately impact organizational performance capacity (see Relationship Mapping, Chapter 7; Rummler and Brache 1995). In short, job analysis is useful in uncovering opportunities for performance improvement and employee growth and development. A typical job analysis reveals five interrelated components: performance outputs, performance activities, job descriptions, performance standards, and competency maps (Table 8.5).

Performance Execution

The next step in the performance engineering blueprint is to examine the performance execution of employees. This can be a straightforward and simple activity if the term performance is properly understood. Moreover, understanding the meaning of performance is essential to executing the performance engineering blueprint.

Let us examine the term *performance*. Perform means "to begin and carry through to completion; to take action in accordance with the requirements of; fulfill. Performance means something performed; an accomplishment" (Rothwell 1996, 26). Thus, performance is synonymous with outcomes, results, or accomplishments. Performance is measured in terms of outcomes such as reduced product costs, increased quality, or increased productivity.

Performance should not be confused with other terms like *behaviors, work activities, duties, responsibilities,* or *competencies*. A behavior is an observable action taken to achieve results whereas a work activity is a task or series of tasks taken to achieve results. A work activity has a definite beginning, middle, and end, while a duty is a moral obligation to perform. Responsibility is an action or a result for which one is accountable, and a competency is an area of knowledge or skill that is critical for producing key performance outputs.

As previously discussed, every job consists of four elements: performance outputs, standards, activities, and competency maps. Once designed and aligned in proper order in the production and service delivery sequence, employees use their competencies to engage in performance activities with the purpose of generating performance outputs at an acceptable performance standard. Performance execution is, quite simply, the implementation of performance activities by employees at all levels in a firm.

Another important and often overused and misunderstood element of performance execution is job descriptions, which demonstrate the relationship between performance outputs and activities. Job descriptions illustrate the most appropriate competencies required to execute a job. They also include the performance standards that determine when performance activities and outputs are generated at an excellent level. Unfortunately, most job descriptions fail to provide this critical information.

With this in mind, effective job descriptions are written to achieve four goals: to clearly identify performance outputs for each job, isolate the performance activities required by employees to produce these deliverables, demonstrate the relationship between activities and outputs, and highlight the performance standards required for activities and deliverables. Quite simply, a job description is a written document that describes an employee's performance activities and deliverables, along with their corresponding standards.

Motivation System. The purpose of any organization is to achieve results, from increasing profitability or improving quality to gaining market share. A clear link must be established between producing positive performance outputs and recognition. A straightforward, commonsense approach useful in enhancing employee performance involves simply notifying employees of results or outputs required, levels of quality needed, and applicable time frames.

Properly designed motivations systems build commitment and improve employee loyalty and gauge employee performance in relationship to performance standards or expectations, directly linking compensation and rewards to actual performance. Performance engineers develop motivation systems that account for myriad needs found within firms.

Historically, motivation systems have been performance based, and have given little consideration to rewarding employees for enhancing their skills and competencies. However, it makes tremendous sense to reward employees for their growth, development, and commitment. At the heart of this approach is a simple shift in philosophy where an organization links the compensation and reward program to employee performance growth and development activities. This is done to encourage continuous growth and development, which increases performance dramatically. In this way, the motivation system becomes a vehicle for ever-increasing employee development as opposed to mere performance achievement. Our intent is not to discount the importance of performance but to clarify that performance without growth and development stagnates or even declines. Shifting the motivation system to encourage employee growth and development ensures that employees' skills and competencies continue to evolve.

Feedback System. For the performance engineering process to function smoothly, managers need to communicate in a way that encourages employees to improve their performance. In simplest terms, performance execution requires managers to provide information about an employee's performance and the consequences of their performance. This is known as feedback and the orderly dissemination of such information throughout the production and service sequence is known as the feedback system.

Employees modify their job-related behavior to optimize performance when they are able to associate their work with specific consequences. However, without frequent accurate performance feedback, employees are far less likely to improve their performance over time. To prevent employees from becoming defensive, managers should provide feedback in a positive manner. Effective feedback is delivered continuously, not as a surprise or one-time event. In other words, performance feedback reinforces the behaviors and actions known by employees so they can quickly recognize them and correct their job performance.

Effective performance engineers encourage managers to secure appropriate and adequate documentation prior to sharing their observations with employees. In short, implementing performance feedback requires evidence of various behaviors and actions. Precise, comprehensive documentation places managers and the organization on solid legal ground if an employee's performance leads to termination.

Although recording every incident of performance feedback is unrealistic, proper and thorough documentation of poor performance assures objectivity in dealing with the problem and the employee. Simultaneously, accurate documentation of good performance justifies assigning new and challenging work for employees. We recently (1999, 74) identified a seven-step process that managers can use to provide their employees with feedback regarding incorrect performance (Table 8.6). It is your responsibility to make certain that these seven steps become standard practice.

We believe that feedback is best administered through performance coaching activities. Performance coaching is a series of one-on-one exchanges with employees to improve performance, resolve problems, and achieve results, which encourages managers to establish positive relationships with their employees, enabling them to become active participants as opposed to passive observers. Performance coaching requires managers to constantly shift from one role to another, helping employees improve and enhance their self-esteem and achieve appropriate business results. In this way, feedback becomes a proactive activity that provides a roadmap for helping employees become productive and successful.

Seven-Step Process Useful in Providing Employees Feedback Regarding Incorrect Performance

1. Demystify the performance problem by telling the employee exactly what was done incorrectly. Whenever possible, provide feedback immediately.

2. Allow the employee to react and respond to feedback, which requires listening to the employee's response and observation of his or her non-verbal behavior.

3. Offer concrete evidence of the poor performance. Be specific and clear in your presentation and attempt to identify the strength(s) possessed by the employee that may compensate for the weakness in performance.

4. Identify the appropriate performance that the employee can demonstrate, which may include exact steps to be followed, changes to be made, or the way to go about improving or ensuring quality.

5. Communicate to the employee the consequences of poor performance (discipline, suspension, termination, and so forth).

6. Make certain the employee understands it is his or her responsibility to correct performance and that he or she has ownership of the problem.

7. Identify ways of improving performance or the skills, knowledge, or both necessary for improvement.

TABLE 8.6   Seven-Step Process Useful in Providing Employees Feedback Regarding Incorrect Performance

Performance Output

Performance outputs refer to accomplishments—the hourly, daily, weekly, monthly, quarterly, or yearly production of employees in a specific job classification (Gilley 1998, 91). They are the tangibles and intangibles employees are paid to produce (for example, the number of successful sales calls made by telemarketing representatives, the number of sales made per month by sales personnel, service claims handled by customer service representatives, and so on).

Performance engineers determine whether employees have generated sufficient performance outputs that meet or exceed standards, whether performance activities were executed properly, and whether employees possess the minimum competencies to accomplish their jobs in a satisfactory manner.

Performance Appraisal.   Performance appraisal is a review process designed to give managers an opportunity to judge the adequacy and quality of employee performance. Additionally, performance appraisals are used to:

1. determine whether employees are producing acceptable performance outputs.
2. determine whether performance meets or exceeds performance standards.
3. determine if employees are performing acceptable activities.
4. identify the level of internal and external client satisfaction with outputs generated by employees.
5. determine how employee performance is helping the department and the organization achieve its strategic business goals and objectives.
6. design a performance improvement plan for employees.
7. confront employee performance and make recommendations for improvement.

In theory, performance appraisals are an effective developmental activity that rewards past performance, improves future performance, and encourages career development. In reality, nothing could be further from the truth. The primary reason for the disparity between performance appraisal theory and practice is in the execution of the performance appraisal process. The first problem is that most organizations rely on performance appraisal or review forms that allow managers to painlessly evaluate their employees by assigning numbers for every possible performance category. By making the process as simple as possible, organizations prohibit managers and employees from thinking developmentally. Such forms are more damaging than beneficial because they prevent managers from working collaboratively with employees in their development. Overcoming this obstacle requires managers to be given the opportunity and freedom to work with their employees to identify performance problems, solutions, and developmental opportunities. Organizations must eliminate useless, wasteful performance appraisal and review forms, and substitute them with an opportunity to conduct developmental evaluations.

The primary purpose of developmental evaluations is to identify the strengths and weaknesses of employees and discuss current and future developmental goals and objectives along with plans to achieve them. They are also an excellent opportunity for reviewing the fit between organizational expectations and those of the employee. As a result, managers and employees can engage in constructive discussion regarding developmental and career planning opportunities. Most critically, developmental evaluations are a means for discussing future growth and development actions to enhance employees' abilities and competencies, as well as their careers. From this perspective, performance growth and development plans become a long-term

Nine Steps in Creating a Developmental Evaluation

1. Gather employee performance data.

2. Compare performance results with performance standards and expectations.

3. Share observations and opinions with employees that include perceptions of their strengths and weaknesses, their record of achieving performance outputs, and their abilities and attitudes toward performance activities.

4. Allow employees to respond to managers' critiques.

5. Discuss manager and employee differences.

6. Discuss development opportunities that will enhance employees' skills and abilities.

7. Identify, isolate, and eliminate performance interference.

8. Create growth and development plans based on employees' strengths.

9. Identify performance consequences that will motivate employees to produce adequate, acceptable performance results.

TABLE 8.7   Nine Steps in Creating a Developmental Evaluation

strategy instead of a quick fix. They help managers isolate obstacles that prevent exemplary performance and identify strategies to overcome them. Thus, developmental evaluations provide formal and summative evaluations of an employee's current performance, skills, and aptitudes designed to help employees adopt corrective actions or identify activities to enhance their future potential. A development evaluation consists of nine easy steps (Table 8.7).

The primary difference between a developmental evaluation and a typical performance appraisal are steps six and eight. Another difference is the tone of the review. Developmental evaluations are much more conversational and free flowing, whereas performance appraisals are sometimes perceived as judgment- and analysis-focused. The purpose of a developmental evaluation is to establish opportunities that enhance performance through continuous employee growth and development rather than to simply review performance execution.

Compensation and Reward System.   Many employees fail to perform adequately because there is a disconnect between what they are rewarded for by the organization and what they do (performance/reward disconnect). For example, many organizations have encouraged teamwork and have spent millions of dollars training their people in the skills, knowledge, and practice of self-directed work teams. Unfortunately, most continue to compensate their employees for individual performance rather than those of the team in which they are members. Quite simply, desired performance behavior (teamwork) will be ignored because another behavior is being rewarded (individual contributions). As LeBoeuf (1985) wrote, the things that get rewarded get done. Is it any wonder that teamwork never improves in these organizations?

A direct correlation must exist between desired performance and rewards received for organizational performance to improve. Failure to reward proper performance leads to undesirable results. Thus, if people are rewarded for the right performance the organization will get the right performance. Another common problem is that many organizations fail to adequately reward employees for their efforts. Consequently, employees often fail to improve their performance. Although this may appear a bit shortsighted on the part of employees, many are convinced that unless the organization is willing to provide financial rewards and incentives, changing their performance is unnecessary. A simple solution to this problem is for organizations to simply notify employees of results or outputs required, establishing the levels of quality needed, identifying when the results or outputs are due, and linking compensations and rewards to the criteria accordingly. By following this formula, organizations are rewarding the things to help them achieve the results they need.

Typically, compensation and reward systems include rewards, incentives, recognition, status, power and authority, responsibilities, or compensation, and are linked to job performance. These reward employees who have performed adequately during a specified period of time.

The formulation of a compensation and reward philosophy is of critical importance to any organization interested in improving employee performance. We believe that establishing a compensation and reward philosophy should be based on rewarding people for the right performance. Quite simply, "the things that get rewarded get done" (LeBoeuf 1985, 9). Using this approach assures an organization that it will secure desired results.

When developing a compensation and reward philosophy, consider the organization's culture, values, and guiding principles along with its strategic business goals and objectives. Without this alignment, compensation and reward systems are doomed to fail.

An effective compensation and reward philosophy is flexible, accounting for the ever-fluctuating nature of the organization, change initiatives, and other important organizationwide activities. When this occurs, the compensation and reward program remains pliable, subject to review, alteration, or redesign, which is an approach that guarantees continuous compensation improvement. An organization's compensation and reward philosophy should take into account each step of the performance engineering process. In this way, a compensation and reward approach allows you to:

- Identify your stakeholder needs and expectations;
- Select appropriate resources useful in increasing productivity;
- Encourage management actions that help build collaborative relationships with employees;
- Produce internal work climates that foster loyalty, harmony, and a sense of belonging;
- Design jobs that produce maximum results at the highest possible level of quality;
- Enhance performance execution through the proper use of the motivation and feedback systems;
- Achieve improved performance outputs by allowing managers to conduct developmental evaluations with employees, and collaboratively create performance growth and development plans designed to enhance performance capacity.

Finally, develop a compensation and reward philosophy to ensure satisfactory results. This can be achieved by focusing the compensation and reward system on long-term solutions, entrepreneurship, leadership, employee performance growth and development, teamwork and cooperation, creativity, and employee commitment and loyalty.

Conclusion

Becoming a performance engineer is a time-consuming, difficult, yet rewarding effort. Successful performance engineers develop specific competencies that enable them to be architects of superior behavior within their firms. The performance improvement model and performance engineering blueprint guide efforts to resolve performance problems and support enhancing organizational results.

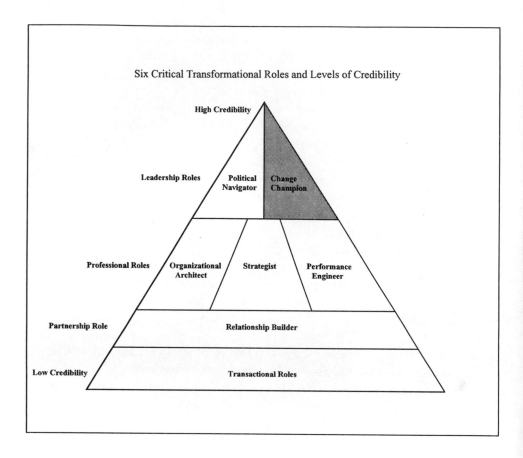

Six Critical Transformational Roles and Levels of Credibility

Change Champion

9

Change champions demonstrate the experience, capability, qualifications, and competence necessary to achieve results in a timely fashion, within budget, and according to quality specifications. Change champions are experts who understand the human and organizational aspects of change—our numerous possible responses (fear, excitement, suspicion) along with procedures available to successfully plan for, communicate, implement, monitor, and evaluate change.

Change champions engage in and are responsible for myriad critical functions within firms, they:

- develop long-range plans included in the broad human resource strategy of the organization, which includes the development of organizationwide change initiatives.
- identify the organization's strengths and weaknesses and create plans for its continuous development.
- identify external threats and opportunities that confront the organization, along with forces or trends impacting it.
- develop guidelines for implementing long-range plans and determine alternative directions for the organization.
- implement analyses that measure the impact of change on the organization.

Regardless of the strategic roles embraced, change champions function first as members of the management team, and second as advocates of performance, productivity improvement, and organizational development through learning, performance, and change. Change champions demonstrate that human resources are critical assets to the organization.

227

Purpose of Change Management

One of the most heated debates among change champions and academics involves whether change management is a contingent or normative process (Burke 1992, 183). The contingent group believes that change champions should allow clients to determine the direction of change, with change champions supporting clients to achieve this end. The normative group believes change champions have a responsibility to recommend specific directions for change. The normative approach addresses organizational values more than any other aspect of the organization's culture because changes in certain operational norms require a value shift that had already been determined (Burke 1992, 196–197). Consequently, the normative constituency promotes a shift toward a more humanistic treatment of all employees characterized by an organizational culture in which growth and development of employees is just as important as improving profits, increasing revenue, or reducing costs. Culture in such organizations exudes equal opportunity and fairness for all employees. Employees feel a sense of ownership of the organization's mission and objectives, and conflict is dealt with openly and systematically, rather than ignored, avoided, or handled in a typical win-lose fashion. Managers in these organizations work in partnership with employees, create work environments conducive for continuous growth and development, and encourage employees to participate in problem solving and decisionmaking.

A normative approach to change management creates an organizational culture in which cooperative behavior is rewarded more frequently than competitive behavior. Communications are emphasized so employees have access to information, especially when it directly affects their jobs or them personally. A normative approach fosters an organizational culture in which rewards are based on both equality-fairness and equity-merit. In this environment employees are given as much autonomy and freedom as possible to ensure both a high degree of individual motivation and accomplishment of organizational objectives.

Change champions holding humanistic values believe that organizations should serve humans, not the reverse. Change champions are supportive of interventions that help employees

- be more involved in decisions that directly affect them;
- be assertive regarding their needs, if not their rights;
- plan their careers;
- become more a part of the work group;
- obtain more interesting jobs or enrich the ones they have;

- have opportunities for additional training, education, and personal development;
- be more involved with their superiors in establishing the objectives and quotas they are expected to reach, and;
- in general, receive respect and fair treatment (Burke 1992, 183).

Over the years, several researchers and authors have identified a number of critical purposes of change management (Burke 1992; Lippitt and Lippitt 1986; Turner 1983; Ulrich 1997). We separated them into three categories: traditional, client oriented, and organizationally oriented (Table 9.1).

Roles and Competencies of a Change Champion

Those making the transition to results-driven HRD rely on four sources of power and influence—brains, heart, courage, and vision. Change champions use brains to understand and intellectually influence decisionmakers, the heart to meaningfully connect with the colleagues, leaders, and employees, the courage to advocate change, and the vision to illustrate what the organization will look like in the future (Gilley, Quatro, Hoekstra, Whittle, and Maycunich 2001). Each of these—brains, heart, courage, and vision—are personal sources of power and influence from which to draw on when operating in the four core roles of a change champion (Figure 9.1):

1. Business partner—master your client's business and the tools of your profession.
2. Servant leader—selflessly serve your client's needs, both personally and professionally.
3. Change expert—exhort your client to strive for excellence throughout the change process.
4. Future shaper—assist your client in defining the long-term future of the organization.

Each of these core roles is interdependent of one another yet independent at the same time. Further, each provides a decidedly different platform from which to lead change. As you progress through each of the core roles, the outcomes are an ever-increasingly broad sphere of influence.

The Business Partner Sphere of Influence

Change champions first demonstrate the capacity to understand, facilitate, and manage change. Quite simply, this requires brain power to build alliances

---

Purposes of Change Management

Traditional Purposes of Change Management

- **Providing Information and Solving Problems**—helping clients define the correct problem, and then work with the problem in such a way that more useful definitions emerge.

- **Conducting Effective Diagnoses and Providing Recommendations**—identifying problems, data gathering, data analysis, and making recommendations, which includes examining the economic conditions facing the organization, analyzing the political and technological status of its industry, determining the appropriateness of the organizational structure, measuring managerial abilities and attitudes, or auditing the organizational culture.

- **Implementing Change**—engaging clients in the change process for the purpose of facilitating a change solution.

Client-Oriented Purposes of Change Management

- **Building Consensus and Commitment**—convincing clients of the steps required in bringing about lasting change, which requires identification of essential decision makers and involving them in the change process.

- **Facilitating Client Learning**—helping clients develop the knowledge and skills needed to adjust to future conditions and address potential problems.

Organizationally Oriented Purposes of Change Management

- **Improving Organizational Effectiveness**—helping organizations adapt future strategies and behavior to change and optimize the contribution of their human resources.

- **Enhancing Organizational Renewal and Performance Capacity**—encouraging a continuous growth and development strategy that enables an organization to enhance it's competitive readiness through the increased performance capability of it's human resources.

- **Improving Organizational Capability**—establishing internal structures and processes that influence its employees to create organization-specific competencies, which enables the organization to adapt to changing client and strategic needs (Ulrich and Lake 1990, 40).

- **Overcoming Employee Depression**—overcoming a psychological condition brought about by under-utilization, apathy, and alienation of employees who feel they are not perceived to be vital, contributing members of the firm (Ulrich 1997).

- **Increasing Employee Productivity and Performance**—providing support for employee excellence through their participation in change initiatives and growth and development activities.

TABLE 9.1   Purposes of Change Management

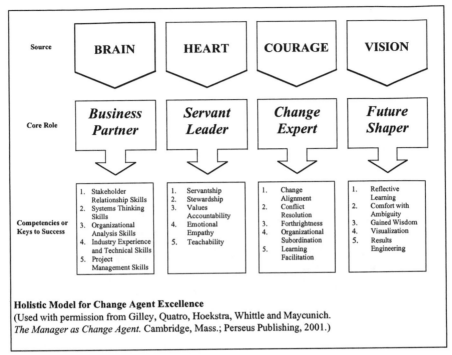

Holistic Model for Change Agent Excellence
(Used with permission from Gilley, Quatro, Hoekstra, Whittle and Maycunich.
The Manager as Change Agent. Cambridge, Mass.; Perseus Publishing, 2001.)

FIGURE 9.1   Holistic Model for Change Agent Excellence

and demonstrate your knowledge of change management, which also serves as the initial source of influence in building business partnerships (Figure 9.2). Without this vital source of power and influence, you are doomed to failure since you will be regarded as superficial and one-dimensional, with recommendations for change perceived as unnecessary, misguided initiatives.

The Servant Leader Sphere of Influence

The heart becomes the source of selflessness necessary for change champions to gain the full commitment and trust of your clients once credible business partnerships are established. The change champions' primary goal as servant leaders is to demonstrate completeness in their approach to organizational life and work—a wholeness that compels clients to become fully engaged during a change initiative and trust that you are committed, first and foremost, to their (the client's) success.

The Change Expert Sphere of Influence

Garnering the commitment and trust of client groups through selflessness earns you the right to employ courage to champion change throughout the

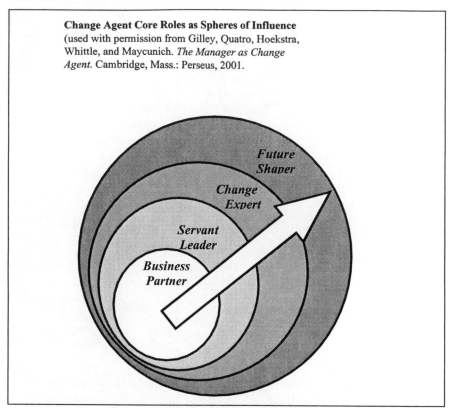

Change Agent Core Roles as Spheres of Influence
(used with permission from Gilley, Quatro, Hoekstra, Whittle, and Maycunich. *The Manager as Change Agent.* Cambridge, Mass.: Perseus, 2001.

Future Shaper

Change Expert

Servant Leader

Business Partner

FIGURE 9.2   Change Agent Core Roles as Spheres of Influence

clients' organization. Here your influence is ever expanding and growing. As a change champion, you are the organization's change representative and greatest proponent.

The Future Shaper Sphere of Influence

This final and greatest sphere of influence allows you to leverage your vision and become a leader in the strategic direction of your organization. To operate in this sphere of influence future shapers demonstrate a proven track record of results over a significant period of time within their client organizations.

Operating in one sphere does not mutually exclude the others, even though change champions initially progress through each of the four core roles successively to achieve increased depth and breadth of influence. For example, once you have performed successfully as a business partner, you continually regress as needed to operate within that sphere; or, at times, concurrently operate in any combination of the four spheres. This dynamic is clearly demonstrated in Figure 9.2, which portrays the core roles as increasingly broad, although not mutually exclusive, spheres of influence (Gilley et al. 2001).

Competencies of a Change Champion

Five competencies are associated with each of the four core roles of a change champion. Each is necessary to become an effective change champion. None can be excluded from your toolkit if your goal is holistic client engagement (Figure 9.1).

Competencies of a Business Partner. Some HRD practitioners lack the competencies for establishing a true business partnership even though they desire to make their organization a better, more effective operation. Gaining credibility as a change champion requires demonstrating the knowledge, skills, and abilities that the organization values. It is absolutely prerequisite to solve problems, create opportunities, capitalize on strategic opportunities, and leverage organizational strengths. To achieve this end, develop skills in stakeholder relationships, system thinking, organizational analysis, industry experience and technical and project management.

- Stakeholder relationship skills—the ability to work with people and to be recognized as someone who adds value to the organization. This requires listening, observing, and empathizing skills, which enables you to really hear what others are saying and to pick up on what is between the lines of a message. Accordingly, the first rule in relationship building with a stakeholder must be listening, truly hearing what stakeholders are saying, both verbally and nonverbally.
- Systems thinking skills—viewing and understanding an organization as an open system requires you to have detailed knowledge of the inputs, throughputs, and outputs of your organization, as well as the critical connections and disconnections existent therein. These characteristics form a framework for appraising an organization's internal environment, isolating performance problems, and identifying relationships critical to organizational effectiveness.
- Organizational analysis skills—identifying the needs of all key decisionmakers, stakeholders, and employees. Additionally, these skills enable you to identify the organization's performance and business needs, as well as its strategic goals and objectives. Consequently, organizational analysis is a process, not an event.

- Industry experience and technical skills—process analysis and redesign, performance management, leadership development, and information systems design and implementation. Further, you also need a related field of experience with significant responsibility.
- Project management skills—planning and identifying objectives and activities that produce a desired result, organizing people to get the job done and directing them by keeping them focused on achieving the results, and measuring the change initiative team's progress and giving them feedback to keep the project moving ahead, constantly monitoring progress toward, and deviation from, the project's goals.

Competencies of a Servant Leader. Determining the motives of others enables you to bring about true individual and organizational transformation. Assessing others' motives requires that you selflessly humble yourself. Consequently, you become a servant leader, focused first and foremost on the success of others, recognizing that your clients' success is, ultimately, your success. Thus, it is an imperative to truly gain the trust and commitment of your clients, which of course is one of the most important goals of change agency. Operating as a servant leader requires you to develop five competencies: servantship, stewardship, values accountability, emotional empathy, and teachability.

- Servantship—demonstrate a servant heart toward others, intentionally serving their needs and goals before your own—making *them* your overriding focus.
- Stewardship—requires that you be held accountable for meeting your clients' needs and ensuring their successes (Block 1999). It also requires you to equip your clients with the knowledge, work skills, and resources necessary for success, helping them develop the authority and autonomy to make significant change-related decisions.
- Values accountability—involves an overt commitment on the part of you to access the *terminal values* (Rokeach 1973) of your clients, to make your values known, and to allow those values to be a constant source of personal and corporate meaning and motivation. It is these terminal values that are most influential and enduring in human beings.
- Emotional empathy—demonstrating that you are empathically attuned to the emotions and feelings of your clients. However, successful change champions understand that change is messy, and at times decidedly

emotional (Jick 1993), especially for your clients, who often don't have the same adaptability to change as you do. These emotions are normal, inevitable, and therefore can not be ignored. More important, practicing emotional empathy raises holistic understanding and engages clients, thereby gaining more change leverage.

- Teachability—creating work environments in which individuals are encouraged to grow and develop. It also involves enhancing your client's readiness to learn and change as well as linking growth and development initiatives to the organization's strategic business goals and objectives.

Competencies of a Change Expert. Becoming a change expert is not for the weak of heart. It requires you to possess the ability to tolerate rejection, even failure, and the courage to confront your organization's powerful immune system. To fulfill the core role of change expert, you must develop change alignment, conflict resolution, forthrightness, organizational subordination, and learning facilitation competencies.

- Change alignment—adopting a change management model that helps you implement, facilitate, and manage change within your organization. One such model was introduced in Chapter 5, which we encouraged you to use when transforming your HRD program from activity-based to results-driven. We discuss the model later in this chapter.
- Conflict resolution—working proactively to both prevent unnecessary conflict and aggressively resolve the inevitable conflicts that do arise. Leveraging conflict in this way depends on your ability to implement the following steps: proactively monitor individual clients and the client organization for sources of conflict, work aggressively to constructively resolve it, bring the parties involved in the conflict together to work through the issue, and ensure that the proposed resolution is implemented immediately. Following this approach elevates you to the vital role of peacemaker (Goleman 1998).
- Forthrightness—assertive and forthright message is nonjudgmental in tone, includes a transparent disclosure of the feelings incited by the behavior, and a clarification of the effects of the client's behavior on the change initiative at hand (Bolton 1986). Quite simply, successful

change champions ensure that they forthrightly address performance and behavior problems among their clients with clarity and with respect. This enhances client understanding of the dysfunctional effects of undesirable behavior and leads to smoother and quicker resolution of the problem.

- Organizational subordination—intentionally prioritizing the contributions, involvement, and loyalty of individual clients above the ingrained organizational system. Thus, you demonstrate organizational subordination by eliminating policies and procedures that interfere with, prevent, or discourage individual client growth and development, as well as eliminating organizational structures that inhibit the progress of the change initiative (Gilley 2002).
- Learning facilitation—having the courage to facilitate learning throughout the organization. Taking on this responsibility requires you to master the art of balancing advocacy—teaching clients, and inquiry—engaging clients in the learning process (Senge 1990, 198). Effective change champions clearly articulate knowledge transfer as a top priority, take advantage of teachable moments, and hold clients accountable for learning. These steps require you to have the courage to ask questions, make connections, and forgive failure.

Competencies of a Future Shaper.   Future shapers are responsible for identifying the impending journey and making midcourse corrections to avoid danger. Future shapers rely on past experiences as a source of information and wisdom. As a visionary, you solicit the wisdom of your clients and examine internal and external environmental conditions before making commitments. Accordingly, you demonstrate faith in others while dynamically balancing optimism and realism, intuition and planning (Quatro, Hoekstra, and Gilley 2002). Future shapers find themselves on a journey that can only be described as a process of "becoming" that involves the development of the competencies of reflective learning, comfort with ambiguity, gained wisdom, visualization, and results engineering.

- Reflective learning—assessing (identifying a gap in present and desired states), challenging (experiencing disequilibrium), and supporting (reflective guidance before, during, and after the experience) (McCauley, Moxley, and Van Velsor 1998).
- Comfort with ambiguity—being at ease with the unknown and relying on your intuition as a guide when critical facts are

unavailable. "The more comfortable you can make yourself with ambiguity, the better leader you will be" (DePree 1992, 57).

- Gained wisdom—relying on others to resolve problems, make recommendations on how to proceed, and to champion. Gained wisdom is evident when you learn to tap into the wisdom of the elders in your organization
- Visualization—identifying future states, connections, and possibilities that others simply cannot see. Then chart a course for change that others can follow in organizations.
- Results engineering—an unyielding commitment to results. You only achieve desired results in concert with your clients. Quite simply, results are ultimately achieved through other people. Thus, you must employ the following components of results engineering: clearly articulate the business-driven need for the change, clearly define the desired deliverables and results, and integrate a performance management process into the change initiative's infrastructure. Once the future reality is identified, you focus with laserlike precision on the journey to that reality.

Responsibilities of a Change Champion

Change champions motivate, inspire, and coach their team members. Active listening skills, as well as the ability to provide meaningful performance feedback, help ensure successful project completion. Effective managers are assertive, not aggressive or submissive, in their interactions with team members and project support groups. That is, change champions confront poor performance and at the same time maintain the self-esteem of team members or support personnel. Communicating tough decisions and being sensitive to the needs of team members and staff remains an effective approach. Interpersonal conflicts over financial and material resources consume precious time and, thus, should be minimized. Finally, change champions remain flexible while performing multiple roles during the process.

To ensure success, change champions maintain the technical competence necessary to complete a complex project. Although no change champion holds all the technical competence necessary to execute every project, each must have the experience and competence to direct, evaluate, and make sound decisions on technical alternatives related to the project. Technical competence includes an understanding of technology, product applications, technological trends and evolutions, and relationships among supporting technologies (Kerzner 1982).

Because change champions direct change initiatives, they must have the leadership and strategic competencies to design, coordinate, control, and implement project plans. Competencies include the ability to envision, design, and communicate the big picture to all members of the project team—which means seeing the forest in spite of the trees. Change leaders demonstrate the ability to ask thought-provoking questions that help team members assigned the project understand their role and responsibilities.

Change champions have the responsibility and authority to complete the project on time, within budget, and according to quality specifications. Change champions must, therefore, delegate the appropriate responsibility and authority to project team members to ensure successful completion. Creation of reporting and control systems alert team members to potential problems, and allow project team members the time necessary to take corrective action when projects appear to be out of control.

Applying the Change Management Process

The change model introduced in Chapter 4 is an effective guide (Figure 9.3) for implementing and managing change initiatives. Although this model was dedicated to the transformation of HRD within your organization, the same steps are applicable for organizationwide change management activities. Apply them accordingly.

Phases of the Change Management Process

To bring about organizational improvement and change, change champions embrace a comprehensive approach that they use over and over. Generally, a ten-step process guides facilitating change initiatives.

Phase 1: Entry—Contact between the change champion and client for an exploratory discussion about the possibility of a change management effort.

Phase 2: Establishing client relationships—the process of exploring the possibilities of a working relationship. The client usually assesses whether your previous experience applies to the present situation, whether you are competent and can be trusted, and most important, whether he or she can relate well with you.

Phase 3: Contracting—the process of negotiating a contract is essentially a statement of agreement that succinctly clarifies what you and the client agree to do respectively.

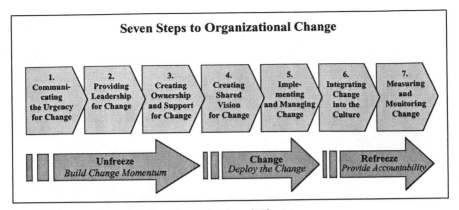

FIGURE 9.3   Seven Steps to Organizational Change

Phase 4: Identifying problems—the principal responsibility of change champions involves identifying the performance, managerial, cultural, or system problem(s) affecting organizational productivity, performance, quality, or competitiveness. These problems are often viewed as the difference between what is and what should be. Consequently, most organizations use the change management process to narrow this gap.

Phase 5: Diagnosing problems—obtaining, organizing, analyzing, interpreting, and evaluating data. Once data are collected, you interpret, categorize, analyze, and summarize to make certain that all information is accounted for. Next, organize the information so that the client can easily understand it, work with it, and take appropriate action.

Phase 6: Identifying root causes—uncovers the real cause of a problem prior to wasting material, financial, and human resources (and possibly fixing the wrong problem).

Phase 7: Providing feedback—presenting preliminary findings to clients. This gives clients an opportunity to examine the data and offer their reactions and opinions, as well as to determine client readiness for change and make certain that the solution is appropriate for the organization.

Phase 8: Planning change—Identifying, evaluating, and selecting solutions. Identify the most appropriate change intervention possible by identifying the sources of organizational problems and matching appropriate solutions to them.

Phase 9: Implementing interventions—an action step requiring application of the solution within the organization.

Phase 10: Evaluating results—determining the overall success of a change initiative based on whether initial goals have been met and the business issue resolved.

Stages of the Organizational Development Process

OD Process	Purpose	Role of Change Agent
1. Entry	First information sharing	To provide information on background, expertise, and experience of client team
2. Establishing Client Relationships	Build synergistic collaborative client relationships	To provide professional background and expertise of change agents
3. Contracting	Sufficient elaboration of needs, interest, fees, services, working conditions, arrangements; and to establish the specific goals and strategies to be used	To specify actual services, fees to be charged, time frame, and actual work conditions, and to agree mutually with the client team on the goals and strategies to be used
4. Identifying Problems	To obtain an unfiltered, undistorted, and objective view of the organization's problems and processes	To clearly identify the performance problem or organizational issue
5. Diagnosing Problems	To obtain, organize, analyze interpret, and evaluate data	To collect data concerning organizational problems and processes, and to provide feedback
6. Identifying Root Causes	To identify root causes of problems	To analyze possible causes of performance and organizational problems, and isolate the most obvious
7. Providing Feedback	To provide timely feedback to client regarding the status of the change initiative and responsibilities	To maintain a clear understanding of the nature and scope of the change initiative and of one's perspective
8. Planning Change	To design a change initiative that will achieve the project goal(s)	To design and develop a change initiative
9. Implementing Interventions	To implement an appropriate intervention	To work with the client team to implement a change intervention
10. Evaluating Results	To determine the effectiveness of intervention strategies, energy, and resources used, as well as the change agent-client system relationship	To gather data on specified targets and report findings to the client

FIGURE 9.4   Stages of the Organizational Development Process

Figure 9.4 provides a brief overview of each of these steps and the change champion's responsibilities during each.

Project Management: Key to Implementing Change Initiatives

Every change initiative is a project to be planned and managed. Thus, it comes as no surprise that effective change champions are competent at managing change initiative projects to evolve to the strategically integrated HRD level.

Project Management

Project management differs from regular management in several ways. First, project management is a comprehensive approach to planning and directing complex activities. Although planning is the cornerstone of success of project management, it is not as critical to regular management. Project management emphasizes results—getting the job done on time, within budget, and with specific controls to gauge progress and provide feedback. Regular management incorporates planning, organizing, directing, and controlling as part of the process of managing people, work flows, and achieving results. Project management uses systems analysis and measurement to make certain that expected results are achieved.

One of the best ways to understand project management is to identify the characteristics of a project. Change initiatives (projects) vary in size and scope—from a simple job redesign to a comprehensive organizational development redesign. A project:

1. is an organized effort with planned activities and schedules;
2. has specific time-bound results;
3. has multiple tasks and roles;
4. has a series of specific yet interdependent tasks;
5. is a one-time effort; and
6. involves many people, usually across functional areas in the organization.

Successful projects exhibit certain characteristics. First, a solid, conceptual plan leads to production of desired results—this means the thinking behind the project makes sense and is easily conveyed to other project team members.

Second, successful projects contain goal and objective statements that are written—in language that is specific, measurable, agreed upon, realistic, timely, and written (S.M.A.R.T.w.). Third, project steps are broken down, measurable, and clear, which helps change champions reduce a large project to micro projects that are much easier to manage and control. Fourth, each step of a project should be discreet, with observable results. Projects are easier to control and quality easier to maintain when observable results have been established. Fifth, sufficient resources (material, financial, and human) should always be available to accomplish the desired objectives. Sixth, every member of the assembled project team should be focused on the desired outcomes. No team member should question or resist the methods chosen to complete the project or meet its objectives. Seventh, the human resources assembled should be competent, qualified, and cooperative. These resources ensure higher quality, promptness, efficiency, and cost control. Finally, successful projects require constant monitoring of outcomes with proper feedback given to project team members. To monitor outcomes, project controls must be identified from the beginning of the project.

Projects are constrained by the organization's need to maintain service, quality, and positive human relations within the firm. Obviously, constraints can hinder progress, achievement of desired outcomes, or both. Consequently, guard against overzealousness when managing projects—always realizing that internal political pressure and politics must be understood and managed.

Project Management Process

Project management is meta–change management and a set of techniques based on the accepted management principles of planning, organizing, directing, and controlling. Each principle is used in combination to reach a desired end result, on time, within budget, and according to established specifications. Project management is also a way of thinking that keeps desired results in focus. Change champions achieve specific objectives using proven tools and techniques such as critical paths (charts), scheduling technologies (Gantt charts), goal and risk analysis, stakeholder analysis, controlling techniques, and project diagrams. Personnel are organized and their efforts directed toward achievement of desired results. Finally, project management requires measurement and evaluation of project objectives against measurable criteria.

Project management involves planning objectives and activities for successful results, organizing people to get things done, directing people to keep them focused on achieving desired results, and measuring progress to provide useful feedback.

Planning.   Planning involves identifying clear, specific goals and objectives, which must be attained on time, within budget, and at a desired level of quality. Work activities to be carried out by members of the project team must be specified, including individual tasks and expected results. Furthermore, specific dates, time, and individuals responsible for producing the desired results must be identified.

To control the outcomes of a project, change champions develop comprehensive plans—no plan means no control. Alternatives must be assessed and more than one way of accomplishing the desired result must be distinguished. This is an effective means by which to guard against unforeseen changes, which can alter the outcome of the project. For example, adjust to unexpected contingencies such as having the funds allocated for completing a project drastically reduced or eliminated. This unforeseen contingency can dramatically affect the quality and timeliness of project outcomes. In fact, it would be nearly impossible to produce the same desired results absent the budget or human resources allocated to accomplish it. Obviously, project quality suffers greatly, as will one's ability to deliver desired results on time. To alleviate the impact of unanticipated difficulties and ensure successful project completion, controls must be built in.

Organizing.   When change champions create a structure used in executing project plans, they are engaged in the process of organizing. Organizing is a set of activities, responsibilities, and authoritative relationships used in implementing the project plan. Organizing includes determining who is responsible for what activities, objectives, and results; who reports to whom; what activities are carried out where in the organization; and who is authorized to make critical project decisions.

Project management entails assembling necessary material and financial resources to carry out work defined in the project plan. Additionally, span of control most appropriate for the project must be identified. That is, too many or too few activities or people can prevent achievement of the desired results.

Change champions identify a principal change champion who is ultimately responsible for achieving project objectives. This individual is accountable for identifying work divisions based on the tasks and activities to be achieved, balancing the authority and responsibility necessary to complete the project, and delegating work to other project team members.

Directing.   Communicating, motivating, coaching, supervising, and providing performance feedback for project team members is a process known as directing. Directing is an ongoing activity, not a singular event. In certain circumstances, directing requires both formal and informal communication, which can include memos, directives, meetings, reports, e-mails, and telephone and informal conversations with project team members as needed.

Change champions are likened to orchestra conductors, who at all times know where they are in the plan and direct each team member to produce a quality performance. One of their chief responsibilities is to build synergy around project outcomes, encouraging participation and ownership during the process.

Controlling. Once human and material resources have been identified and assembled into a workable structure, it will be necessary to observe, monitor, and control that structure as the project progress. Actual results must be compared to plan results, and their discrepancies isolated. Based on the feedback obtained, make decisions necessary to narrow the gap between expectations and performance.

To minimize discrepancies between actual and desired performance, change champions possess knowledge of performance measurement as well as a clear, specific understanding of their client's expectations. Establishment of proper reporting relationships at specific points throughout the project provides an early warning of discrepancies that may threaten project outcomes. These controls allow the time necessary to redesign or adjust the project and its activities to produce deliverables on time, within budget, and at quality specifications. Project success depends greatly on the quality and quantity of checks and balances during execution. Checks and balances guarantee continuous improvement of change champions, project team members, and others involved in planning and controlling the project.

The project management process involves complete and specific identification of expected operations and results. Project management includes systematic measurement of actual progress compared to expectations to identify deviations. Decisionmaking activities used in correcting and redirecting the project keep it on track.

Finally, change champions constantly guard against the failure of a change initiative. In Table 9.2, we outline several reasons why change initiatives fail. The presence of any or all of these conditions dooms the change initiative to failure—which is an unpleasant experience for all involved. In the case of results-driven HRD, each change initiative failure negatively impacts the image and credibility of HRD programs and its professionals. By implementing a systematic process designed to overcome these failures, change initiatives will be delivered on time, within budget, and at desired levels of quality. An effective process consists of eight phases, which include change initiative visual-

> **Ten Reasons Why Change Initiatives Fail**
>
> 1. The change initiative is a solution in search of a problem.
>
> 2. Only the change initiative team is interested in the end result.
>
> 3. No one is in charge.
>
> 4. The change initiative plan lacks structure.
>
> 5. The change initiative plan lacks details.
>
> 6. The change initiative is underbudgeted.
>
> 7. Insufficient resources are allocated.
>
> 8. The change initiative is not tracked against its plan.
>
> 9. The change initiative team is not communicating.
>
> 10. The change initiative strays from its original goals.
>
> (Bienkowski 1989, 99)

TABLE 9.2   Ten Reasons Why Change Initiatives Fail

ization, definition, planning, leadership, implementation, controls, termination, and evaluation.

The Eight Phases of Implementing and Managing Change Initiatives

Implementing and managing change initiatives consists of eight phases. Each phase helps break down large, unmanageable change initiatives into small parts, which can be more easily mastered. As a result, change champions can systematically design, develop, implement, manage, and evaluate change initiative outcomes. This eight-phase process also provides a means of visualizing change initiative planning activities.

Phase 1: Change Initiative Visualization

One of the most effective tools for helping change champions think through a change initiative is visualization. It helps you consider the major components of a change initiative and its corresponding subparts, and shows the relationship between the parts and the subparts. In other words, visualization is a tool that creates a picture of change initiative activities and tasks. Figure 9.5 is a representation of visualization, depicting the relationship between multiple tasks, their dependency and interdependency, and task relationships from beginning to end. Visualization can be used to help delegate various tasks and activities so that the change initiative takes the form of a series of minitasks rather than one large, unmanageable undertaking. Visualization also allows you to think about the dependency relationship among the parts and subparts before a change initiative is begun. The arrows represent functional dependencies in which one part relies on another for one or more of its necessary inputs.

Sometimes it is useful to diagram a change initiative in greater detail that helps identify the resources needed for change initiative completion. Visualization allows this to occur by breaking down complex sections of the change initiative into visual subparts, thus enabling demonstration of their dependency and codependency. Such visualizations allow you to better communicate with team members about their responsibilities. Finally, by breaking a change initiative into subparts, tasks can be delegated to team members easily, who serve as mini-project managers.

Phase 2: Change Initiative Definition

The first task facing a change champion is to separate the change initiative into parts and subparts, which form sets of interrelated work packages. A work package is a group of tasks or activities that an individual can complete (Gilley and Coffern 1994). A work package consists of tasks, which are continuous activities, each of which is assigned to a single individual. Deliverables for each work package are clearly defined and measurable according to established standards and change initiative controls. Each work package has a scheduled start and end date for each task included. Finally, work packages are designed in such a way that preceding and succeeding work packages are identified. In other words, a logical flow exists for completing activities within each work package.

To illustrate work packages, let us consider a common example—that of building a home. Home construction comprises literally thousands of activities and steps, each of which can be assigned to individual workers such as carpenters, bricklayers, electricians, plumbers, roofers, drywallers, painters, and finish carpenters. Each of these individuals is responsible for activities in their area of expertise (work packages). The building contractor (change

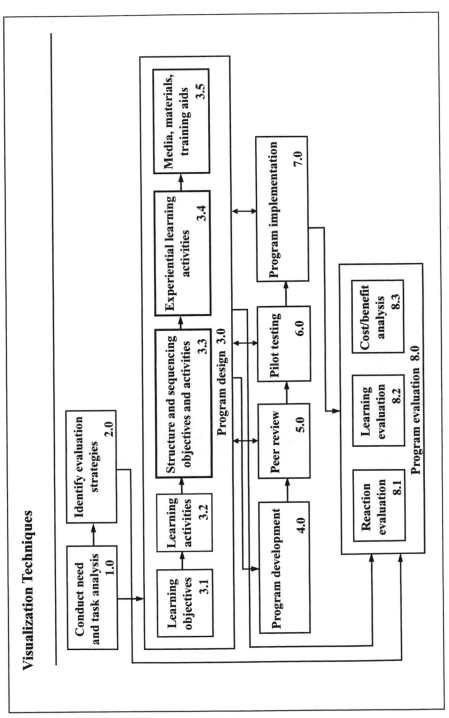

FIGURE 9.5   Visualization Techniques

champion) schedules and coordinates work activities in what is deemed a logical, efficient manner. In this way, a large, nearly unmanageable initiative (building a home) can be broken down into manageable subparts assigned to specialized workers (subcontractors). If managed correctly, the home building project should be completed by the deadline, under or at budget, and at quality specifications. Simply put, work packages are groups of activities or tasks that, when linked together, produce a projected outcome.

Phase 3: Change Initiative Planning

Change initiative planning includes all tasks and activities necessary to achieve change initiative goals, and sets objectives relative to schedules, costs, and quality. With ultimate objectives in mind, alternatives are identified that could include different tasks or activities. Five change initiative planning tools and techniques are available for use in transforming large, unmanageable change initiatives into smaller, more negotiable efforts. They include:

1. goal analysis
2. risk analysis
3. stakeholder analysis
4. scheduling technologies
5. input process and output analysis

Goal Analysis. Every change initiative contains one or several goals to be accomplished. The goal is a global statement of purpose and direction to which all objectives, activities, and tasks point. Goals serve the following functions: they define outcomes in terms of end products or services; act as a continual point of reference for settling disputes and misunderstandings about the change initiative; are the guides that keep all objectives and other associated work on track (Weiss and Wysocki 1992). Two additional functions include enabling you, your clients, and team members to stay focused on desired results and creating commitment and agreement about change initiative outcomes.

One of the best ways to capture the change initiative goal is to consider the statement of results. Goal statements help team members and clients know when the change initiative is finished. That is, change initiative goals show everyone involved what the end looks like.

Again, effectively written goals are specific, measurable, attainable, realistic, time-based, and written (S.M.A.R.T.w.). Goals that meet S.M.A.R.T.w. criteria are more easily communicated to clients, and serve to better manage and control change initiative outcomes. When goals are written in such a way that they can be measured, evaluating results is also easier.

Change initiative goals written with end results in mind and meeting the S.M.A.R.T.w. criteria help clients understand what's in it for them. End-user satisfaction remains a critical component in goal development. The first step in goal identification is consideration of clients' expectations, which requires two-way communications between you and your clients. Change champions speak with other team members about the goal and the most efficient means by which to execute change assignment. In fact, formulating goals is as much an excuse to develop a dialogue with end users and team members as it is to identify the ultimate outcome of the change initiative.

Risk Analysis.   Every change initiative, regardless of size and scope, has risk associated with it. Consequently, you need to identify risks associated with completing a change initiative, allowing contemplation of what might go wrong or what undesirable results might occur by accomplishing the change initiative goal. When completing this activity, three constraints require consideration—schedule, cost, and quality—which serve as constant reminders of the most important criteria used in measuring a change initiative's success.

Change champions are responsible for examining the effects of limited resources on change initiative completion. Accordingly, they identify the optimal resources needed to realistically complete a change initiative, as well as consequences surrounding failure to secure those resources.

Change champions consider what problems or delays might jeopardize the change initiative. Since delays seriously affect project execution, including budget and scheduling quality, the impact of cost overruns or missed deadlines should not be discounted. These outcomes negatively influence one's personal and professional credibility, and can severely impact current and future change initiative outcomes.

Addressing these issues enables you to be better prepared to identify backup strategies to be employed before the change initiative begins. By considering risks prior to implementation, adjustments may be made to scheduling and budgeting, allocation of additional resources, or negotiation of additional time to complete the change initiative. Analysis identifies discrepancies between clients' expectations and actual execution before the change initiative begins—which promotes better change initiative control. Consequently, you can produce better quality deliverables within the budgets available.

Stakeholder Analysis.   Stakeholder analysis is another decisionmaking tool you can use to better plan change initiatives, understand planning obligations and tactics when dealing with clients, and improve communications between change initiative team members, clients, and individuals who stand to gain or lose as a result of the change initiative. Each of these groups is a stakeholder. The purposes of stakeholder analysis are to:

- Enable change champions to identify groups that must be interacted with to meet change initiative goals.
- Develop strategies and tactics to effectively negotiate competing goals and interests among the different groups.
- Identify each group's strategic interest in the change initiative to negotiate common interests.
- Help change champions better allocate resources to deal with differing constituencies (Weiss and Wysocki 1992).

The first step in conducting a stakeholder analysis entails identifying all parties who have something to gain or lose as a result of the change initiative (stakeholders). Second, the interests or expectations of each stakeholder in the change initiative must be identified, thereby providing a baseline for all future decisionmaking and action. Third, identify the action sequences they plan to follow to meet the interests or expectations of each stakeholder. Stakeholder analysis is a powerful tool that helps maintain customer service focus during the implementation and management of a change initiative.

Scheduling Technologies.   One of the most difficult aspects of change management is identifying all change initiative activities and determining their task dependency, which is the primary purpose of creating a change initiative schedule. Another equally important aim is to identify when resources are needed. When these two components have been determined, you can schedule tasks in their proper sequence and allocate resources for maximum efficiency.

The most common type of scheduling format is the Gantt (bar) chart. Although simple to draw, they capture a great deal of information about the change initiative plan. Gantt charts are useful when overviewing a change initiative with clients, and are a quick management tool for use in checking change initiative progress. Gantt charts consist of three parts: a time line, a list of activities or tasks, and a bar for each activity (the length of which represents the time estimate for each activity or task). Each bar depicts the start and end times for a task or activity. The bar chart also demonstrates which tasks cannot start until other tasks are completed.

It was once said that a picture is worth a thousand words—which is quite true of Gantt charts. Drawn on a single page, team members and clients can

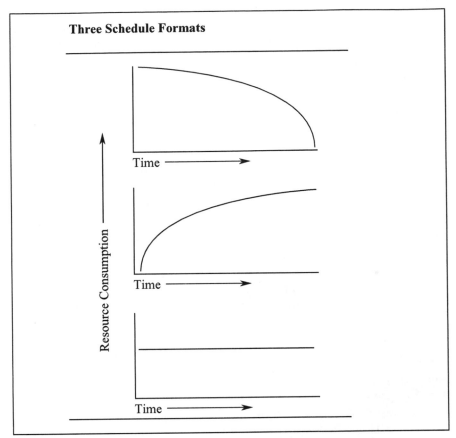

Three Schedule Formats

FIGURE 9.6   Three Schedule Formats

view the entire change initiative at a glance. This change initiative planning tool conveys a considerable amount of information about the change initiative, its complexities, and possible problem areas.

Human and material resources can be used quite differently during the change initiative. They can be used early in the change initiative (front-loaded), late in a change initiative (rear-loaded), or on a constant basis (level-loaded) (Figure 9.6). Each of these represents a type of schedule that can be used when planning change initiative outcomes.

With front-loaded schedules most of the material and human resources are consumed and tasks are completed in the early phases of the change initiative—which means resources are used as early in the change initiative as possible. One risk associated with front-loaded scheduling is that tasks, activities, or both are completed so early in the change initiative that the information developed may need to be reviewed or revised later in the change initiative.

Front-loaded schedules can also cause team members some concern, as they may be nervous about doing tasks too early in the life of the change initiative. Another risk associated with front-loaded schedules is that team members who complete tasks or activities early may be feel disassociated or abandoned as the change initiative moves forward.

Rear-loaded schedules provide for resource allocation and task completion at the very end of the change initiative time line—which fosters change initiative synergy and energy. In other words, tremendous activity is occurring and team members are abuzz over the completion of the change initiative. This type of schedule does, however, have several risks associated with it. The most notable risk is task slippage, which can jeopardize change initiative outcomes. Consequently, make certain that team members adhere strictly to change initiative time lines since no additional time remains to complete tasks. Another risk associated with rear-loaded schedules is that they create a tremendous amount of stress among team members. Stress results from a seemingly overwhelming number of tasks facing the team, as well as fear of reduced quality associated with completing so many tasks so late in the change initiative. Cost overruns are most common with this type of schedule due to failure to allocate sufficient resources. Additional resources are often required to meet change initiative deadlines. These allocations may entail paying over time or increased bonuses to accomplish the same change initiative objectives.

The most common type of change initiative schedule is level-loaded. In practice, it is not the most realistic schedule because resources are seldom available in a uniform fashion. However, it is most commonly used during change initiative proposals to demonstrate how a change initiative is to be completed. Level-loaded schedules use resources and complete tasks equally from the beginning to the end of the change initiative. It allows team members to complete tasks in a linear fashion in what we call the domino effect. That is, one human resource can be assigned to complete all tasks within the change initiative from beginning to end.

Front- and rear-loaded schedules require allocating multiple resources to carry out multiple tasks simultaneously. When level-loaded schedules are used, it is almost impossible to complete multiple tasks at the same time; consequently, they are often considered unrealistic. The biggest advantage of level-loaded schedules is that they provide change initiative continuity from beginning to end.

On the surface, change initiative scheduling seems relatively simple. Unfortunately, some constraints make the process difficult and often lead to less-than-ideal schedules (Table 9.3). Any and all of these constraints can prevent

Scheduling Constraints

- The availability of a particular resource during a change initiative

- Demands on resource needs for other, present, or future change initiatives

- Different or conflicting demands by you for other resources

- A desire to avoid extensive work overloads for a particular individual

- Resource availability to complete a particular task

- Budgetary constraints

- Desire to lessen write-offs or budget overruns

- Integration and use of other change initiatives using the same resource

- Reasonable time for doing activities that are uncertain

- Technical constraints that may need extra time

- Difficulties inherent in scheduling far in advance.

(Gilley and Coffern, 1994)

TABLE 9.3   Scheduling Constraints

you from producing change initiatives on time, within budget, and up to quality standards. Consequently, these constraints should be taken into consideration prior to creating a change initiative schedule.

Input, Process, and Output Analysis.   Input, process, and output analysis (IPO) names the resources needed to complete a task or activity, the process by which they achieve its outcome, and a list of each intended outcome produced if the process is successful. IPO analyses are designed for each major part or subpart of the change initiative. They can be used to communicate to clients and team members the steps required for change initiative completion, which can be very helpful when training new employees.

IPO analyses are the blueprint, or schematic, for the change initiative and help break down large, unmanageable change initiatives into smaller, mini–change initiatives. As a result, you can delegate tasks and activities to members of the change initiative team, who become mini-you. IPO analysis greatly enhances control and management of a change initiative and helps increase involvement of clients and team members. Using goal and risk analysis, stakeholder analysis, scheduling technologies, and IPO analysis helps you accurately define the change initiative before it begins. Such knowledge fosters planning of more effective, efficient change initiatives, as well as communicates to clients and team members the desired outcomes and activities of the change initiative. These analyses also allow for corrections, additions, or deletions before allocation of expensive, limited financial, material, and human resources. In combination, these five tools promote better change management—that is, remaining within budget, on time, and at desired quality levels.

Phase 4: Change Initiative Leadership

Managing a change initiative effectively requires adopting a leadership style that both motivates and empowers change initiative team members, and monitors and guides their progress. Change champions treat change initiative team members with respect, listening to their opinions and ideas until you fully understand their respective points of view.

When conflict arises, your views, needs, and feelings must be expressed assertively, not submissively or aggressively. When communicating assertively, change champions exhibit self-respect, at the same time demonstrating understanding and acceptance of your team members. However, they are clear in their assertions, opinions, and requests for more and better performance. That is, assertive change champions stand up for their own rights yet express their personal needs, values, concerns, and ideas in a direct and appropriate way. Although meeting your own needs (for example, properly implemented change) do not violate those of your team members. True assertiveness is a way of behaving that affirms your individual worth and dignity and simultaneously confirming and maintaining the worth and dignity of change initiative team members. In Table 9.4, we provide twelve guidelines for effective change management leadership, which serve as a resource for managing people during change initiatives.

Communication. Clear communications is the key to successfully managing human resources during change initiatives. All change initiative team members must be fully aware of the change's purpose, plan of action, current status, expected results, and their own roles and responsibilities. Effective and timely communications should be provided throughout the change initiative. This may include team meetings, one-on-ones with various change initiative members, memorandums, e-mails, voice-mails, and the like. Communications planning serves as a powerful tool to schedule appropriate, timely communiqués capable of keeping all participants well informed.

Twelve Guidelines for Effective Change Management Leadership

1. Do not overdirect, overobserve, or overreport.

2. Recognize differences in individuals. Hold a keen appreciation for each person's unique characteristics.

3. Help subordinates see problems as change opportunities.

4. Encourage employees to think more creatively and consider the types of creative contributions they would most like to make during the change initiative.

5. Encourage self-directed work teams and behaviors during the change initiative.

6. Respond positively to ideas rather than negatively.

7. Accept mistakes and errors as learning opportunities.

8. Create positive work environments where failure is not punished, but viewed as a way of improving future performance.

9. Be a resource person rather than a controller — a helper rather than a boss.

10. Insulate your employees from outside problems or internal organizational politics.

11. Participate in professional development activities that enhance creative abilities.

12. Make certain that innovative ideas are forwarded to superiors within the organization with your full support and backing.

   (Raudsepp 1987)

TABLE 9.4   Twelve Guidelines for Effective Change Management Leadership

Barriers to Effective Communications

Numerous barriers often block change initiative communications, although they may be avoided if recognized. Common barriers to effective communications include bias, stereotyping, information overload, noise, and use of slang. Sometimes the most innocent, well-intended comments backfire, preventing change initiative team members from embracing change, trying new skills, resolving conflicts, or solving problems. Furthermore, employee confidence suffers, along with self-esteem. Some poorly informed or ineffective change champions believe that advising, ordering, moralizing, questioning, or threatening change initiative team members improves their overall performance. In reality, these behaviors often backfire, producing negative results.

Certain techniques cause performance to decline. For example, limited emotional involvement while addressing employee performance problems or conflicts may communicate lack of concern or involvement for the well-being of the change initiative team members. As a result, team members resist logical, well-thought-out feedback as well as reassurances that change initiative outcomes will indeed be achieved.

Occasionally, some change champions distract team members by diverting their attention to unrelated or unimportant issues, rather than dealing directly with the performance concerns, feelings, or change initiative issues. When any of these barriers to communications are present, open and honest interaction seldom exists. Consequently, team members are reluctant to discuss problems or concerns with change initiative managers, resulting in failure to achieve change initiative outcomes.

Phase 5: Change Initiative Implementation

Change initiative implementation is a straightforward process that includes execution of all tasks and activities using the tools and techniques already discussed in the first four phases of change management. In other words, implementation is simply the "just do it" part of change management. However, guard against procrastination or other diversions that prevent completion of change initiatives on time, and make certain that team members are performing in an acceptable manner.

Phase 6: Change Initiative Controls

Regardless of how complete and accurate change initiative planning has been, a number of events will always prevent the initiative from being completed as planned. What can go wrong will, and usually at the most inopportune time. Occasionally, as the old saying goes, they come in threes. Ultimately, contingencies threaten change initiative success. The acid test of any change champion is his or her ability to detect problems and take appropriate, corrective action, keeping the change initiative on schedule, within budget, and completed according to quality specifications.

Predicting or controlling unforeseen events is the purpose of change initiative controls, which are designed to focus on one or more of three components of a change initiative: performance levels, costs, and time schedules (Weiss and Wysocki 1992). The primary reasons for change initiative controls are to:

- Track change initiative progress.
- Detect variance from the change initiative plan.
- Take corrective action.

Proposed Schedule/Plan Change Worksheet			
	Impact on...		
Proposed Change	**Schedule?**	**Cost?**	**Quality?**

FIGURE 9.7   Change Worksheet

Track Change Initiative Progress.   One method of tracking progress entails creating a periodic (weekly or monthly) reporting system that lists the status of every activity in a change initiative. These reports summarize progress for a specified period of time and identify any areas of concern or difficulty. These reports can be used for part or all of the change initiative.

Detect Variance from the Change Initiative Plan.   One of the most important functions of change initiative control involves detecting variances from the change initiative plan—allowing you the time to take corrective action. Figure 9.7 is a simple variance report that provides your team members the opportunity to work closely with you to identify proposed changes that impact schedules, costs, and quality. By using these reports, you are not encouraging variances in the original change initiative plan, but are providing team members an opportunity to discuss unforeseen contingencies and unexpected changes, early enough such that appropriate actions can be taken. This tool is extremely important for large, complex change initiatives with a number of material and human resources to be coordinated and controlled over an extended period of time. Finally, these reports reduce the number of questions regarding the implementation or clarification of activities or tasks, and are a more formalized dialogue than random discussions in the hallways and corridors of one's organization.

Take Corrective Action.   A significant variance from the change initiative plan forces corrective action. The change initiative's complexity determines the number of what-ifs to be considered. The necessity of taking corrective action is most acute when change initiatives appear to be falling behind schedule, thus jeopardizing budgeting or quality of the deliverable. To get the change initiative back on schedule, human and material resources may require reallocation, and alternatives identified. Regardless of the contingency or problem that surfaces, use change initiative controls to make adjustments.

Two types of controls can be used to ensure that change initiatives remain on track: steering controls and go/no go controls.

Steering Controls

When a change initiative reaches a critical checkpoint, it is time to compare the change initiative's current status with its plan. If activities or tasks do not meet specifications, a set of corrective actions known as steering controls should be implemented. Steering controls are designed to redirect and steer tasks and activities in such a way that they adhere to the change initiative plan and its corresponding schedule. They answer the question "What if?" and are most useful when critical decisions must be made at key points within the change initiative. Steering controls should be identified before the change initiative begins, and serve as soundings along the way.

Let us provide an illustration of the importance of steering controls. When a ship captain sails from England to Australia, a number of conditions must be taken into account prior to launching. These conditions may include water currents, wind conditions, future weather systems, weight and size of the vessel, number of passengers, cargo weight and placement, and geographic variations beneath the water's surface. Each of these conditions can greatly influence the captain's selected route. While sailing, the captain continuously adjusts his charted course, unlike automobile travel that follows a linear connection from one point to another. At certain points along the route, the captain determines whether he or she is on schedule and is at the appropriate geographical point. Measurements are taken to determine whether the ship is on course. If off course, adjustments will be made to return the ship to the appropriate course, or an acceptable alternative to reach the ultimate destination will be chosen. These soundings, or checkpoints, may occur several times during the sailing excursion. As one might imagine, the more complex the route, the more soundings (checkpoints) will be necessary. This is an excellent example of steering controls. The ship captain functions as the quintessential change initiative manager. The change initiative plan is the sailing course, which includes a number of activities. Soundings are change initiative controls. No ship captain would set sail without establishing a course of action and identifying steering controls. It makes tremendous sense, therefore, to embark on performance improvement and organizational development change initiatives after establishing the same kinds of safeguards.

Go/No Go Controls

A go/no go control is similar to a steering control, but the corrective action involved is different. When a go/no go control is used, you must determine whether it makes sound financial and business sense to continue the change initiative. That is, you use these controls to determine whether the change initiative should be abandoned prior to committing additional financial and human resources. Go/no go controls allow the reallocation of financial, material, and human resources to other change initiatives with greater potential for success. The most important purpose of go/no go controls is to provide you the opportunity to terminate change initiatives that do not have a high probability of success. In this way, personal and professional credibility is preserved.

Change Initiative Budgeting. Although change initiative budgets are typically developed during the planning phase, they are so critical to the outcomes of an initiative that they should be a type of change initiative control. In this way, change initiative budgets influence whether change initiative outcomes are on time and within quality specifications. Underfunded change initiatives are destined to produce inferior results. Change champions are responsible for negotiation of a budgeting level appropriate to achieve desired outcomes.

Budgets are developed when all costs germane to completing the change initiative are considered. To maximize control, budgets should be built at the component level of the change initiative, which ensures budgetary linkage to a part and its subparts. In other words, change initiative budgets should be built from the inside out. When this approach is used, a more exacting accountability of costs can be realized, allowing you to examine the budgetary costs at a micro level within the change initiative, rather than at a macro level. Summarizing component-level budgets highlights the overall costs of the change initiative.

Five different types of costs are build in to budgets:

1. Direct costs—all items directly attributable to the change initiative, its parts and/or subparts (for example, equipment, travel expenses, supplies, tools, or dedicated human resources).
2. Indirect costs—items difficult to assign to specific change initiatives, parts, or subparts (such as heating, electricity, insurance, or other overhead expenses).
3. Fixed costs—items that do not vary regardless of their use (for example, rent expense, computer equipment, or certain types of human resources such as administrative assistants).
4. Variable costs—items that vary with their usage (long-distance telephone calls, copying, or other disposable materials).
5. Allocated costs—items already paid for by the organization (such as salaries and benefits).

Change initiative budgeting remains one of the most critical elements of change management, and is used to determine whether a change initiative has been completed successfully. Budgets should be carefully developed and adhered to strictly, with adjustments made only when quality of the change initiative deliverables is in jeopardy.

Phase 7: Change Initiative Termination

Although it makes sense to plan, implement, and control change initiative outcomes, it also makes sense to properly terminate a change initiative. In many situations, change initiative termination determines how people feel about the change initiative's outcomes. In Table 9.5, we provide the rationale for terminating a change initiative.

Additionally, the three types of change initiative terminations are extinction, inclusion, and integration (Meredith and Mantel 1989). Each of these types of terminations helps you determine the change initiative's acceptance within the organization.

The most formal change initiative termination is extinction, which implies that change initiative activities as scheduled are either successfully or unsuc-

Rationale for Terminating a Change Initiative

1. To formally close outside contractual relationships with suppliers, customers, and other budgeted parties who expect an early, agreed-upon termination of their services.

2. To formally terminate change initiative team members' assignments.

3. To obtain client acceptance of change initiative outcomes and deliverables.

4. To ensure that all deliverables have been installed and implemented according to time, budget, and quality specifications.

5. To ensure that adequate change initiative documentation and baseline information are in place to facilitate interactions or changes that may need to occur in the future.

6. To issue or obtain sign-offs on the final report or change initiative status which show that contracted deliverables have been satisfactorily implemented.

7. To terminate all interior and exterior relationships.

(Weiss and Wysocki 1992)

TABLE 9.5   Rationale for Terminating a Change Initiative

cessfully completed, and the decision to terminate is agreed upon by all parties. When a change initiative has been extinguished prior to its completion, stress and feelings of inadequacy may result on the part of change initiative team members, managers, and clients since their time, energy, and effort have, for all practical purposes, been undermined.

Change initiative termination by inclusion means the change initiative is a success and has been institutionalized into the organization (Weiss and Wysocki 1992). Termination by inclusion implies that a transformation has occurred within the organization, and that significant changes are occurring or are scheduled to occur as a result.

Change initiative termination by integration is a business as usual approach. In other words, the change initiative simply ends, and successful deliverables are shared within the organization. Change initiative equipment, materials, and human resources are redistributed back into the organization, to be reassigned to new change initiatives. Little fanfare or celebration occurs during this type of change initiative termination, which is seen as an everyday occurrence.

It is extremely important to know when a change initiative should be terminated, especially when there is a departure from the published or planned dates and deadlines set forth in the original change initiative plan. A number

Checklist for Change Initiative Termination

- Has the change initiative lost its key champion or internal advocate?

- Is the change initiative team enthusiastic about change initiative deliverables?

- Does it seem likely that the change initiative will achieve the minimal goals set for it?

- Could the change initiative be outsourced without loss of quality or extensive financial costs?

- Is the change initiative team still innovative, or have they gone stale?

- Is organizational support for change initiative deliverables enthusiastic?

- Is organizational support significant for change initiative success?

- Is the change initiative still consistent with organizational strategic business goals and objectives?

- Is management sufficiently enthusiastic about the change initiative to support its implementation?

- Does the change initiative have the support of all departments needed to implement it (important during organizational development interventions)?

- Is the current change initiative team properly qualified to continue the change initiative?

- Does the organization have the required skills to achieve full implementation of the change initiative?

- Is the scope of the change initiative consistent with the organization's vision, mission, and guiding principles?

(Meredith and Mantel 1989)

TABLE 9.6   Checklist for Change Initiative Termination

of important guidelines have been developed, which serve as a checklist in determining when a change initiative should be terminated (Table 9.6).

Phase 8: Change Initiative Evaluation

Determining a change initiative's success entails ascertaining how well change initiative goals and activities have been achieved by measuring them against the original change initiative plan, budget, time deadlines, quality of deliverables specifications, and client satisfaction. The most important questions to be answered are:

- Was the change initiative goal achieved?
- Was change initiative work completed on time, within budget, and according to quality specifications?
- Was the client satisfied with change initiative results? (Weiss and Wysocki 1992).

These questions drive the postimplementation evaluation in such a way that you and team members learn from their successes and failures. It is extremely important to have a postmortem discussion about how well the change initiative was managed, coordinated, and implemented. Such meetings should be informal affairs allowing individuals to share their opinions and ideas freely. In this way, assemblies will be perceived as learning experiences rather than fault-gathering activities—resulting in a great deal of shared learning. It is important to remember that people have dedicated many hours to the successful execution and completion of a change initiative; therefore, it makes sense to celebrate its success or discuss its failures. Otherwise, team members feel a sense of loss or inadequacy as a result of the lack of closure.

Conclusion

Change management is, indeed, one of the most important tools available to improve the image and credibility of HRD programs, its professionals, interventions, and consulting services. Change initiatives provide an opportunity to develop strategic business partnerships, performance improvement, and organizational development partnerships throughout the firm. Change champions remember that the eyes of the organization are on them during a change, especially when plans are being championed by senior management or key influencers within the firm. Consequently, change management and execution are crucial as HRD programs struggle to evolve to the strategically integrated level.

Every change champion is a project manager, although many lack a practical approach and techniques for completing a project efficiently. Few know how to plan and manage a project, even though every performance improvement and organizational development intervention is a project, to be managed, implemented, and evaluated. Thus, it comes as no surprise that change champions must become competent at managing projects to evolve to the strategically integrated HRD level.

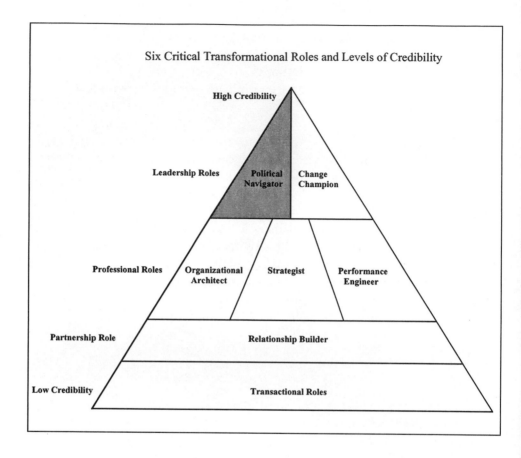

Six Critical Transformational Roles and Levels of Credibility

High Credibility

Leadership Roles — Political Navigator | Change Champion

Professional Roles — Organizational Architect | Strategist | Performance Engineer

Partnership Role — Relationship Builder

Low Credibility — Transactional Roles

10

Political Navigator

Political navigators negotiate organizational obstacle courses on a daily basis. The complex natures of politics forces navigators to draw on a multitude of skills and abilities to successfully maneuver through and manage organizational obstacles and opportunities. Using the bicycle analogy, political navigators employ both front and back wheel skills to develop credibility. Political savvy represents front wheel competencies whereas professional and organizational competence and expertise are back wheel skills.

Professional and Organizational Competence and Expertise

Demonstrating professional and organizational competence and expertise are essential to building credibility and a reputation with key decisionmakers for problem-solving problems, performance improvement, or change implementation. Political navigators demonstrate business acumen and address clients' attitudes toward HRD, which establishes a level of credibility that becomes a source of power from which to make recommendations, provide suggestions, and share ideas useful to the firm.

Strategy 1: Demonstrating Business Acumen

Although many HRD professionals are experts in HRD practices, this is of little value to the organization unless you are able to demonstrate understanding of business concepts, methodologies, practices, and operations—in short, business acumen. Political navigators think like their clients, understand how things get done inside the organization, and how and why decisions are made. Effective political navigators have a solid understanding of common practices of finance, marketing, manufacturing, management, organizational behavior, economics, quantitative analysis, decision theory, operations, and business strategy. Knowledge of business fundamentals, systems theory, organizational culture, and politics reveals understanding of organizational philosophy that guide business action. These are common themes in any MBA program throughout the world. Thorough business understanding enables you to adapt your practices and activities to changing business and economic conditions. This understanding also guides your generation of pertinent, practical solutions for your clients.

One of the first steps in developing business acumen is to learn the language of the organization. This can be accomplished by reading the organization's annual report; attending some trade shows associated with the organization's business or products; scheduling short informational interviews with leading business managers to get their take on where the company is headed; visiting the marketing department to obtain copies of product brochures and sales collateral; and reading the organization's press releases (Fuller and Farrington 1999).

Another way of demonstrating business acumen is by understanding the needs and expectations of your stakeholders. Effective political navigators adapt their practices, procedures, products, innovations, and services based on this knowledge—which allows them to better service their clients. Business acumen provides you the credibility to promote business initiatives that help the organization improve its competitive readiness, performance capacity, and renewal capabilities. Thus, business acumen allows you to be a member of the organizational family responsible for its improvement.

The purpose of strategically integrated HRD is to help the organization improve business results, therefore political navigators acquire knowledge of the organization and its industry. The following activities build this knowledge base:

- Describing the type of business that the organization is operating;
- Identifying the three top-selling products or services and the three most profitable products or services;
- Describing the three newest products or services;
- Analyzing the financial condition of the organization and comparing it with last year's results;
- Identifying the organization's top three competitors;
- Identifying the major trends in the organization and its industry (Fuller and Farrington 1999, 191);
- Identifying the organization's strengths, weaknesses, opportunities, and threats;
- Isolating the firm's core competencies.

These activities increase your understanding of the organization and its industry. If you are unable to readily address these questions, create a development plan that gets you up to speed on the organization and its industry. This may include reading the annual reports for the last three years to identify the condition of the organization, its practices, financial health, and focus.

Next, develop a working knowledge of the departments, divisions, and units within the organization. Since each group has its own mission, processes, and perspectives, political architects discover their performance issues, major initiatives, and performance problems. Quite simply, you forge links with all the different parts of the organization. By doing so, you understand the services that HRD provides, what HRD can do for clients, and what HRD might need to ask them to do in the future.

Excellent opportunities exist to improve the organization's strength and viability through awareness of the financial and business issues facing the organization, understanding client needs and expectations, and creating long-term solutions to difficult problems. Insight and operational understanding of the business maximize your ability to improve the firm's performance. Three subroles reveal your business understanding: scout, strategic partner, and systems linker.

Scouts operate as visionaries within the organization, maneuvering through obstacles, seeking viable paths, and guiding the organization through uncharted territory in the quest for improvement. In short, you lead the organization into areas it has not gone before by providing an understanding of future events, trends, and relationships, both internal and external. In the scout subrole, you generate innovative solutions to complex problems, set priorities, synthesize client input, translate these into action plans, and direct the organization toward achieving its business goals. This, of course, cannot occur without developing a keen understanding of business operations, systems theory, and financial management.

Strategic partners communicate benefits that change strategies and innovations provide the organization. You understand the critical factors affecting organizational competitiveness and possess a thorough understanding of business fundamentals, core processes, operations, and procedures.

Political navigators serve as systems linkers to unify myriad divisions, departments, units, and functions that work in harmony to achieve efficient, effective business results. These groups are aligned to a common set of guiding principles that define the organization's direction and provide its purpose and focus. You help members of the organization pull in the same direction to achieve a common set of business results. Your effectiveness is measured by the ability to establish connections between departments by communicating the value and importance of teamwork.

Strategy 2: Addressing Client's Attitudes Toward HRD

Results-driven political navigators focus attention on improving performance, solving problems, facilitating change, and improving business results. The philosophy is one of helping the organization achieve business results through human resources. This requires you to address four attitudes that clients have toward HRD, which are no trust, no need, no help, or no support.

Attitude 1: No Trust.   Often, political navigators possess little or no history or involvement with certain clients. As a result, these clients are often skeptical of your motives or distrusting of your recommendations. This attitude may be the result of a bad experience with HRD.

When lack of trust exists between you and the client, an open and honest discussion about performance problems and developmental needs must occur. As a result, this becomes the first phase in the political and relationship process: developing rapport with clients.

Attitude 2: No Need.   Another attitude that clients have toward HRD is that of no need, which occurs when clients do not perceive that a problem or opportunity exists. This may also be brought about by past failure to adequately examine the client's situation before recommending a solution, resulting in a recommendation not viewed as credible by the client. You must, therefore, enlighten clients to the potentials and pitfalls looming ahead and analyze their situation thoroughly before making a recommendation. This, then, becomes the second phase of the political and relationship process: discovering performance and developmental needs of clients.

Attitude 3: No Help.   A third attitude common among HRD clients is known as no help. Under this condition, clients are skeptical of the solutions being recommended because they have a different perspective of the problems. This condition often exists because some HRD practitioners do not base their recommendations on identified performance problems and developmental needs discovered during analysis. An even more serious problem occurs when HRD practitioners (activity-based HRD programs) avoid this phase altogether, which results in nothing on which to base recommendations other than lucky guessing. Therefore, they are no help to the client. This becomes the focus of the third phase of the political and relationship process: presenting targeted solutions to clients.

Attitude 4: No Support.   Many activity-based HRD programs have a single solution to very complex problems: offer training. Many training programs are not designed to improve performance or satisfy developmental needs because problems or opportunities are too complex to be resolved through a simple solution like training. Many HRD practitioners fail to develop learning transfer strategies that reinforce behavioral change and skill acquisition. These factors combine to produce the fourth attitude toward HRD: no support.

Political navigators understand that clients use HRD services to solve performance problems, satisfy developmental needs, or implement change initiatives. Dissatisfaction with HRD solutions creates bad feelings toward the HRD program and its practitioners. This causes the no trust attitude to resurface and so hurts HRD within the organization. Political navigators are very supportive of client decisions and satisfy unhappy clients. This is the fourth phase of the political and relationship process: supporting client decision and conclusion with appropriate actions.

Strategy 3: Enhancing Credibility Through Meetings

Building credibility requires you to interact with potential clients. This generally occurs through meetings and one-to-one exchanges. Each of these mediums provides opportunities to showcase your competencies and expertise. Meetings pose prime opportunities to use a method that communicates your goal for the meeting, its purpose, and the benefit that both parties will receive as a result, referred to as the goal agenda benefit method (GAB). This procedure communicates your empathy for the client and your appreciation for the client's problems and needs. GAB helps clients gain confidence in you as a person who wants to assist. GAB statements describe

- Why you are there.
- How you would like to proceed.
- The potential benefit to clients for spending time with you.

Goal Statements.   Goal statements inform clients of the specific reason or objective for your meeting. Communicate the purpose of the meeting involves sharing your motives with clients, which helps them understand your true problem-solving purpose. Clients can then judge whether the development of a relationship will be beneficial.

Goal statements answer the question, Why you are there? An example is: "My goal today is to share some information about myself, my colleagues in HRD, our program, and the consulting services we offer. I would also like to find out more about you and your department's issues, problems, and needs. Is that agreeable with you?"

Agenda Statements. Agenda statements tell the client what you are going to do and suggest a procedure or way to do it. They answer the question, "How will we proceed?" Disclosing the agenda you intend to follow reduces tension because it helps the client know what to expect. It also reinforces your problem-solving purpose because it describes the steps you will follow toward a goal. An example is "I would like to begin by discussing the professional background of my colleagues and myself. Next, I would like to overview several possible alternatives and explain their purposes. Finally, I would like to get to know you better, and obtain a thorough understanding of your situation, your people, and their professional development needs."

Benefit Statements. Benefit statements reveal how the meeting will benefit both you and the client. They answer the question, "How will we both benefit from spending time together?" You might say, for example, "We hope you will learn something about us, we'll learn something about you, and together we'll determine whether our group is a potential resource for meeting your department's performance problems and developmental needs."

Politically Savvy Strategies

Organizations are comprised of a myriad of individuals with different perspectives, assumptions, experiences, personalities, agendas, goals, and ambitions. Therefore, it is essential that you develop the "front wheel" skills appropriate to effective work with people to achieve desired outcomes. Political navigators develop an understanding of the political arena in which the organization conducts business. Absent these skills and insights, you will fail to develop the type of influence necessary to bring about long-term systemic change.

Strategy 1: Understanding Power

Power is the ability to control other people. It is distributed both formally and informally. The most common type of formal power stems from the legitimate authority structure of the organization, and typically involves line/staff and specific reporting relationships. Power is distributed informally through work groups, teams, and special assignments. Power comes to people for various reasons. In 1959, French and Raven identified five key reasons for power:

1. Legitimate power, usually called authority, flows from a person's position in the organization.
2. Reward power stems from the leader's ability to control rewards given to other people.
3. Coercive power depends on the ability to punish others.
4. Expert power is due to special skill or knowledge.
5. Referent power depends on appeal, magnetism, charisma.

The first three are typically formal sources of power whereas the last two are informal sources. Since they are all common in every organization, it is useful to recognize their existence and associate each source with specific individuals within the organization. Armed with this awareness, you can better prepare for interactions with such individuals to maximize your influence with them. This knowledge is invaluable when building a guiding coalition responsible for implementing and managing change and is also helpful when identifying individuals that are influential through the organization, both formally and informally. Finally, these five sources of power are directly parallel to the organizational chart. Consequently political architects identify patterns and symbols of each of these types of power so that you can respond accordingly.

Becoming an effective political navigator involves increasing your personal power, which enhances your position or provides you an opportunity to make connections with individuals who can assist you in your quest for political influence. Let's examine several other sources of power identified by Reardon (2000, 153–177).

The *power of relevance* involves developing power based on what you do within the organization. Jobs, positions, and skills that can be linked to the priorities of the organization as well as link to it strategic business goals and objectives are more relevant than those that are less well matched. For this reason alone, results-driven HRD programs are more powerful than activity-based ones. Simply stated, results-driven HRD programs are directly linked to the priorities of the organization; activity-based ones are not.

The *power of centrality* entails receiving power that accrues from occupying central positions in important networks, such as strategic planning committees, senior management planning teams, and reporting relationships (for example, executives and senior managers). Regardless, your involvement is such that high-level discussions and interactions will provide you invaluable information and help in establishing trusting relationships that enhance your influence within the organization.

The *power of career cachet* involves deriving power from holding an appreciated occupation. This is similar to the power of relevance although it differs in the following way. The power of career cachet refers to occupations that have a positive stigma. Thus, the perceptions that others have of an occupation will determine its importance within the organization regardless of whether it is directly linked to its priorities. Positions that are positively perceived are considered essential and others are not.

Activity-based HRD is not perceived as vital to enhancing revenue, increasing profitability, improving market share, or maximizing profits. As a result, its practitioners are often referred to as trainers. In fact, this is often considered a negative title within many organizations because these individuals are deemed a cost to the firm. On the other hand, the very reference to result-based HRD sends a message through the organization. It is clear that you are in the business to produce results, which is exactly the connotation needed to elevate HRD within the organization.

The *power of autonomy* involves the degree of freedom, discretion, and independence that you are allowed to exercise in your current position. Jobs with the most autonomy have the most power. The greater the autonomy the stronger the indication that the leaders of the organizations trust you and are granting you the right to exercise your judgment on the job.

Transformational roles possess much greater autonomy than transactional ones, which is evident in the type of activities promoted throughout the organization. As a transformational HRD professional, you engage in organizational analysis activities (Chapter 6), strategic planning assignments (Chapter 7), performance management interventions (Chapter 8), and change management initiatives (Chapter 9). These are complex and complicated projects that require a great deal of autonomy. On the other hand, transactional roles primarily are responsible for the design, development, implementation, and evaluation of training programs and needs assessment activities. These are task-based assignments that require little autonomy or independent thinking. Over time, such assignments will limit your influence within the organization and lock you into response-oriented interactions in which you serve at the pleasure of others in the organization.

The *power of expertise* involves demonstrating the proficiency and aptitude necessary to perform a series of tasks or performance activities that others cannot. Individuals who exhibit expertise are given special status in a work group or organization and are excellent candidates when developing best practices, exploratory procedures, and efficiencies.

As a transformational HRD professional, you have the opportunity to demonstrate your organizational analysis, strategic planning, performance management, and change management expertise. These are valuable skills that help the organization achieve its business results. Therefore, promote these competencies and advocate their use within the organization.

The *power of dedication* demonstrates long-term tenure or commitment to an organization. These individuals possess an extensive organizational memory and understand the importance of institutional history. They are helpful in identifying penetration points where change has the most likelihood of success.

This is a situational source of power. Some will be able to use this source of power because they have a long tenure with their present organization, while others will not. Those who have been in their organizations a short while (less than two years) offer another value, which can be a source of power—objectivity. Those with their organization a short while provide an unbiased perspective. Internal loyalties, organizational culture, corporate traditions, vested interest, or personal bias does not influence such a perspective, allowing straightforward and candid observations and instincts, regardless of the potential outcome.

The *power of positive impression* involves looking the part, which is very important in convincing others that you belong in the executive boardroom. This is why dressing for success and demonstrating proper etiquette is so critical to upward mobility. People who present themselves in a polished manner have an easier time building positive relationships with others. Therefore, the more you look and act the part of a competent professional the more likely others will treat you that way. It is that simple.

The *power of high confidence* involves being at ease under extremely stressful conditions. When a person remains cool under pressure, it improves his or her position within a group. Others realize that such a person is not going to fracture when the going gets tough. Consequently, others rely on such a person under the most difficult conditions.

Quite simply, you cannot let them see you sweat. Remain calm under the worst circumstances and be assertive and forthright. Additionally, be smooth and relaxed in your delivery, which includes question-and-answer sessions, presentations, focus groups, and analysis activities (needs, performance, and organizational). In this way, you reflect a poised and polished demeanor that others perceive as confident and competent.

You have one of two ways of using each of the sources of power. You can either demonstrate each of these sources of power in your daily HRD practice or identify individuals who can leverage their specific power when implementing change within the organization. The former will elevate your position within the organization and the latter will enhance your relationship with the person being asked to leverage their specific power. In either case, you have made significant political gains within the organization.

Strategy 2: Understanding Your Political Style

Discovering your political style may advance your career and enable you to defend yourself against others wishing to cause you harm. This can be of benefit when you wish to advance your ideas, recommendations, or solutions. Four different political styles can be identified:

- The purist believes in getting ahead through hard work, declines to participate in politics, and is honest (sometime naively so).
- The team player believes in getting ahead by working well with others, participating in politics to advance the goals of the group, and puts group needs ahead of personal needs.
- The street fighter is an individualist who believes that the best way to get ahead is through the use of rough tactics, is willing to use politics to gain an advantage, watches his or her back, pushes hard to get personal goals achieved, and is slow to trust others.
- The maneuverer is an individualist, one who believes in getting ahead by playing political games in a skillful, unobtrusive manner—not in the habit of using politics to advance personal objectives or personal agendas, looks for ulterior motives in others, has little regard for sanctioned rules, and is considered a smooth operator (Reardon 2001, 24–30).

One cannot become an effective political player unless you are aware of your style.

Strategy 3: Identifying an Organization's Political Climate

An important ingredient of establishing credibility in an organization is developing the ability to identify the type of political arena you are in. To do so, closely observe the interactions, conflicts, and behaviors of organizational members. From this activity, four political arenas emerge:

- *Minimally politicized organization* consists of atmospheres that are amicable in which conflict is rare. In such organizations, camaraderie is common and competition among coworkers is discouraged. People treat each other with positive regard, are considerate, and do not often resort to underhanded politics. Purists work best in this type of organizational environment.
- *Moderately politicized organization* operates on a set of well-understood rules and formalities. Conflicts are not usual, although they tend to be moderate. Additionally, unsanctioned means of achieving individual and group goals are not unusual although if detected, they would be denied as having taken place. This is because leaders in this type of an organization prefer to convey the impression that everything is done by the rules. Organizations such as this suffer from a kind of schizophrenia in which they expect one thing (performance/behavior) and reward another (Reardon 2001, 15). Team players work best in this type of organizational environment.
- *Highly politicized organization* often suffers from frequent conflict because formally sanctioned rules are seldom invoked. It is common to classify employees as part of an in-group or out-group, which creates an environment of the haves versus the have-nots. Reporting relationships are very formal and hierarchical. Thus few people have the opportunity to interact with executives and senior managers except members of the same group. Working in this type of organization is highly stressful and turnover is common. Street fighters and maneuverers work best in this type of organizational environment.
- *Pathologically politicized organization* is seldom productive because daily interaction is fractious (Reardon 2001, 18). Further, conflict is common and most performance goals are achieved by going around the formal procedures of the organization. As a result, distrust among employees is high and they spend masses of time watching their backs to avoid negative repercussions and reprisals. None of the styles is a best fit in pathological organizations, for obvious reasons (Reardon 2001, 13–18).

Once you identify the type of political environment in which you will reside, next identify the danger signs of political decay.

Strategy 4: Identifying Political Land Mines

One of the worst feelings a person can experience follows hearing a phrase like, "We need to talk" or "I need to see you right away." Immediately, you begin negative internal self-talk, asking things such as, "What have I done wrong?" or "What is the problem?" In most cases, everything is fine although these types of messages send you into a mental state that causes you to spend unnecessary energy worrying about nothing.

Others need to avoid delivering ambiguous statements because they are problematic and can cause undue stress, although most people need a radar system for detecting when politics gets heavy-handed (Reardon 2001). This is important to avoid serious political situations that diminish your credibility, influence, and effectiveness. Although these are unfortunate outcomes, sometimes these situations can cost you your job. So it is imperative that you develop a sixth sense for such political land mines.

People play several games that indicate their true intentions. For example, some people use a technique known as the frozen-out strategy in which they purposefully leave you off a major project even though you should be participating. Individuals who have difficulty with confrontation or lack the ability to be direct often use this technique. Others use this technique to assert their power and authority or as a means of putting someone in their place.

Another example is when a person makes a concerted effort to alter his or her colleagues' opinions regarding your competencies and abilities. This is known as poisoning the well. It is effective because you cannot defend or refute the negative statements. Unless someone informs you that such statements are being made, your reputation may be damaged forever.

Some people use a technique known as damning with faint praise, which involves a halfhearted effort at praising rather than communicating exactly what one feels or believes. The person receiving the message is on his or her own to figure out the hidden agenda. This technique is effective because the recipient of the message typically interrupts the statement in the worst possible way, which ultimately diminishes your reputation, credibility, or influence. In fact, this is exactly what the sender of the message desires.

Public put-downs are not as common in most professional environments as other techniques, although they do occur. These are overt insults, interruptions, patronizing comments, blocking behaviors, or criticisms in which another party is challenging publicly your abilities, competencies, and thinking. If and when these occur, the political environment has evolved to a hostile state that can leave lasting scars and evoke emotional damage. Sometimes public put-downs occur because the aggressor lacks political or interpersonal skills. They also occur when the aggressor is attempting to destroy your reputation, credibility, or influence.

One of the most difficult political land mines is one in which a person intentionally conveys that a condition exists when in reality another condition is present. This deceitful and manipulative technique is known as faking left, going right (Reardon 2001, 141). It is serious because it sets you up for failure especially when such information is critical to the future strategy that you employ. In short, this technique makes you look foolish and you have no way of explaining or defending your actions or decisions.

Most of these political land mines are covert and difficult to isolate. Therefore, your primary strategy for evading them is political awareness and observation. In this way, you are constantly looking for the conditions where land mines are present. Quite simply, your best defense is to demonstrate that you are an alert political adversary, one ready for any contingency.

Strategy 5: Developing a Politically Savvy Approach

Several techniques demonstrate a politically savvy approach. Let's examine a few.

- Practice reciprocity—treat people the way you want to be treated. In this way, others reciprocate like behavior. In other words, if you treat another person with dignity and respect, he or she will typically treat you in a similar manner.
- Observe, observe, observe—pay attention to your environment, the interaction between people, and their patterns. By doing so, you will gather a wealth of information to make important decisions and avoid political land mines.
- Even your worst political adversary is a human being—befriend your political enemies so that you can discover mutual ground from which to build a working relationship.
- Identify the power—determine who in the organization has the power to make decisions and get things done. Identify individuals who have access to powerful individuals. Once identified, create a positive relationship with these individuals.

- Identify coalitions—isolate individuals who have developed alliances with powerful people in the organization. This helps identify individuals who can introduce you to important decisionmakers and opinion leaders.
- Do the unexpected—do things that others do not expect. This includes demonstrating talents, abilities, and skills that others are not familiar with. In this way, you become a mystery to others, which can increase their interest in you as a person and as a professional.
- Build rapport with the right people—make connections with people who are able to grant you permission to participate in high-profile projects and change initiatives.
- Be nice and friendly—be nice and friendly to people who otherwise do not care for you; sometime in the future they will notice and reciprocate the behavior. People are drawn to people who reach out and appear to be open and warm.
- Develop contacts—engage in overt efforts to develop rapport with people who can help you succeed in the organization. In most cases, this is a long-term strategy that requires building a broad network of contacts.
- Build a coalition—build your own network of contacts throughout your career; partner with people who can provide advice, introductions, and assistance.
- Avoid public confrontations—never allow yourself to engage in public displays of aggressiveness or hostility. Always confront people in private, and do so in a tactful, intelligent manner.
- Pick your battles—select the battles on which you are willing to spend precious emotional resources and do so in a balanced and frugal manner. Avoid the combat-ready approach; it diminishes your energy and effectiveness.
- Stand your ground—be willing to fight vigorously for important, value-based issues. Remember that political aggressors will avoid you much like most animals avoid tenacious wolverines and badgers— they understand that a serious confrontation with such an animal is just too painful.
- Keep your powder dry—maintain readiness for political action. Never take things for granted and be ready to engage in the political game at a moment's notice.
- If you declare war: Play to win—there is no such thing as a neat, well-mannered, polite war. The same is true in politics. Play to win if you

decide to take someone on who is preventing you from achieving your goals.

- Do not sit on a lead—means never take anything for granted. This includes relationships, connections, and how others perceive you. Always enter the political arena believing that you are behind and must play harder and smarter than the other person.
- Know when to fold them—understand when you are out of numbers or do not have the support needed to successfully accomplish your goals. Initiate a graceful retreat under these conditions, and live to fight another day, hopefully under better and more manageable circumstances.
- Seek the high ground—identify when conditions are right to initiate a political action or seek support for an idea or recommendation.
- Develop favor banks—do favors for others much like making a deposit in a savings account. Over time, the principal and interest grow to a point where you can cash in and take advantage of an opportunity.
- Keep your distance—avoid getting too close to other organizational members. Share just enough of yourself to be effective; never get too intimately involved with people who can affect your career and livelihood.
- Play it close to the vest—share just enough information so that others support you and open doors for you. Never let others know everything you are thinking and feeling. Like playing poker, never show another player your cards. If you do, they have the advantage.
- Develop finesse—create a polished and professional approach to playing politics. This involves studying others who have mastered the art of political gamesmanship.

Conclusion

Politics often possesses a negative image in most of our minds; however, it is an important ingredient to the success of transformational HRD professionals. It is therefore essential that you develop organizational competence and political savvy to be an effective leader in your organization.

References

Anderson, R. W. "The Future of Human Resources: Forging Ahead or Falling Behind?" In *Tomorrow's HR Management: 48 Thought Leaders Call for Change*, ed. D. Ulrich, M. R. Losey, and G. Lake, pp. 146–154. New York: Wiley and Sons, 1997.

Argyris, C., and D. Schon. *Organizational Learning II: A Theory of Action Perspective*. Reading, Mass.: Addison-Wesley, 1996.

Bellman, G. "Partnership Phase: Forming Partnerships." In *Moving from Training to Performance: A Practical Guide*, ed. D. G. Robinson and J. C. Robinson, pp. 39–53. San Francisco: Berrett-Koehler, 1998.

Bibler, R. S. *The Arthur Young Management Guide to Mergers and Acquisition*. New York: Wiley and Sons, 1989.

Biekowski, D. "Ten Causes of Project Bust." *Computerworld* 4 (1989): 99.

Bierema, L. L. "Human Resource Development for Humans: Moving Beyond Performance Paradigms on Workplace Development." In *2000 Handbook of Adult and Continuing Education*, ed. S. B. Merriam. San Francisco: Jossey-Bass, 2000.

Block, P. *Flawless Consulting: A Guide to Getting Your Expertise Used*. San Diego: Pfeiffer, 1999.

Bolton, R. *People Skills: How to Assert Yourself, Listen to Others, and Resolve Conflicts*. New York: Simon and Schuster, 1986.

Bolton, R., and D. Grover Bolton. *People Styles at Work: Making Bad Relationships Good and Good Relationships Better*. New York: AMACOM, 1996.

Boyett, J. H., and J. T. Boyett. *Beyond Workplace 2000: Essential Strategies for the New American Corporation*. New York: Dutton, 1995.

Brethower, D. M. "General Systems Theory and Behavioral Psychology." In *Handbook of Human Performance Technology: Improving Individual and Organizational Performance Worldwide*, ed. H. D. Stolovitch and E. J. Keeps, pp. 67–81. San Francisco: Jossey-Bass, 1999.

Brinkerhoff, R. O. "Measurement Phase: Evaluating Effectiveness of Performance Improvement Projects." In *Moving from Training to Performance: A Practical Guide*, ed. D. G. Robinson and J. C. Robinson, pp. 147–174. San Francisco: Berrett-Koehler, 1998.

Brinkerhoff, R. O., and A. M. Apking. *High Impact Learning: Strategies for Leveraging Business Results from Training*. Cambridge, Mass.: Perseus, 2001.

Brinkerhoff, R. O., and S. J. Gill. *The Learning Alliance*. San Francisco: Jossey-Bass, 1994.

Broad, M., and J. Newstrom. *Transfer of Training. Action-Packed Strategies to Ensure High Payoff from Training Investment.* Reading, Mass.: Addison-Wesley, 1992.

Brookfield, S. D. "Uncovering Assumptions: The Key to Reflective Practice." *Adult Learning* 16, no. 1 (1992): 13–18.

Buckingham, M., and D. O. Clifton. *Now, Discover Your Strengths.* New York: Free Press, 2001.

Buckingham, M., and C. Coffman. *First, Break All the Rules: What the World's Greatest Managers Do Differently.* New York: Simon and Schuster, 1999.

Burke, W. W. *Organizational Development: A Process of Learning and Changing.* Reading, Mass.: Addison-Wesley, 1992.

Cameron, K. "Critical Questions in Assessing Organizational Effectiveness." *Organizational Dynamics* 9, no. 2 (1980): 66–80.

Cascio, W. F. *Managing Human Resources: Productivity, Quality of Work Life, Profits.* New York: McGraw-Hill, 1997.

Clifton, D. O., and P. Nelson. *Soar with Your Strengths.* New York: Delacorte, 1992.

Collins, J. *Good to Great: Why Some Companies Make the Leap . . . and Others Don't.* New York: HarperBusiness, 2001.

Collins, J., and J. L. Porras. *Built to Last: Successful Habits of Visionary Companies.* New York: HarperBusiness, 1994.

Conner, D. *Managing at the Speed of Change.* New York: Villard Books, 1992.

Dean, P. J. *Performance Engineering at Work.* Washington, D.C.: International Board of Standards for Training, Performance, and Instruction, IBSTPI Publications, and International Society for Performance Improvement, 1999.

De Pree, M. *Leadership Jazz.* New York: Dell Publishing, 1992.

Dyer, W. G. "Team Building: A Microcosm of the Past, Present, and Future of OD." *Academy of Management OD Newsletter* 4 (1989): 7–8.

Fallon, T., and R. O. Brinkerhoff. *Framework for Organizational Effectiveness.* Paper presented at the American Society for Training and Development International Conference, 1996.

Feldman, D. C. "A Contingency Theory of Socialization." *Administrative Science Quarterly* 21, no. 9 (1967): 434–435.

French, J. R. P., and B. H. Raven. "The Bases of Social Power." In *Studies of Social Power,* ed. Dowin Cartwright. Ann Arbor: University of Michigan Press, 1959.

French, W. L., and C. H. Bell. *Organization Development: Behavioral Science Interventions for Organizational Improvement.* 6th ed. Englewood Cliffs, N.J.: Prentice-Hall, 1998.

French, W. L., C. H. Bell Jr., and R. A. Zawacki. *Organizational Development: Behavioral Science Interventions for Organizational Improvement.* Englewood Cliffs, N.J.: Prentice-Hall, 1999.

Fuller, J., and J. Farrington. *From Training to Performance Improvement: Navigating the Transition.* San Francisco: Jossey-Bass, 1999.

Gibson, J. L., J. M. Ivancevich and J. H. Donnelly. *Organizations: Behavior, Structure, Process.* 9th ed. New York: McGraw-Hill, 1999.

Gilbert, T. F. *Human Competence: Engineering Worthy Performance.* New York: McGraw-Hill, 1978.

_____. *Human Competence: Engineering Worthy Performance.* Tribute ed. Washington, D.C.: ISPI, 1996.

Gill, S. J. "Shifting Gears for High Performance." *Training and Development Journal* 49, no. 5 (1995): 25–31.

Gilley, J. W. *Strategic Planning for Human Resource Development.* Alexandria, Va.: American Society for Training and Development Press, 1992.

_____. *Improving HRD Practice.* Malabar, Fla.: Krieger, 1998.

Gilley, J. W., and N. W. Boughton. *Stop Managing, Start Coaching: How Performance Coaching Can Enhance Commitment and Improve Productivity.* New York: McGraw-Hill, 1996.

Gilley, J. W., N. W. Boughton, and A. Maycunich. *The Performance Challenge: Developing Management Systems to Make Employees Your Greatest Asset.* Cambridge, Mass.: Perseus, 1999.

Gilley, J. W., and A. J. Coffern. *Internal Consulting for HRD Professionals: Tools, Techniques, and Strategies for Improving Organizational Performance.* New York: McGraw-Hill, 1994.

Gilley, J. W., S. A. Eggland, and A. Maycunich Gilley. *Principles of Human Resource Development.* 2d ed. Cambridge, Mass.: Perseus, 2002.

Gilley, J. W., and A. Maycunich. *Strategically Integrated HRD: Partnering to Maximize Organizational Performance.* Cambridge, Mass.: Perseus, 1998.

_____. *Organizational Learning, Performance, and Change: An Introduction to Strategic HRD.* Cambridge, Mass.: Perseus, 2000a.

_____. *Beyond the Learning Organization: Creating a Culture of Continuous and Development Through State-of-the-Art Human Resource Practices.* Cambridge, Mass.: Perseus, 2000b.

Gilley, J. W., S. Quatro, E. Hoekstra, D. D. Whittle, and A. Maycunich, A. *The Manager as Change Agent: A Practical Guide for Developing High Performance People and Organizations.* Cambridge, Mass.: Perseus, 2001.

Goleman, D. *Working with Emotional Intelligence.* New York: Bantam Books, 1998.

Greenleaf, R. K. *On Becoming a Servant Leader.* San Francisco: Jossey-Bass, 1996.

Guba, E. G., and Y. S. Lincoln. *Effective Evaluation: Improving the Usefulness of Evaluation Results Through Responsive and Naturalistic Approaches.* San Francisco: Jossey-Bass, 1998.

Hale, J. *The Performance Consultant's Fieldbook: Tools and Techniques for Improving Organizations and People.* San Francisco: Jossey-Bass and Pfeiffer, 1998.

Harless, J. H. *An Ounce of Analysis: Is Worth a Pound of Objectives.* Newman, Ga.: Harless Performance Guild, 1974.

Jacobs, R. *Human Performance Technology: A Systems-Based Field for the Training and Development Profession.* Columbus: ERIC Clearinghouse on Adult, Career, and Vocational Education, National Center for Research in Vocational Education, Ohio State University, 1987.

Jewell, S. F., and D. O. Jewell. "Organization Design." In *Handbook of Human Performance Technology: A Comprehensive Guide for Analyzing and Solving Performance Problems in Organizations,* ed. H. D. Stolovitch and E. J. Keeps, pp. 211–232. San Francisco: Jossey-Bass, 1992.

Kaufman, R., A. M. Rojas, and H. Mayer. *Needs Assessment: A User's Guide.* Englewood Cliffs, N.J.: Educational Technology Publications, 1992.

Killion. J. P., and G. Todnem. "A Process for Personal Theory Building." *Educational Leadership* 48, no. 6 (1991): 14–16.

Kline, P., and B. Saunders. *Ten Steps to a Learning Organization.* Arlington, Va.: Great Ocean Publishers, 1998.

Knowles, M. S. *Self-Directed Learning.* New York: Association Press, 1975.

Kotter, J. P. *Leading Change.* Boston: Harvard Business School Press, 1996.

Kotter, J. P., and J. L. Heskett. *Corporate Culture and Performance.* New York: Free Press, 1992.

LeBoeuf, M. *Getting Results: The Secret to Motivating Yourself and Others.* New York: Berkeley Books, 1985.

Levy, A. "Second-Order Planned Change: Definition and Conceptualization." *Organizational Dynamics* 15, no. 1 (1986): 5–20.

Lewin, K. *Field Theory in Social Science.* New York: Harper, 1951.

Lippitt, G., and R. Lippitt. *The Consulting Process in Action.* 2d ed. San Diego: University Associates, 1986.

Mager, R. F. *Preparing Instructional Objectives.* 2d ed. Belmont, Calif.: Fearon, 1975.

Marquardt, M. J. *Building the Learning Organization.* New York: McGraw-Hill, 1996.

———. *Action Learning in Action: Transforming Problems and People for World-Class Organizational Learning.* Palo Alto, Calif.: Davies-Black Publishing, 1999.

Marquardt, M.J., and A. Reynolds. *The Global Learning Organization.* Burr Ridge, Ill.: Irwin, 1994.

Maxwell, J. C. *The 21 Irrefutable Laws of Leadership: Follow Them and People Will Follow You.* Nashville, Tenn.: Thomas Nelson Publishers, 1998.

McCauley, C. D., R. S. Moxley, and E. Van Velsor. *Handbook of Leadership Development [Center for Creative Leadership].* San Francisco: Jossey-Bass, 1998.

McLagan, P. "Models for HRD practice." *Training and Development Journal* 43, no. 9 (1989): 49–59.

McLagan, P., and R. Bedrick. *Model for Excellence.* Alexandria, Va.: ASTD, 1983.

Meredith, J. R., and S. J. Mantel. *Project Management: A Managerial Approach.* New York: Wiley and Sons, 1989.

Merrill, D., and R. Reid. *Personal Styles and Effective Performance.* Radnor, Pa.: Chilton, 1981.

Mezirow, J. *Transformative Dimensions of Adult Learning.* San Francisco: Jossey-Bass, 1991.

Michael, D. N. *On Learning to Plan—and Planning to Learn: The Social Psychology of Changing Toward Future-Responsive Social Learning.* San Francisco: Jossey-Bass, 1973.

Mink, O. G., P. W. Esterhuysen, B. P. Mink, and K. Q. Owen. *Change at Work: A Comprehensive Management Process for Transforming Organizations.* San Francisco: Jossey-Bass, 1993.

Morris, L. "Development Strategies for the Knowledge Era." In *Learning Organizations: Developing Cultures for Tomorrow's Workplace,* ed. S. Chawla and J. Renesch, pp. 323–336. Portland, Oreg.: Productivity Press, 1995.

Nadler, D. A. *Champion for Change: How CEOs and Their Companies Are Mastering the Skills of Radical Change.* San Francisco: Jossey-Bass, 1998.

Neilsen, E. H. *Becoming an OD Practitioner.* Englewood Cliffs, N.J.: Prentice-Hall, 1984.

Nilson, C. *The Performance Consulting Toolbook: Tools for Trainers in a Performance Consulting Role.* New York: McGraw-Hill, 1999.

Patterson, J. *Coming Clean About Organizational Change.* Arlington, Va.: American Association of School Administrators, 1997.

Preskill, H. "The Use of Critical Incidents to Foster Reflection and Learning in HRD." *Human Resource Development Quarterly* 7, no. 4 (1996): 335–347.

Preskill, H., and R. T. Torres. *Evaluative Inquiry for Learning in Organizations.* Thousand Oaks, Calif.: Sage, 1999.

Quatro, S. A., E. Hoekstra, and J. W. Gilley. "Holistic Model for Change Agent Excellence: Core Roles and Competencies for Successful Change Agency." In *Changing the Way We Manage Change: The Consultants Speak,* ed. R. Sims. Westport, Conn.: Quorum Books, 2002.

Raudsepp, E. "Managers as Leaders." In *Handbook for Creative Managers,* ed. R. L. Kuhn, pp. 173–182. New York: McGraw-Hill, 1987.

Reardon, K. K. *The Secret Handshake: Mastering the Politics of the Business Inner Circle.* New York: Doubleday, 2001.

Redding, J. *Strategic Readiness: The Making of the Learning Organization.* San Francisco: Jossey-Bass, 1994.

Revans, R. Keynote presentation at the 1994 Academy of Human Resource Development annual meeting.

Robb, J. "The Job of a Performance Consultant." In *Moving from Training to Performance: A Practical Guide,* ed. D. G. Robinson and J. C. Robinson, pp. 229–255. San Francisco: Berrett-Koehler, 1998.

Robinson, D. G., and J. C. Robinson. *Training for Impact: How to Link Training to Business Needs and Measure the Results.* San Francisco: Jossey-Bass, 1989.

_____. *Performance Consulting: Moving Beyond Training.* San Francisco: Berrett-Koehler, 1996.

Rogers, C. R. *On Becoming a Person.* Boston: Houghton Mifflin, 1961.

Rolls, J. "The Transformational Leader: The Wellspring of the Learning Organization." In *Learning Organizations: Developing Cultures for Tomorrow's Workplace,* ed. S. Chawla and J. Renesch, pp.101–110. Portland, Oreg.: Productivity Press, 1995.

Rosenberg, M. J. "Human Performance Technology: Foundation for Human Performance Improvement." In *The ASTD Models for Human Performance Improvement. Roles, Com-*

petencies, and Outputs, ed. W. Rothwell. Alexandria, Va.: American Society for Training and Development, 1996.

Rossett, A. "Analysis for Human Performance Technology." In *Handbook of Human Performance Technology: Improving Individual and Organizational Performance Worldwide,* ed. H. D. Stolovitch and E. J. Keeps, pp. 139–162. San Francisco: Jossey-Bass, 1999a.

———. *First Things Fast: A Handbook for Performance Analysis.* San Francisco: Pfeiffer, 1999b.

Rothwell, W. *Beyond Training and Development: State-of-the-Art Strategies for Enhancing Human Performance.* New York: AMACOM, 1996.

Rothwell, W., and R. Cookson. *Beyond Instruction: Comprehensive Program Planning for Business and Education.* San Francisco: Jossey-Bass, 1997.

Rummler, G. "The Three Levels of Alignment." In *Moving from Training to Performance: A Practical Guide,* ed. D. G. Robinson and J. C. Robinson, pp. 13–35. San Francisco: Berrett-Koehler, 1998.

Rummler, G. A., and A. P. Brache. "Transforming Organizations Through Human Performance Technology." In *Handbook of Human Performance Technology: A Comprehensive Guide for Analyzing and Solving Performance Problems in Organizations,* ed. H. D. Stolovitch and E. J. Keeps, pp. 32–49. San Francisco: Jossey-Bass, 1992.

———. *Improving Performance: How to Manage the White Spaces on the Organizational Chart.* San Francisco: Jossey-Bass, 1995.

Schein, E. H. *Organizational Culture and Leadership.* San Francisco: Jossey-Bass, 1992.

Schneider, B., and A. Konz. "Strategic Job Analysis." *Human Resource Management* 28, no. 2 (1989): 51–63.

Schwandt, D. R. "Learning as an Organization: A Journey into Chaos." In *Learning Organizations: Developing Cultures for Tomorrow's Workplace,* ed. S. Chawla and J. Renesch, pp. 365–380. Portland, Oreg.: Productivity Press, 1995.

Schwinn, D. *The Interactive Project Learning Model.* Concept paper. Jackson, Mich.: Transformation, Inc., 1996.

Senge, P. M. *The Fifth Discipline: The Art and Practice of the Learning Organization.* New York: Doubleday, 1990.

Silber, K. "Intervening at Different Levels in Organizations." In *Handbook of Human Performance Technology: A Comprehensive Guide for Analyzing and Solving Performance Problems in Organizations,* ed. H. D. Stolovitch and E. J. Keeps, pp. 50–65. San Francisco: Jossey-Bass, 1992.

Simerly, R. *Strategic Planning and Leadership in Continuing Education.* San Francisco: Jossey-Bass, 1987.

Simonsen, P. *Promoting a Developmental Culture in Your Organization: Using Career Development as a Change Agent.* Palo Atlo, Calif.: Davies-Black Publishing, 1997.

Sink, D. L. "Success Strategies for the Human Performance Technologist." In *Handbook of Human Performance Technology: A Comprehensive Guide for Analyzing and Solving Performance Problems in Organizations,* ed. H. D. Stolovitch and E. J. Keeps, pp. 564–575. San Francisco: Jossey-Bass, 1992.

Smith, K. K. "Philosophical Problems in Thinking About Organizational Change." In *Change in Organizations*, ed. P. S. Goodman and Associates, pp. 316–374. San Francisco: Jossey-Bass, 1982.

Stolovitch, H. D., and E. J. Keeps, eds. *Handbook of Human Performance Technology: A Comprehensive Guide for Analyzing and Solving Performance Problems in Organizations.* San Francisco: Jossey- Bass, 1992.

_____. *Handbook of Human Performance Technology: Improving Individual and Organizational Performance Worldwide.* San Francisco: Jossey-Bass, 1999.

Stolovitch, H. D., E. J. Keeps, and D. Rodrigue. "Skill Sets, Characteristics, and Values for the Human Performance Technologist." In *Handbook of Human Performance Technology: Improving Individual and Organizational Performance Worldwide*, ed. H. D. Stolovitch and E. J. Keeps, pp. 651–697. San Francisco: Jossey-Bass, 1999.

Stufflebeam, D. L. "Toward a Science of Education Evaluation." *Educational Technology* 7, no. 14 (1975).

Tichy, N. M. "GE's Crotonvule: A Staging Ground for Corporate Revolution." *Academy of Management Executive* 102 (1989).

Torres, R. T., H. Preskill, and M. E. Piontek. *Evaluation strategies for Communicating and Reporting: Enhancing Learning in Organizations.* Thousand Oaks, Calif.: Sage, 1996.

Treacy, T., and F. Wiersema. *The Discipline of Market Leaders: Choose Your Customers, Narrow Your Focus, Dominate Your Market.* Cambridge, Mass.: Perseus, 1997.

Turner, A. N. "Consulting Is More Than Giving Advice." *Harvard Business Review* 61, no. 5 (1983): 120–129.

Ulrich, D. *Human Resource Champions.* Boston: Harvard Business School Press, 1997.

_____. "A New Mandate for Human Resources." *Harvard Business Review* 76, no. 1 (1998): 124-134.

Ulrich, D., and D. Lake. *Organizational Capability: Competing from the Inside Out.* New York: John Wiley and Sons, 1990.

Vaile, R. *Learning as a Way of Being.* San Francisco: Jossey-Bass, 1996.

Walton, J. *Strategic Human Resource Development.* New York: Financial Times/Prentice-Hall, 1999.

Watkins, K. E., and V. J. Marsick. *Sculpting the Learning Organization: Lessons in the Art and Science of Systematic Change.* San Francisco: Jossey-Bass, 1993.

Weiss, J. W., and R. K. Wysocki. *5-Phase Project Management: A Practical Planning and Implementation Guide.* Cambridge, Mass.: Perseus, 1992.

Wilson, L. *Changing the Game: The New Way to Sell.* New York: Fireside, 1987.

Index